GLOBAL ENTREPRENEURSHIP

Entrepreneurs around the world are encouraged and held up as the new deliverers of economic growth in turbulent times. Entrepreneurship is taught globally, but often without much reference to the truly global array of cases and examples that can provide helpful insights for international students in particular.

This collection brings together expert entrepreneurship scholars to provide a collection of global case studies around entrepreneurial firms worldwide. This unique educational resource covers a broad range of topics of relevance to understand entrepreneurship, including corporate, social and indigenous entrepreneurship.

This book provides entrepreneurship educators with reliable cases suitable for classroom discussion, analysis or even for assessment purposes. Instructors teaching this subject will be able to use the book as a stand-alone reference or as an ideal supplement for many introductory texts in entrepreneurship.

James Hayton is Professor at Warwick Business School, UK. He is Editor-in-Chief of the journal *Human Resource Management*, an Editor of *Entrepreneurship Theory and Practice* and is a member of the editorial boards for many other journals. He is the co-editor of another Routledge title, *Global Human Resource Management Casebook*.

Carlo Salvato is Associate Professor of Business Strategy at Bocconi University, Italy.

Mathew J. Manimala is Professor of Organizational Behaviour and Human Resource Management at the Indian Institute of Management, Bangalore, India.

Leading scholars have highlighted attention to context as an important focus for the 'next act' of entrepreneurship scholarship. In this volume, the editors have collected a range of intriguing case studies from around the globe, showcasing entrepreneurship in all its variety. Apart from the main focus on country settings, the collection captures an array of industry, governance and firm development stage contexts, and success as well as failure. The cases provide valuable illustrations that put flesh to the bones of abstracted, theoretical notions. This makes it a significant companion text for courses in entrepreneurship, and especially those focusing on international issues.

Per Davidsson, Professor, Queensland
University of Technology, Australia

This volume represents a great initiative by the Ambassadors Program of the Entrepreneurship Division of the Academy of Management. The contributions provide a much needed insightful resource for both research and teaching that will enhance our understanding of the variety of contexts in which entrepreneurship occurs.

Mike Wright, Professor, University of Ghent, Belgium

With the ever growing worldwide interest in entrepreneurship, Hayton, Salvato and Manimala have put together an outstanding collection of cases that capture the diversity of settings, managerial and entrepreneurial issues, and organizational practices around the globe. Well researched and documented, these cases provide a rich basis to teach about (and learn from) different actions that entrepreneurs undertake. I compliment the authors and editors on a great book that will make the study of entrepreneurship fun and informative. I highly recommend this wonderful book.

Shaker A. Zahra, Professor, University of Minnesota, USA

This book is filled with a remarkable set of cases from all over the world. Thought-provoking and informative, this is an eminently readable text with case illustrations across a broad spectrum of issues. This is a great primer for students, faculty and entrepreneurs interested in international new ventures.

Harry J. Sapienza, Professor, Carlson School of Management,
University of Minnesota, USA

Entrepreneurial behaviors emerge and develop in a wide variety of situations and contexts. This new book edited by James Hayton, Carlo Salvato and Mathew Manimala is centered on this environmental and contextual dimension of entre-preneurship. The book offers relevant and insightful case studies of entrepreneurial firms operating in different regions of the world. It will certainly be a reference for those interested in getting a better understanding of the interplay between institutional, environmental and organizational factors, and its effects on the development of entrepreneurial firms.

Alain Fayolle, Professor and Director of the Entrepreneurship
Research Centre, Emlyon Business School, France

GLOBAL ENTREPRENEURSHIP

Case studies of entrepreneurial firms operating around the world

Edited by
James Hayton, Carlo Salvato and
Mathew J. Manimala

Routledge
Taylor & Francis Group

LONDON AND NEW YORK

First published 2015
by Routledge
2 Park Square, Milton Park, Abingdon, Oxon OX14 4RN

Simultaneously published in the USA and Canada
by Routledge
711 Third Avenue, New York, NY 10017

Routledge is an imprint of the Taylor & Francis Group, an informa business

British Library Cataloguing in Publication Data
A catalogue record for this book is available from the British Library

Library of Congress Cataloging in Publication Data
Global entrepreneurship: case studies of entrepreneurial firms operating
  around the world/edited by James Hayton, Carlo Salvato, Mathew J.
  Manimala. – First Edition.
  pages cm
  1. International business enterprises – Management – Case studies.
  2. Small business – Management – Case studies. I. Hayton, James C.,
  editor of compilation. II. Salvato, Carlo, editor of compilation.
  III. Manimala, Mathew J., 1950– editor of compilation.
  HD62.4.G54334 2014
  658.4'21 – dc23
  2014016354

ISBN: 978-0-415-70323-9 (hbk)
ISBN: 978-0-415-70324-6 (pbk)
ISBN: 978-0-203-79478-4 (ebk)

Typeset in Bembo and Stone Sans
by Florence Production Ltd, Stoodleigh, Devon, UK

MIX
Paper from
responsible sources
FSC
www.fsc.org   FSC® C013604

Printed and bound by CPI Group (UK) Ltd, Croydon, CR0 4YY

CONTENTS

FIGURES

TABLES

CONTRIBUTORS

Kevin Au earned his Ph.D. in management/international business at the University of British Columbia. Professor Au founded and directs the Center for Entrepreneurship and the Centre for Family Enterprising and Business Advising at the Chinese University of Hong Kong. He also serves as Associate Director of the MBA Programmes. His research interests include international management, entrepreneurship, family business, social network and cross-cultural research methodology. Kevin has extensive publications and served on the editorial boards of several academic journals. His edited book *Family Enterprising in Asia: Exploring Transgenerational Entrepreneurship in Family Firms* is forthcoming. Kevin has consulted both government and business corporations, including the Central Policy Unit, Hong Kong Cyberport, Credit Suisse and a number of startups.

Urs Baldegger is Professor for Entrepreneurship and Chairholder of the Van Riemsdijk Endowed Chair at Liechtenstein University. Before that, he was Professor for Entrepreneurship at the HTW University Chur, Switzerland, and Research Assistant and Lecturer at the University of St Gallen, Switzerland, where he was also awarded his doctorate. Next to his academic career, Prof. Baldegger holds extensive experience as corporate consultant and member of the supervisory board of several young as well as of established companies. His research interests mainly lie in the fields of Entrepreneurship Education, Transformation Processes as well as in the intersection between management and psychology.

Vladimír Bartošek, Ph.D., graduated with an MA in Economics at the Faculty of Business and Management, Brno University of Technology. His postgraduate study was carried out at the Faculty of Business and Management, Brno University of Technology, in the field of operation management and logistics management; here he also obtained his Ph.D. In 2006 he took part in a six-month research fellowship in the UK, at Liverpool Hope University. He is a senior lecturer and vice-director of the Department of Management at the Faculty of Business and Management, specializing in the fields of logistics management and information systems of manufacturing companies.

Sanjay Bhowmick has been teaching courses in strategy, entrepreneurship and innovation, as well as finance and entrepreneurial finance, at the University of Auckland, the Foundation for Liberal and Management Education in India, and now at Newcastle Business School, Northumbria University, UK. He has an MBA from the University of Delhi and a Ph.D. from the University of Auckland. Sanjay is an achievement motivation trainer and conducts entrepreneurship development programmes with existing and aspiring entrepreneurs. Before academia, Sanjay has had senior management experience in banking, consulting and venture capital. His theory-building research interests lie in entrepreneurship, firm internationalization and social cause venturing.

Maryse Brand earned a Ph.D. in economics at the University of Groningen in the Netherlands with a dissertation in the field of business-to-business marketing. After her Ph.D., she worked for a number of years as a small business consultant. At present, Maryse is Associate Professor of Small Business and Entrepreneurship at the Faculty of Economics and Business in Groningen. Maryse is a member of the review board of the *Journal of Small Business Management* and has published in peer-reviewed journals, including *Entrepreneurship, Theory and Practice, Journal of Small Business Management, Small Business Economics* and *Management International Review*. Her interests focus on strategic small business topics such as internationalization, cooperation, franchising, strategic HRM and innovation adoption.

Cagri Bulut is Associate Prof. and Dr of Management in the Business Administration Department at Yasar University, Turkey. Cagri Bulut has a B.Sc. in Economics from Istanbul University, an M.Sc. in Strategy and a Ph.D. in Business Administration from Gebze Institute of Technology (GIT), Turkey. Before joining Yasar University, he served as postdoctoral Economist at the Food and Agriculture Organization of The United Nations, CountrySTAT Project. Cagri has written for a wide range of publications on Strategy and Management of Innovation and Corporate Entrepreneurship. His research particularly focused on culture-based strategic orientations and firm performance, Social and Technological Innovations, Intrapreneurship and Intellectual Capital Management. Besides supervising many Ph.D. students, Calgri has been visiting professor in a number of European countries, such as Italy, Portugal, Slovenia and Germany. He has taken part in many projects, some funded by the Scientific and Technological Research Council of Turkey (TUBITAK) and ISI-FRAUNHOFER. Outside the university, Cagri is a member of the Entrepreneurship Education Commission at TUBITAK, a council member of the Third Council of the Ministry of Science, Technology and Industry of Turkey; he has represented the Republic of Turkey in the OECD, and in many other organizations supporting entrepreneurship. He is the co-editor of Yasar university journal, and a member of reviewer and editorial boards for prominent business journals. Dr Bulut is Ambassador of the Academy of Management, Entrepreneurship Division, Turkey.

Jeremy Cheng holds an MBA with Distinction from Victoria University of Wellington, an MA in Linguistics and a BSSc in Psychology from the Chinese University of Hong Kong (CUHK). He is now an Ed.D. candidate at the University of Bristol. Jeremy is currently an Executive Officer at CUHK where he is responsible for developing and running executive education programmes. His partners include overseas universities and multinational companies. He is also involved in the Business School's new initiatives in Kuwait. Jeremy is a member of the CUHK Research Team of Successful Transgenerational Entrepreneurship Practices and the Family Firm Institute. He is also a Chartered Marketer with the Chartered Institute of Marketing.

Evelien Croonen earned a Ph.D. in Management at the University of Groningen in the Netherlands with a dissertation titled 'Strategic Interactions in Franchise Relationships'. Currently, Evelien is an Assistant Professor at the Department of Innovation Management and Strategy of the Faculty of Economics and Business at the University of Groningen. She mainly teaches about small business strategy and management, entrepreneurship, innovation and franchising. Her research is focused on franchising, and more specifically on strategy, management and performance on both the level of franchise systems and the level of units/franchisees. Evelien has published in peer-reviewed journals, including *Entrepreneurship, Theory and Practice*, *Journal of Small Business Management* and *Journal of Business Ethics*.

Alfredo De Massis is Director of the Centre for Family Business at IEED, Lancaster University Management School (UK), and a former Professor at the University of Bergamo (Italy), where he co-founded the Center for Young and Family Enterprise (CYFE), which he ran as Deputy Director until September 2013. He serves as Chair of the European Leadership Council and Global Board Member of the Global STEP Project for Family Enterprising. His research interests include innovation management and organizational goal-setting in family firms. On these topics, he has published widely in leading academic and professional journals, including *Entrepreneurship Theory and Practice*, *Journal of Product Innovation Management*, *Journal of Small Business Management* and *Family Business Review*. He has been TOFT Professor at CeFEO/JIBS (Sweden), and a management consultant in Accenture and SCS Consulting.

Clay Dibrell is an Associate Professor of Management at the University of Mississippi, a research fellow with the Australian Centre for Family Business at Bond University, and a US Fulbright Scholar. He earned his Ph.D. from the University of Memphis where he majored in Strategic Management and minored in International Business. Areas of research interest include innovation, stewardship and family enterprises. His research has been published in leading academic journals, including *Entrepreneurship Theory and Practice*, *Journal of Small Business Management*, *Family Business Review*, *Journal of Family Business Strategy*, *Journal of Business Research*, *Small Business Economics* and *Journal of World Business*.

Ahmet Murat Fiş received his Ph.D. in Management from Sabancı University (2009). Dr Fiş is Assistant Professor in Entrepreneurship, and currently serves as Head of the Entrepreneurship Department, and Coordinator of the Master in Entrepreneurship Program at Özyeğin University. Dr Fiş's interdisciplinary research interests include entrepreneurship, the effects of organizational culture on various organizational phenomenon, and strategic orientations and the firm-wide outcomes of these strategic orientations. His recent research focuses on corporate entrepreneurship in particular, in which he aims to reveal the underlying factors behind firm-level entrepreneurship and its outcomes. He has presented his work at various national and international conferences, and has a book chapter besides articles published in refereed journals. His teaching interests parallel his research concentration.

Elias Hadjielias is Lecturer in Entrepreneurship at the University of Central Lancashire, Cyprus (UCLan Cyprus). He has a Ph.D. from Lancaster University (UK) in 'Cooperation and Collective Entrepreneurial Learning in Family Business Organizations'. Elias is Course Leader of BA (Hons) Business Administration and Director of CEDAR, the Centre of Entrepreneurial Development, Alliance and Research at UCLan Cyprus. Elias teaches entrepreneurship and management at both the postgraduate and undergraduate levels. His research interests revolve around collective entrepreneurship, entrepreneurial learning, family business, and intra and inter-group cooperation. He has also consulting experience in startups and new venture development.

Søren Henning Jensen holds a B.Sc. EBA, an M.Sc. in Business Administration and Strategic Management and a Ph.D. from Copenhagen Business School (CBS), where he currently works as Associate Professor in Strategy and Leadership. He has conducted research in entrepreneurship, looking to shed further light on issues such as entrepreneurial orientation, differences in family and non-family firms and entrepreneurship in knowledge-intensive companies. Søren Henning Jensen has published a book and several articles based on his research. In addition to his research activities, he is managing a master's programme in International Marketing and Management (IMM). He also teaches strategy, leadership and innovation management on both master's and executive programmes.

Sascha Kraus is Professor for Entrepreneurship at the University of Liechtenstein and Extraordinary Chairholder/Professor for Entrepreneurship at Utrecht University, the Netherlands. He is also Guest Professor at Twente University, the Netherlands, and the Autonomous University of Barcelona, Spain. Before his current positions, he was Evald and Hilda Nissi Foundation International Fellow at the University of Vaasa, Finland, and Substitute Professor at the Salzburg University of Applied Sciences, Austria.

Clare Kurian is a doctoral candidate in the area of organizational behaviour and human resource management at the Indian Institute of Management, Bangalore. She also holds a bachelor's degree in technology from the National Institute of Technology, Calicut. Her current research interests focus on topics such as human resource policies and planning in emerging economies, strategic human resource management, leadership, employee engagement and organizational socialization. Prior to her doctoral work, she worked for almost four years in the IT software industry.

Mathew J. Manimala is a Professor of Organization Behaviour and Chairperson-OBHRM Area at the Indian Institute of Management Bangalore (IIMB), India. At IIMB he has worked closely with the N. S. Raghavan Centre for Entrepreneurial Learning (NSRCEL) primarily to build the research competencies of the Centre during its early years, when he served as the Jamuna Raghavan Chair Professor of Entrepreneurship for two terms and as the Chairperson of NSRCEL for one term. He has received several academic honours, including a Certificate of Distinction for Outstanding Research in the Field of New Enterprise Development (Heizer Award) from the Academy of Management. He is a member of the editorial board of several journals and the Editor of *South Asian Journal of Management*.

Tommaso Minola is co-founder and Deputy Director of the Center for Young and Family Enterprise (CYFE) at the University of Bergamo (Italy), and national representative for the GUESSS (Global University Entrepreneurial Spirit Students' Survey) consortium. He performs research in Entrepreneurship, Family Business and Technological Innovation, looking at how entrepreneurs benefit from family as a unique resource during venturing, innovation and strategic renewal processes. His works appeared in refereed entrepreneurship and innovation journals, such as *R&D Management, Journal of Technology Transfer, International Journal of Entrepreneurship and Innovation Management, International Journal of Small Business and Entrepreneurship*. He is Director of the Go.In' International Entrepreneurship Course at the University of Bergamo School of Management and has been supporting small and medium enterprises and new firms' development through innovation and new technologies.

John M. Mueller is a doctoral candidate majoring in Entrepreneurship at the University of Louisville. His research interests include entrepreneurial finance, and technology and sport entrepreneurship, with his dissertation addressing whether it is beneficial for new firms to be resourceful in their financing. He has founded several businesses in the software and golf industries. Before entering the entrepreneur ranks, he worked at the executive level as well as in the operational ranks, including programming and testing software applications. His work experiences have allowed him to live and work in the United States, Europe, the Middle East and Africa, including serving as a US representative to South African companies in the capacity of adviser and consultant on business linkages, partnering and financing for small and medium businesses.

Henrietta Onwuegbuzie is currently the Academic Director for the Owner-Manager Programme and Project Director for the Impact Investing policy initiative at the Lagos Business School. She has an M.Sc. in Economics and Business Administration from the University of Navarre in Spain and an MBA from Lagos Business School. Prior to joining the LBS faculty, she managed non-profit educational projects for the development of women in different states in Nigeria. Subsequently, she worked in the banking sector with key responsibilities in corporate banking. Henrietta is a member of the Governing Council of the African Forum in Brussels, and sits on the Board of a number of Nigerian companies. She was recently conferred the 2013 African Women Development Champion Award by the Centre for Economic and Leadership Development.

Panikkos Poutziouris is Professor of Entrepreneurship and Family Business at the University of Central Lancashire, Cyprus (UCLan Cyprus), the Enterprising British University in Cyprus. Panikkos is Head of the School of Business and Management and Chair of CEDAR, the Centre of Entrepreneurial Development, Alliance and Research at UCLan Cyprus. He has served for almost two decades on the Faculty of Manchester Business School, University of Manchester (UK) as Fellow in SME Management, Senior Lecturer in Entrepreneurship and Visiting Associate Professor for Family Business Initiatives. Professor Poutziouris lectures, coaches, researches, publishes and advises internationally on Entrepreneurship and Strategic Development of Family Businesses and Business Families.

Martina Rašticová, Ph.D., is a social and organizational psychologist. She graduated from Masaryk University, Brno, in 2004 (Ph.D. studies). In 2006 and 2007 she received a scholarship at George Washington University, Washington, DC, USA. She is currently leading the Institute of Management at the Faculty of Business and Management of Brno University of Technology. Her professional interests includes diversity management, social and cross-cultural psychology, and leadership. She regularly publishes in Czech and international scientific journals.

Neusa Maria Bastos F. Santos is a Full Professor of Management and Organization at the School of Business of the Pontificial Catholic University of São Paulo (PUCSP). She was a Fulbright Scholar (CIES) at the Gerald Ross Business School, University of Michigan, and Visiting Professor at McGill University, Canada, under the Faculty Research Program sponsored by the International Council of Canadian Studies (ICCS). She received her Ph.D. from the University of São Paulo (USP). Dr Santos also serves as the Director of the Master Program in Accounting and

Finance at PUCSP. Her research interests are focused on entrepreneurship in its forms and approaches, and their consequences in the workplace, organization and society, cross-cultural management, corporate culture and governance. Her work has appeared in many academic journals, including *Career Development International, Women in Management Review, Management Research News, Employee Relations* and in Brazilian leading journals.

Carlos Eduardo de Sousa is currently a Ph.D. student in the Management Department at Pontifícia Universidade Católica de São Paulo (PUC/SP), Brazil. His work focuses on research that involves issues of fairness, equity and morality in organizational interactions and behaviour. His three main topics of interest are diversity, organizational justice and ethical behaviour. In 2008, he received his master's degree in Education from Harvard University, USA. Carlo has served in different academic commissions, including Harvard's Student Government Association (Vice President, Diversity), Harvard's Office of Student Affairs (Multi-cultural Advisory Council member) and the Harvard Graduate Council. Carlos is currently a Jorge Paulo Lemann Fellow and member of the Academy of Management.

Carlos Denner dos Santos Jr is an Adjunct Professor of the Department of Management at the Universidade de Brasília (UnB), Brazil. He has previously worked as a Research Fellow in the Horizon Digital Economy Research Institute at the University of Nottingham, UK. Carlos earned his Master's in Strategic Management from Universidade Federal de Minas Gerais (UFMG), Brazil; Ph.D. in Management Information Systems as a Fulbright Scholar from Southern Illinois University at Carbondale, USA; and post-doctorate in Computer Science from the Universidade de São Paulo (USP), Brazil. His research interests include Open Innovation, Free and Open Source Software, Adoption and Diffusion of Information Technology and Innovation, Statistical Methods, and Organizational Theory.

Roberto Fernandes dos Santos received his Ph.D. and master's degree in Controllership and Accounting from the Universidade de São Paulo, Brazil, and his bachelor's degrees in Engineering, Business Administration and Accounting from the same university. Dr Santos is a Full Professor at the Pontifícia Universidade Católica de São Paulo (PUC/SP), Brazil, where he serves on the Graduate Studies in Controllership and Finance; he is also a professor in the undergraduate degree in Controllership and Accounting from the Universidade de São Paulo. He also serves as the Director of the Master Program in Accounting and Finance at PUC/SP. Dr Santos has extensive professional experience in Controllership, working in important multinational groups in Brazil.

Arnis Sauka joined SSE Riga as a research fellow in 2005. At the beginning of 2008 Arnis Sauka earned a Ph.D. in Business Administration (*magna cum laude*) from the University of Siegen (Germany). Prior to that, Arnis was a visiting Ph.D. candidate at Jönköping International Business School (Sweden) and a teaching fellow at SSEES/University College London (UK). From 2011 to 2013 Arnis was Academic Vice-Rector at Ventspils University College where he established the Centre for Entrepreneurship Innovation and Regional Development. His research findings have been published in a number of peer-reviewed books and journals, and presented at numerous European and North American conferences. His main research interests include productive and unproductive entrepreneurship, business startups, growth and exits, entrepreneurship policy-making and entrepreneurship in transition context.

Duygu Seckin Halac is a graduate business student at the Graduate School of Yasar University, Turkey.

Chellie Spiller, of Ngāti Kahungunu and Pākehā lineage, researches, writes and lectures at the University of Auckland Business School. Her Ph.D. investigated how Māori businesses create authentic and sustainable wealth and well-being. Chellie was a Fulbright Senior Scholar at the Harvard Kennedy School and the University of Arizona between November 2011 and March 2012. She is a recipient of a 2011 Dame Mira Szászy Māori Alumni Award, 2011 National Māori Academic Excellence Award, and 2010 AuSM Best Lecturer Award, AUT University. Her publications reflect an abiding respect for authentic leadership, indigenous entrepreneurship, and relational well-being and wealth. Chellie has two books forthcoming, one on indigenous spiritualties at work and the other on wayfinding and the craft of celestial navigation.

Janine Swail is a lecturer in Innovation and Entrepreneurship at Nottingham University Business School within the University of Nottingham Institute for Enterprise and Innovation (UNIEI). Prior to joining UNIEI in February 2013 she was a lecturer in Entrepreneurship at Newcastle University Business School (2007–2013) and completed her Ph.D. in gender and nascent entrepreneurship at the University of Ulster (2003–2007). Janine's research interests are in nascent entrepreneurship, and in particular how women navigate the entrepreneurial process. She is also interested in the role of media and culture in influencing entrepreneurial intentions, particularly among young people. She is currently on the Board of Trustees for the Institute of Small Business and Entrepreneurship (ISBE), which is the network for people and organizations involved in small business and entrepreneurship research, policy, education, support and advice.

Christine Vallaster is Associate Professor at the University of Liechtenstein. She received her postdoctoral lecture qualification (Habilitation) from the University of Innsbruck, Austria. She publishes regularly in academic journals, including *Business Horizons, European Journal of Management, Journal of Marketing Management* and *Qualitative Research: An International Journal*. For practitioners, her contributions appeared in journals like *Harvard Business Manager*. Additionally, she works as a consultant.

Kishinchand Poornima Wasdani is a doctoral scholar at the Department of Management Studies, Indian Institute of Science (IISc), Bangalore, India. Prior to joining the doctoral programme of IISc, she has worked as Assistant Professor at Saint Gits College of Engineering, Kerala, India. She is also the Associate Editor of *South Asian Journal of Management*. Her research interest is in the area of Entrepreneurship, especially the sources and process of Opportunity Recognition in the different stages of venture creation and management.

Friederike Welter is President of the IfM Bonn (Institut für Mittelstandsforschung) and Professor for SME management and entrepreneurship at the University of Siegen, Germany. She is Visiting Professor at Jönköping International Business School in Sweden and at the Small Business Research Centre at Kingston University in Kingston, UK. Her research interests are entrepreneurial behaviour and policies in different contexts and women entrepreneurship. Friederike is on the review board of several leading entrepreneurship journals as well as editor of *Entrepreneurship Theory and Practice*. She is a Fellow of the European Council of Small Business and Entrepreneurship (ECSB) and Wilford L. White Fellow of the International Council of Small Business (ICSB).

PREFACE

Economic development is a priority for all nations, which they try to achieve primarily by promoting entrepreneurship and new venture creation. This is important even for the developed nations, as the economy would stagnate if there were no new ventures. New ventures in an economy serve a function similar to that of new sprouts in an ecosystem. While the new venture creation is primarily a function of the entrepreneurial orientation and volition of the individual, the survival and growth of the venture will depend largely on the quality of the entrepreneurial environment in a country or the 'entrepreneurial framework conditions' (EFCs), as they are designated by the Global Entrepreneurship Monitor (GEM) project. The GEM 2013 document defines nine such EFCs, which are as follows: (1) financial support to new firms; (2) government policy on new firms; (3) government programmes for new firms; (4) education and training support; (5) research and development transfer; (6) commercial, legal and professional infrastructure; (7) market openness and ease of entry; (8) adequacy of physical infrastructure; (9) appropriateness of social and cultural norms.[1]

The above list of factors is illustrative of the complexity of the entrepreneurial environment and its 'difficult-to-predict' impact on new venture creation. More importantly, these factors and their relative strengths and weaknesses will vary significantly across nations and therefore may have differential impact on the creation, survival and growth of new ventures. In an era of globalization, it would be useful for all concerned (entrepreneurs, researchers, consultants as well as policy-makers) to appreciate the characteristics of the entrepreneurial environment and relate them to entrepreneurial actions in different countries. It is with the intention of painting a broad scenario of entrepreneurship in different countries that we have undertaken a project to publish a case-book containing entrepreneurship cases from different countries. Accordingly, we have assembled such cases on fifteen different enterprises from as many different countries. Authors invited to contribute are all members of

TABLE 0.1 Cases and issues along with the countries of origin and industries

Chapter no.	Country & Case	Industry	Topics/issues
1	**Brazil** Business incubation and the PipeWay business case	Oil and gas (pipeline inspection and repairs)	• Niche-based service ventures • Startups competing with MNCs • Strategies for capability building – internal development versus acquisition
2	**Cyprus** From family business to business family: the strategic development of Zorbas – Master Bakers	Bakery	• Family business – growth and professionalization • Entrepreneurship as a process • Social responsibility of business
3	**Czech Republic** ALUCAST s.r.o.	Aluminium casting	• High-tech ventures and technology upgradation • Environmental issues and CSR in new-venture creation • Quality and capability development in SMEs • Succession planning
4	**Denmark** Noma	Restaurant	• Ethnic business • Expertise development • Enterprise growth • Internationalization
5	**Hong Kong** AML	Engineering (manufacturing)	• Family business – professionalization and succession management • Enterprise growth and internationalization • Fostering entrepreneurship in family firm
6	**India** Terumo-Penpol	Biomedical devices (manufacturing)	• R&D-based startup in a developing economy • Ecosystem for high-tech entrepreneurship • Startup phases and processes • Growth and internationalization
7	**Italy** Italcementi Group	Cement (manufacturing)	• Transgenerational family entrepreneurship

TABLE 0.1 *continued*

Chapter no.	Country & Case	Industry	Topics/issues
			• Social innovation as entrepreneurial outcome • Environmental and sustainability issues • Industry–government collaboration in CSR
8	**Latvia** Furnitura Ltd	Furniture and home interiors	• Business failure versus entrepreneurial failure • Strategies for expansion and growth • Management education/ experience and new venture creation
9	**Liechtenstein** The Liechtenstein Brewing Co.	Brewery	• Marketing of new venture product: entry strategies for small-country product in big-country market • Competing with MNCs – pricing strategy • Internationalization
10	**Netherlands**	Eat & Enjoy	• Food and cooking products • Strategic management of new ventures • Franchising • Internationalization • Business failure
11	**New Zealand** Whale Watch Kaikoura	Eco-tourism	• Community entrepreneurship • Eco-friendly business • Entrepreneurship and regional development • Alternate business strategies • Sustainable business growth
12	**Nigeria** Indigenous entrepreneurship in Nigeria: growing from scratch	Automobile spare parts (import, retail, wholesale and manufacture)	• Entrepreneurship training – apprenticeship versus classroom instruction • Family business • Professionalization of family business • Growth and diversification

TABLE 0.1 *continued*

Chapter no.	Country & Case	Industry	Topics/issues
13	**Turkey** The Academy of Culinary Arts	Vocational training	• Academic/institutional entrepreneurship • Social entrepreneurship • Growth strategies • Internationalization
14	**United Kingdom** Barefruit Products: a case of entrepreneurial failure in the UK agri-food sector	Agri-food	• Business plans and planned business • Systematic search for business opportunities • Training for venture creation • Business failures and learning from them
15	**USA** Wynkoop Brewing Company	Craft brewery	• Entrepreneurship and community development • Green business • Lifestyle business • Growth strategies for traditional/lifestyle business

the 'Ambassadors' Program' of the Entrepreneurship Division of the Academy of Management. The titles of the cases, along with the countries and industries they represent and the topics and issues discussed in them, are given in Table 0.1.

The cases are drawn from countries that are at various levels of economic development, broadly classified as developed and developing. Within the latter, one could make further classifications such as emerging (e.g. Brazil, India) and transitional (e.g. Czech Republic, Latvia) economies. There are also wide variations in the geographical sizes and population of these countries. The principality of Liechtenstein, with an area of 160 sq km and a population of about 35,000 is the smallest. In contrast, countries such as the United States, Brazil and India are large in terms of land area as well as population. Obviously, the entrepreneurial opportunities and constraints under such vastly varying business environments would be of a different nature.

The industries represented in this volume of cases also offer some variety. It is not surprising that many of them are low-tech ventures such as breweries, bakeries, restaurants, food products and the like, especially because entrepreneurs sometimes use low-tech startups as an entry strategy where the chances and costs of failure are likely to be low. Among the high-tech ones are products/services such as biomedical devices, high-precision casting, advanced machine tools and engineering plastics, and pipeline inspection and repair using robots. There are also interesting combinations of low-tech products with high-tech processes, as in the case of Furnitura (the Latvian enterprise), where the product (furniture and home interiors) are traditional but the order placing by customers and subsequently the custom manufacturing of the order are computer controlled. About two-thirds of the cases included in this volume are product companies. Although the service companies are few, they represent some unique and emerging services such as robotic inspection and repair of oil and gas pipelines (Brazil), vocational training (Turkey) and eco-tourism (New Zealand).

The cases discuss a large number of themes and issues concerning new venture creation. The dominant ones are: management of family business with special emphasis on transgenerational growth, professionalization and succession management; strategies for marketing new venture products and services, especially when competing with large and established players, including multinational companies; strategies for growth, especially through expansion, diversification, franchising and internationalization; developing and retaining human capital as required for the various stages in the startup and growth of the enterprise; corporate social responsibility of entrepreneurial ventures and family business, which is demonstrated through the development of green and sustainable ventures developed in collaboration with and for the benefit of local communities with the objective of regional development; technology development, management and upgradation, especially in the context of R&D-based or niche-based startups; the role of management education/experience as well as entrepreneurship education and training in facilitating opportunity identification, business planning, startup processes and growth management; business failures as distinct from entrepreneurial failures and the possibilities of learning from them.

The last-mentioned issue (business failure) could be seen as a special feature of this volume. Case-books about entrepreneurs often tend to be the documentation of success stories. While it is a legitimate exercise from the perspective of presenting role models to potential entrepreneurs as well as for highlighting the success factors to enlighten policy-makers, it should not be forgotten that business failures are a fact of life. In fact, they are more common than successes – according to various estimates presented in an article recently published in *The Wall Street Journal*,[2] about 40 per cent of new ventures fail within three years and about 65 per cent fail within ten years, not counting the stagnant and the loss-making survivors. It would therefore be an educative experience to look at failure cases, so we have included three of them (that is, the cases from Latvia, the Netherlands and the United Kingdom). Entrepreneurs themselves claim to have learned a lot from their failure experiences, which are not unusual even for successful ones. It should be noted that business failures need not always lead to entrepreneurial failures.

It is our ardent hope that the wide range of countries, industries, themes and issues represented in this case-book would help our readers to appreciate the complexity of interactions among the various constituents of the entrepreneurial ecosystem. This book will be a source of useful insights to entrepreneurs, entrepreneurship educators at all levels (undergraduate, graduate and executive), researchers and policy-makers, especially for those involved with the process of internationalization of entrepreneurial ventures, which in fact is a recurring theme in these cases, and a fitting one too in this era of globalization. We dedicate this volume to the international entrepreneurs (both existing and intending ones) and thank the contributing authors from fifteen different countries for making this case-book possible.

Notes

1 Available online at: www.gemconsortium.org (accessed 27 January 2014).
2 Available online at: http://online.wsj.com/news/articles/SB1000087239639044372020 4578004980476429190 (accessed 28 January 2014).

1

BUSINESS INCUBATION AND THE PIPEWAY BUSINESS CASE IN BRAZIL

Neusa Maria Bastos F. Santos, Carlos Eduardo de Sousa, Carlos Denner dos Santos Jr and Roberto Fernandes Santos

Entrepreneurs often face the challenge of leveraging resources to advance novel business ideas and develop their business. Entrepreneurial initiatives often demand new spaces that can both shelter the development and accelerate the consolidation of innovative businesses. In Brazil, ever since 1984, parks for the development of technology have been created in order to address these issues by hosting technology-based companies that were constituted through agreements with the National Council for Scientific and Technological Development (CNPq). These parks were first founded in specific cities such as São Carlos in the state of São Paulo, Joinville in the state of Santa Catarina, Campina Grande in the state of Paraíba, Manaus in the state of Amazonas and Santa Maria in the state of Rio Grande do Sul. These early experiments led to the creation of new parks in many different regions of Brazil.

With the creation of industrial clusters and technology parks, the emergence of the concept of incubators for technology-based companies was a natural consequence. Business incubators are non-profit organizations where a flexible and supportive environment is established to help not only the emergence but also the growth of enterprises (Dornelas, 2002). As the name implies, business incubators are designed to provide a nurturing environment for the growth and development of starting enterprises, hence promoting entrepreneurship, business formation and innovation. These incubators help their entrepreneurial companies by providing them with business infrastructure (e.g. affordable workspace, shared facilities), knowledge base for learning and researching (e.g. counseling, training, information), and access to professional networks and community involvement (Lalkaka, 2003).

The Batavia Industrial Center, located in the Finger Lakes region of Upstate New York, is widely recognized as the first business incubator, founded in 1959

(Adkins, 2002). The Mancuso family purchased an old manufacturing plant in hopes to rent it to a single tenant and eventually decided to divide the space up into smaller offices that could be used by small companies. At the time, Joseph Mancuso decided to provide these small enterprises not only with accounting help but also to assist them with raising capital and other business assistance services (Adkins, 2002). Since then, the idea of aggregating young companies under one roof and providing them with the conditions for survival and growth has gained great popularity.

Business incubation has experienced rapid worldwide growth over the years. The National Business Incubation Association (NBIA) reports that, by 1980, there were 12–15 incubators operating in the United States. As of 2006, there were over 1,400 business incubators in North America and about 7,000 incubators worldwide (Knopp, 2007).

With the help of incubators, entrepreneurs are better equipped with a comprehensive service portfolio to turn their business ideas into successful companies potentially capable of long-term survival and sustainable growth. In fact, research conducted by the NBIA, the University of Michigan, the Southern Technology Council, and Ohio University[1] has shown that business incubators reduce the risk of business failures. Business incubators also have a tremendous potential for regional development, job and wealth creation, and entrepreneurship promotion.

A growing number of incubators in Brazil turn enterprises into successful companies, such as the case of focus PipeWay, a company initially hosted by the incubator Pontifical Catholic University in Rio de Janeiro (PUC-RIO). The PUC-RIO incubator is a national reference in the promotion of entrepreneurship and welcomed this new enterprise constituted in 1998. PipeWay demonstrated that its success was the product of PUC-RIO incubator's support combined with its own unique vision and entrepreneurial behavior. As a result, PipeWay was accredited with the ANPROTEC award for being the best incubated company of the year 2000.

Entrepreneurship in Brazil

Entrepreneurship has become essential for the growth and development of countries, especially because of its potential to impact a country's competitiveness and rate of new jobs creation (Amorós *et al.*, 2011). In the 2010 edition of the Global Entrepreneurship Monitor Brazil report (GEM/Brazil report[2]), a comprehensive assessment of the current entrepreneurial activity, aspirations and attitudes of individuals across Brazil was reported. Given the importance of entrepreneurship for the well-being of a society, the picture of entrepreneurial activity in Brazil painted by the GEM assessment proves informative. Understanding the trends of entrepreneurial activity in Brazil may help diagnose the future economic health of the country.

Total Early-Stage Entrepreneurial Activity (TEA)

The TEA index is a measure of the percentage of a country's working population (ages 18–64) currently involved in the creation of new business enterprises (i.e. businesses with less than 42 months of existence). The 2010 GEM Brazil report shows a national TEA index of 17.5 percent, the equivalent of 21.1 million Brazilian entrepreneurs in 2010. Among the countries that constitute not only the Group of Twenty Finance Ministers and Central Bank Governors (also known as the G-20) but also the BRIC countries (i.e. Brazil, Russia, India and China), Brazil stands as having the largest TEA, followed by China with a TEA index of 14.4 percent and Argentina with 14.2 percent.

Entrepreneurial attitudes and perceptions

The GEM Global Report (Kelley *et al.*, 2010) summarizes the importance of a society's entrepreneurial attitudes:

- A society can benefit from people who are able to recognize valuable business opportunities, and who perceive they have the required skills to exploit them. Moreover, if the economy in general has positive attitudes toward entrepreneurship, this will generate cultural support, financial resources, networking benefits and various other forms of assistance to current and potential entrepreneurs (p. 17).
- Among Brazilians, the GEM measured the perception of *opportunities and intentions to start a business*. On average, it found that the percentage of the country's adult population, ages 18–64, that believed there would be good opportunities for starting a business in their area equals 48.1 percent. The GEM also assessed *fear of failure*, finding that only 33.2 percent of working Brazilians fear starting a business. As for the *perceptions about entrepreneurship* measure, the GEM found that: (1) entrepreneurship in 2010 was a desirable career choice for more than 78 percent of the Brazilian respondents; (2) Brazil's perceptions regarding the status of an entrepreneur were the highest (79 percent) in the efficiency-driven Latin American countries; and (3) the perception of media attention given to entrepreneurs was also high, with 81.1 percent of participants responding that they constantly see stories of successful entrepreneurs being reported by the media.

Entrepreneurial aspirations

One of the most significant GEM measures used to assess the entrepreneurial aspirations of entrepreneurs about their new business is job creation. Among Brazilian entrepreneurs, 36 percent of the respondents had no expectation of creating new jobs within the following 5 years, and 23 percent had the goal of generating 6 or more job opportunities within the same time period. This means that in the next

5 years, of the 21.1 million Brazilian entrepreneurs in 2010, 4.9 million believe they will be able to generate 6 or more job opportunities. This represents a 15.2 percent increase in the percentage of the aspiration relative to the previous year (GEM Brazil Report, p. 11).

Conditions surrounding entrepreneurship in Brazil

Although Brazil is a very promising emerging market with an enthusiastic entrepreneurial mindset, there is significant room for improvement, particularly in the policy realm. In 2011, Brazil ranked 126 out of 183 economies in the *Ease of Doing Business* index calculated by the World Bank's Doing Business project (World Bank, 2011). The same report indicates that starting a business in Brazil takes 120 days, which represents double the average amount of time for Latin American and Caribbean countries, and is far worse than the average 13 days for the member countries of the Organization for Economic Co-operation and Development (OECD countries). According to the 2010 GEM Brazil Report, Brazilian entrepreneurs also face the lack of governmental policies and programs for entrepreneurship support, a complex tax system and difficulties in access to loans. Moreover, entrepreneurship (lack of) education is also a limiting factor. Nevertheless, specialists particularly emphasize social and cultural norms as well as a favorable economic environment as some significant positive conditions surrounding entrepreneurship in Brazil.

The country's economic growth has had a tremendous impact on factors surrounding entrepreneurship in Brazil. The country's levels of necessity versus opportunity-based entrepreneurship demonstrate this. The proportion of startup entrepreneurs who have identified their motives as based on necessity decreased from 5.9 percent to 5.4 percent relative to 2009; on the other hand, a more stable market, with controlled inflation and economic growth has enabled opportunity-based businesses to thrive.

The PipeWay business case

Historical background

PipeWay Ltd is in the business of inspecting and cleaning gas and oil pipelines. PipeWay's history starts in the labs of the Pontifical Catholic University of Rio de Janeiro (PUC–RIO), where a conjoint research project was underway with the support of Petrobras, a Brazilian company with operations that cover extraction, refinery and distribution of oil and gas in every continent. Initially, Petrobras provided the technology through licensing and sponsorship, and PUC-RIO researchers entered with expertise and innovative approaches for pipeline inspection. As this partnership evolved and more ideas were generated, the researchers applied for support from the Genesis business incubator at PUC-RIO (a national reference in the promotion of entrepreneurship), where the company was then created in

1998, enjoying infrastructure and managerial support until its "graduation" in 1999 (Simoes, 2005). From that moment on, PipeWay, Petrobras and Genesis formed a network of organizations that would result in the development of many innovative products and processes that led to the international success of PipeWay.

Details of the PipeWay business case

PipeWay's pipeline inspection gauges (PIGs) are robots that have the capability of autonomously running through the pipelines to identify leakages, corrosion and other anomalies using ultrasound and magnetic technology for about 48 hours uninterruptedly (Costa, 2010). The data collected by the robot sensors are stored in the embedded computer with real-time software while the pipeline is inspected. After the robot is retrieved from the inspection, the data collected are transferred to a computer equipped with the tool that configures the robot, generates reports and allows the visualization of the anomalies identified in the inspection (i.e. an information system to support decision-making).

The computer model in the proprietary information system developed by PipeWay presents the defects in three dimensions, according to the shape of the magnetic field created and read by the robot in the pipeline (flux signal characteristics), and informs the exact location of these defects (Gloria *et al.*, 2009). Based on that report and the severity of the anomalies, engineers can evaluate the status of the pipelines to plan maintenance activities, and prevent accidents and damages, saving financial and environmental costs, and minimizing human exposition to hazardous conditions (Silva *et al.*, 2004). PipeWay is the only manufacturer of PIGs in the whole southern hemisphere (Costa, 2010).

PipeWay's business model and competitive success are based on meeting clients' specific needs. PipeWay does not sell robots; it offers information as a service, which requires working closely with the client to identify specific pipeline characteristics and then customize the robots to work in their unique settings (Simoes, 2005). Dealing with customers individually, PipeWay is capable of gathering timely data and providing the client with valuable and trustworthy information that can be used to monitor pipes for effective planning of maintenance activities and logistics. To maintain this customer-oriented business model, PipeWay is required to innovate in order to expand its customer base, as its operations and products need to be adapted and reinvented every time a client with unique needs is to be serviced. However, that is a rewarding challenge to face, and PipeWay, aimed at growth and internationalization, has developed this competence to diagnose and innovate that is perhaps the source of its competitive advantage. The trigger for the learning process of this competence has roots in the very early times of the company.

Since its germination stage, PipeWay works closely with future clients to identify needs and opportunities to innovate, offering customized services. In the interactions with Petrobras in the late 80s, during the "lab days," the founders of PipeWay identified two important needs that were not met by the market at the time (Costa, 2010). The need to develop a 3-inch PIG, as the smallest available in the market was of 4 inches and thus could not fit many pipes, especially those in Canada (Silva *et al.*, 2001), and the need of having a multisensor magnetic PIG that could be more precise in describing anomalies. PipeWay created the 3-inch and the multisensor PIGs, fulfilling Petrobras's demand and a gap in the market, thereby opening its own niche by differentiation and allowing the company to attract about $1.2 million in investments from public research institutions and be exempted from taxes in 2004.[3]

This early success taught PipeWay the valuable lesson that its customers vary in needs, and pipes in diameter and thickness, requiring tailored services and products developed on demand (Simoes, 2005). In such a market, attempts to standardize and sell products for gains of scale are likely to fail, and success is based on continuous development and improvement.[4] This pressure to innovate generates opportunities for research, and the development of new products becomes a natural consequence. Accordingly, PipeWay has also created a robot that inspects the pipeline externally, as some oil companies have pipelines with shapes that make them "non-piggable" —that is, PipeWay found out that its current technology did not allow for internal inspection of wavy pipes by doing research with the customer, and, innovatively, once more, created a new product around an unmet need. Curiously, this line of products is named "GIP," the inverse of "PIG," which inspects pipelines internally. Many other products were developed (e.g. the ultrasound-based scanner), and this increasing spectrum of robots has allowed PipeWay to expand its customer base and internationalize its operations by creating a subsidiary in alliance with other countries' companies, such as the PipeWay International Inc. founded in the United States, and PipeWay Argentina (Costa, 2010).

In 2008, 60 percent of PipeWay's revenue stream came from overseas, whereas in 1999 this number was of about 4 percent. Currently, PipeWay has about 40 different PIGs and over 80 employees; it is doing business in more than 10 countries, where another number of indirect jobs were created, and had sales in the order of $6 million in 2010, which accounts for 80 percent of the Brazilian market and half of this country's pipelines.[5]

PipeWay invests 10 percent of its revenues on average in research and development, and is planning to increase this percentage to around 12 percent, thanks to its market orientation and the characteristics of its employees and owners, who are capable of transforming ideas into products. To achieve such level of success in understanding and meeting its market-changing demands, PipeWay counts with a highly educated team of directors, who are engineers and physicists with master's and Ph.D. degrees. Besides that, PipeWay opted for an internal organizational structure with only a few levels of hierarchy (directors and collaborators), allowing for a fast and noiseless communication that leads to effective decision-making processes. Furthermore, to meet the specific challenges of continuous innovation, PipeWay focuses on building close relationships with customers and various organizations. Nowadays, it collaborates with about 13 organizations, ranging from universities, research centers, associations and private companies. This configuration affects the bottom line of the business, keeping PipeWay ahead of its competitors and opening new markets constantly.

The outcomes in the case company

PipeWay began its operations in a small room with only seven employees in the Genesis business incubator at PUC-RIO. Today, the company operates in a large facility, where a team of about dozens of specialists, technical experts and researchers develop and produce its tools for pipeline inspections (e.g. PIGs, GIPs, and others). PipeWay maintains strong relationships with many research centers, including Cenpes of Petrobras. As we discussed, per year, PipeWay invests around 12 percent of its revenues in studies of new technologies. Thanks to his innovative ideas and entrepreneurial spirit, José Augusto Pereira da Silva (PipeWay's cofounder and CEO) received many awards, including being named the Ernst and Young Entrepreneur of the Year in 2003 (emerging category). After being accredited with the ANPROTEC Award as the best incubated company of the year 2000, PipeWay was more recently presented with the FINEP award for Technological Innovation in 2004. PipeWay received this national accolade in the Small Company category by the hands of Brazil's president at the time, Luiz Inácio Lula da Silva.

In the global market, PipeWay has also achieved noteworthy influence. PipeWay initially entered the Latin American market through its network of relationships in Argentina, which spread to Uruguay and later helped PipeWay to win contracts with Chile, Bolivia and Venezuela, among others (Magacho and Costa, 2010). This internationalization of PipeWay was a natural consequence of the evolution of its tools and the profits generated from its international contracts. Currently, PipeWay has great interest in the US market, demonstrated through the creation of its subsidiary, PipeWay International Inc.

PipeWay's growth and success has an interesting effect that goes beyond the benefits for the company itself. As several of PipeWay's products were developed conjointly with Petrobras and Genesis, royalties are constantly paid to these partners (Simoes, 2005; Costa, 2010). This scheme of technology licensing adopted by PipeWay, Genesis and Petrobras allows the reinvestment in innovation, as Genesis incubates several new ideas to transform them in companies, and Petrobras faces the research challenge of constantly finding and extracting oil safely for the environment and society in new and adverse conditions. Having these indirect effects, PipeWay's success creates the opportunity for new ideas to be tested and flourish in the marketplace, giving rise to products, processes and companies that together create innovative services and thus benefit the economy in general. Nevertheless, PipeWay's competitive environment is complex and uncertain, as its competitors are also in the quest for innovation, and the recent run towards alternative sources of energy can threaten the long-term existence of this niche of gas and oil pipelines. How PipeWay should address these new challenges ahead have no easy answer, but it seems appropriate to assume that the company should continue to monitor the business environment at the same time that it invests in the development of its collaborators' and partners' capabilities to nurture the network of organizations it thrives to continue to be at the hub of.

PipeWay's future: directions and challenges

One area that PipeWay seeks constant improvement is in the compilation and presentation of the data its robots gather during the inspection. An inspection may result in over one million corrosion defects, which makes organizing and prioritizing their treatment according to severity a complex and time-consuming computational task. Hence, one of PipeWay's challenges is to optimize this process by means of automation without jeopardizing safety, accuracy and timeliness of the information it sells to clients. PipeWay is in an information-intensive business, and thus its decision support systems and their embedded models must be under constant improvement. This area is particularly suitable to the creation of research and development teams with expertise in statistics and management information systems, as it is probably outside PipeWay's core competencies.

PipeWay's computer models are based on data, and the quality of that data influences directly the value of the information that is later generated based on it. The magnetic technology with sensors adopted to accomplish the data-collection task is another area that PipeWay needs to study and improve continuously. As explained before, it was improving this exact industry process by adding more sensors to the robots that PipeWay made its way to success. Accordingly, a disruption in this area by a competitor, such as adding the capability of recording short movies to the robots, which would bring the area of computer vision into the business, may affect PipeWay's future market performance. Like PipeWay, the other stakeholders in the business of pipeline inspection and cleaning, which include Bucker Hughes, BJ Services and GE Oil and Gas, are very active and innovative. To illustrate this point, one can verify that a search with the string "pipeline pig cleaning" on the website Patents.com returns over 40 results, with patents dated back to the 1980s. This gives an indication that there is a lot of interest and research activity out there in the business processes that PipeWay is specialized in.

Another area that PipeWay has to monitor is the characteristics of the pipelines currently under development, as the location of oil might change in the near future as the most accessible oil fields dry up. For example, Petrobras is looking into the development of ultra-deep water pipelines right now. Can PipeWay's processes operate in such conditions of pressure and temperature? Possibly, adaptations will be required to meet these new needs. Fortunately, PipeWay has already managed to build many partnerships that were capable of addressing these types of research challenges and, therefore, to assemble others should not be especially problematic for the company, as it also has the personnel capabilities required.

Finally, there is the recent wave of preference for greener sources of energy, which could materialize and become mainstream, affecting PipeWay's operations deeply. However, PipeWay is already considering several of these future scenarios, and has developed PIGs that are very versatile. With that built-in flexibility, PipeWay believes that its robots could be easily adapted to work in ethanol and water pipelines, a new niche that is being seriously considered by the managers.[6] According to them, up to 50 percent of the water in cities is wasted due to pipeline leakages. This forward thinking and constant market monitoring that allows innovative and timely responses seem to be PipeWay's most valuable strength. Only the future can tell if PipeWay will ever find a competitor that matches these competencies.

Case study questions

1   What factors probably led PipeWay to win so many awards, as well as national and international recognition? Why are these factors so important?

2   The case of PipeWay shows that startups can compete with Brazilian multinationals. Taking into consideration a successful entrepreneurial process, which step of this process was the most important for PipeWay (innovation, business plan, capitalization, or other)? Why?

3   What role did the Genesis business incubator at PUC-RIO have on the success of PipeWay? If you had a great business idea, would you rather use an incubator to start your own company or try to advance a business plan on your own? Why?

4   Should PipeWay try to build internal capabilities or partner with other organizations to acquire the needed know-how to continue to have a competitive advantage in the monitoring of pipelines business? What are the risks of sharing knowledge with partners in this market? What about the advantages? Is there space for a conjoint research and development project for PipeWay and its partners?

Notes

1   University of Michigan, National Business Incubation Association, Ohio University, and Southern Technology Council (1997). *Business Incubation Works: The Results of the Impact of Incubator Investments Study*. Athens, Ohio: NBIA Publications.

2   Available online at: www.gemconsortium.org/docs/451/gem-brazil-2010-report-portuguese

3   Available online at: www.firjan.org.br/lumis/portal/file/fileDownload.jsp?fileId=2C90 8CE9215B0DC4012163E32E004395

4   Available online at: www.ipea.gov.br/sites/000/2/meide/apresentacoes/Painal-PipeWay. pdf

5   Available online at: www.valor.com.br/empresas/1000462/incubadora-ensina-visao-comercial-pesquisador

6   Available online at: www.PipeWay.com.br/cgi/cgilua.exe/sys/start.htm?infoid=215&op =pt&sid=30

References

Adkins, D. (2002). *A Brief History of Business Incubation in the United States*. Athens, OH: NBIA Publications.

Amorós, J. E., Fernández, C. and Tapia, J. (2011). Quantifying the relationship between entrepreneurship and competitiveness development stages in Latin America. *International Entrepreneurship and Management Journal*, 1–22.

Costa, M.P. (2010). The internationalization process of a Brazilian company: PipeWay Engineering case study. M.Sc. dissertation, Rio de Janeiro: Departamento de Administração, Pontifícia Universidade Católica do Rio (PUC-RIO), p. 139.

Dornelas, J.C.A. (2002). *Planejando Incubadoras de Empresas*. Rio de Janeiro: Campus.

Gloria, N., Areiza, M., Miranda, I. and Rebello, J. (2009). Development of a magnetic sensor for detection and sizing of internal pipeline corrosion defects. *NDT & E International*, 42 (8), 669–677.

Kelley, D.J., Bosma, N. and Amorós, J.E. (2010). Global Entrepreneurship Monitor 2010 Executive Report, 16. Global Entrepreneurship Research Association.

Knopp, L. (2007). *2006 State of the Business Incubation Industry*. Athens, OH: NBIA Publications. Retrieved from: www.nbia.org/resource_library/faq/#3

Lalkaka, R. (2003). Business incubators in developing countries: characteristics and performance. *International Journal of Entrepreneurship and Innovation Management*, 3(1/2), 31–55.

Magacho, L.A. and Costa, M.P. (2010). The internationalization case of PipeWay Engenharia. Paper presented at the Triple Helix Conference, Madrid. Retrieved from: www.lasalleparquedeinnovacion.es/noticias/Documents/2010.10.22%20VIII%20Conference%20Triple%20Helix.%20Book%20of%20Abstracts.pdf#page=211

Silva, J., Antunes, R. and Afonso, O. (2004). A smart location system. Proceedings of the International Pipeline Conference (ASME). Inspection Techniques. Alberta, Canada.

Silva, J., Pinho, A. and Miguel. (2001). Tool for geometric inspection of 3" pipelines. Brazilian Petroleum and Gas Institute – IBP. 3rd seminar on pipeline. Rio de Janeiro, Brazil.

Simoes, M. (2005). The growth of small companies of technological base: the PipeWay case. M.Sc. dissertation, Rio de Janeiro: Departamento de Administração, Pontifícia Universidade Católica do Rio (PUC-RIO).

World Bank. (2011). *Economy Rankings*. Retrieved January 31, 2012, from: www.doing business.org/rankings

2

FROM FAMILY BUSINESS TO BUSINESS FAMILY

The strategic development of Zorbas – Master Bakers – Cyprus

Panikkos Poutziouris and Elias Hadjielias

The business had been very successful so far and General Manager Demetris Zorbas was feeling very proud about it. Thirty-seven years after the establishment of the Zorbas enterprise, Demetris leaned back in his chair and reflected on the key turning points and practices that had been instrumental in transforming the small neighbourhood bakery into a large enterprise:

> It was a time that we understood that we needed to expand further, to create better prospects for our business. The bakery business in Cyprus was becoming saturated and increasingly competitive. We needed to act fast to ensure that we would maintain and strengthen further our market position and our financial sustainability. This is when the developments at that time with the establishment of the Stock Exchange in Cyprus created for us the perfect opportunity. As soon as we became public we secured the resources that we needed to expand our enterprise and build the Zorbas business, as all people know it today . . . Among others, it was quite clear for all the decision-makers that any new endeavours would have to build on and expand our core bakery business and diversify with new business models.

A. Zorbas & Sons Ltd (hereinafter referred to as Zorbas Ltd) is a family business with the ownership and management being in the hands of Zorbas family members, who are the key decision-makers in the firm. The family's commitment and love of the bakery business and the need to strengthen and develop the business further created a powerful impetus for pursuing long-term growth through entrepreneurial action that would build on the core business. The situation today, though, does not reflect the conditions at the start, when owner-manager Andreas Zorbas was striving to sustain his small corner-store bakery to secure an income for his family.

Demetris emphasized that what they had managed to achieve was a small miracle, if one considered that their business was once a neighbourhood bakery. 'It was a great accomplishment. We really transformed this business into a role model for the industry,' he added.

From artisan to a group of companies

At the early stage of venturing, Andreas Zorbas laid the foundation for a step-by-step business development – to trade quality bakery products in parallel with his farming venture. It is axiomatic how he managed to do this, given the hard economic and social conditions during the early start of the business. 'Once we reach 100 loaves, the Zorbas family will start our own independent baking venture', senior Andreas Zorbas included in the terms of engagement with local suppliers and trading partners. That milestone was surpassed and the Zorbas independent bakery was established in 1975. That was the end of the beginning. Andreas Zorbas's children had also made a large contribution to the creation of the Zorbas miracle. Without their ongoing desire and commitment to secure the longevity of their family's business, the growth of the business through entrepreneurialism would not have been possible.

Since 1975, the small corner-store bakery that was once established in the village of Athienou in Larnaka[1] experienced a phenomenal growth and it is today the largest bakery business in Cyprus. During the journey of the Zorbas business, the company became public in 2000 and was listed on the Cyprus Stock Exchange. Twelve years later, the family bought back in full the shares that had been issued to the public, and the business returned to the private ownership of the Zorbas family.

The company runs three high-tech production units in the Aradhippou Industrial Estate in Larnaka and operates 51 retail bakery stores all over Cyprus. It employs 1,300 people (including full-time and pro-rata employees), generating more than €70 million in revenue. Apart from the production, distribution and trading of bakery and confectionery goods, Zorbas Ltd conducts activities in a range of related and unrelated industries, including homemade cooked food, catering services, pizza, preparation of coffee, salads and sandwiches, the installation and maintenance of cooling systems, and rental of investment property. The structure of the company is based on functional departmentalization and activities are grouped into the following key functions: Sales, HR, Development, Finance, IT, Hygiene, Trade, and Production and Logistics (Figure 2.1 provides the company's organizational chart).

The startup, growth and transformation of Zorbas's bakery business occurred within relatively restricted boundaries and under adverse economic conditions. When the business was first established in 1975, the conditions were anything else but business friendly. There was an environment overwhelmed by poverty, unemployment and general economic instability. It was just a year after the 1974

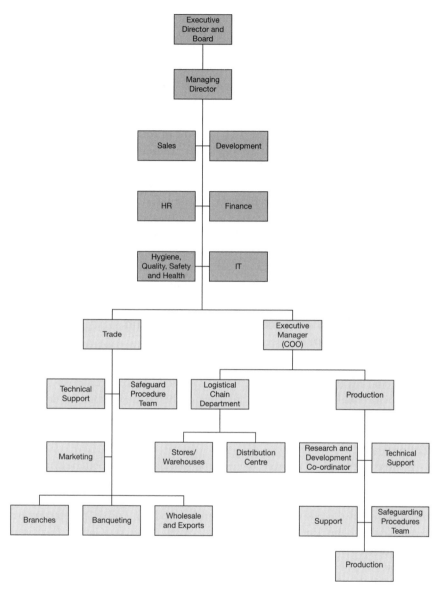

FIGURE 2.1 Organizational chart of Zorbas Ltd, 2012

Turkish invasion of Cyprus that resulted in the division of the island and the forced migration of a number of Greek Cypriots from the occupied north to the south. Other restrictions to the growth of the firm included doing business in a relatively small market and a small industry context. Cyprus is a small European Union nation, located in the eastern Mediterranean basin in south-eastern Europe, of just 840,407 inhabitants.[2] While bakery manufacturing is one of the largest industries in the country, the gross output of that sector is just €340 million.[3] Cyprus depends heavily on the service sector, which accounts for nearly four-fifths of a GDP that reached €15.1 billion in 2011.[4] The country's manufacturing industry is quite small, accounting for just 6 per cent of the country's GDP in 2011.[4] Becoming a business that employs 1,300 people means a great deal in a country where the vast majority of businesses are small enterprises. Specifically, micro-enterprises that employ fewer than 10 persons account for 94.1 per cent of total businesses, while other small enterprises (i.e. fewer than 50 employees according to the EU definition) constitute another 5 per cent of the business population.[5]

Despite not representing the average growth path and size of firms in the country, Zorbas Ltd is a family firm that is the most common form of enterprise in Cyprus. Family firms are very prolific in Cyprus and are estimated to represent 80 per cent of all enterprises[6] in the country. Family members are typically in dominant control of both ownership and management across the generations, which is also the case with Zorbas Ltd that is a second-generation owned and managed family business in the hands of Andreas Zorbas's offspring.

The Zorbas family ownership, management and entrepreneurialism

The company is owned and managed by the Zorbas family – the founder, Andreas Zorbas, and his three sons, Costas, Anastasios and Demetris. Andreas's sons are the key shareholders and executive directors of the business, while his daughter, Evanthia, who is also involved in management, does not have an executive position or shares in the business (see Figure 2.2 for the genealogical tree of the Zorbas family).

Andreas Zorbas was the sole owner (100 per cent) of the business up until the year 2000 when the company became public and the family relinquished 49.9 per cent of the company's shares. The year 2000 was also a year of ownership restructuring of the business, with the founder, Andreas Zorbas, transferring his shareholding to his three sons. Today, the three brothers (Costas, Anastasios and Demetris) are in full control of the business, buying back all the shares initially issued to the public during the Initial Public Offering (IPO). All brothers hold an identical shareholding, each being in ownership of one-third of the company's shares.

Andreas Zorbas was the first CEO of the company and in 1989 passed the baton to his eldest son, Costas. Today, Costas is the company's CEO, assisted by his brother Demetris who holds the General Manager's position. Their brother Anastasios is the Production Director. Despite withdrawing from top management, Andreas Zorbas as Honorary Chairman remains engaged in the business, and as Executive Director attends key meetings where strategic development issues are discussed and decided (Table 2.1 provides details regarding the structure of the company's Board of Directors in 2012).

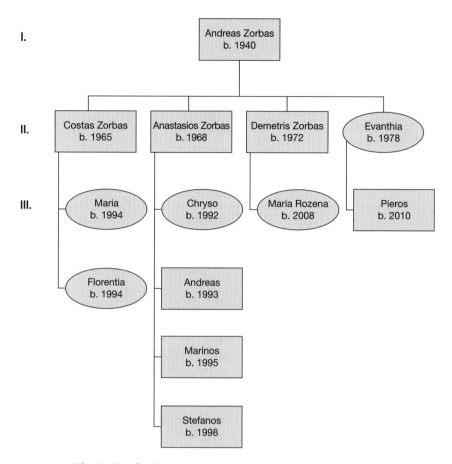

FIGURE 2.2 The Zorbas family tree

TABLE 2.1 Zorbas Ltd: Board of Directors, 2012

Name	Status	Position
Costas Zorbas	Family	Chairman
Andreas Zorbas	Family	Executive – Honorary Chairman
Demetris Zorbas	Family	Executive Director
Anastasios Zorbas	Family	Executive Director
Tasos Anastasiou	Non-family	Non-executive
Panayiotis Athienitis	Non-family	Non-executive
Michaelis Papadopoulos	Non-family	Non-executive

Apart from the four aforementioned family owner-managers, the board encompasses three independent non-family directors from diverse fields. The board and the participation of non-family directors resulted from the company's IPO in 2000. Despite the fact that the company's shares ceased to be traded on the Stock Exchange as of October 2012, the structure of the board remains unaltered as a result of the family's desire to keep the business going in the same professional manner as before. While a number of non-family board members are present, Andreas Zorbas and his three sons are the only Executive Directors of the business. Non-family board members hold non-executive positions, reflecting the intention of the Zorbas family to keep full control of the business.

As senior Andreas Zorbas was withdrawing from duty, his children in partnership were steering the business across new growth avenues. Costas, Demetris and Anastasios had been involved during their teenage years. They gradually entered the business after their education and military service, and climbed the managerial ladder of the family firm. In the 1990s, they had won the mandate (and voting power) to launch the transformation of the family business into a business family – broadening the strategic growth map.

The company would have not grown, though, if the founder was not a capable businessman, manager and entrepreneur. The conditions during the early start were such that the possibilities for entrepreneurial actions were restricted due to the small size of the firm and the limited financial resources that were available for investment purposes. However, Andreas managed to build the foundations of a promising business and transferred to his sons a growth-inspired enterprise.

Apart from attending a number of seminars in the field of bakery manufacturing, Andreas Zorbas had no specialist education that would help him to think and act managerially or strategically. He is a person with substantial experience in the production and distribution of a range of products such as milk and bread. He is an artisan entrepreneur mastering the market. Andreas Zorbas has been endowed with foresight, creativity and drive that were necessary to pioneer with the Zorbas model of bakery business. This involves an extensive network of small bakeries, which revolve around centralization, standardization and value-chain activities that built economies both of scale and scope. Senior Andreas has also been blessed by his enterprising children: his three sons and daughter adopted his entrepreneurial zeal. They follow in the footsteps of their father, who nurtured them to face the challenges of growing the family business.

Today, Costas, Anastasios and Demetris co-own and co-manage the business, shaping the entity's strategic moves. The business is found at a different stage of development, compared with the era when senior Andreas was in leadership. His sons succeeded in transforming the promising family bakery business to a group of integrated enterprises. The involvement and commitment of the enterprising Zorbas family has played a key role in the provision of valuable resources and capabilities to the growing enterprise.

While the company is still a family partnership, the three brothers have already started to address the challenges of bringing the next generation into the business.

The next critical juncture for both the family and the business is how to plan for the meritocratic criteria that will determine which members of the third generation will be joining the growing firm.

From past to present: Zorbas's entrepreneurial development

Zorbas Ltd is a highly entrepreneurial business. Within a period of 36 years, the company changed radically, moving from a corner-store bakery to a large corporation. The company has been entrepreneurial since its inception. However, the notable growth of the firm started 20 years after its establishment, when the family members increasingly felt the pressures of a maturing bakery market, which threatened the longevity of their business. Demetris reflected that:

> When the business was first established in 1975, bakery business in Cyprus was a neighbourhood business. Every bakery was a small unit, supplying nearby neighbourhoods with bread and other traditional bakery products. It was during the mid-1990s when the bakery industry became quite popular. More and more businesses entered the market, and expanded their operations beyond neighbourhoods. In the late 1990s we started feeling the pressure of doing something more than basic bakery production, to avoid having all our eggs in one basket.

Prior to the late 1990s, the business was exhibiting a narrow record of entrepreneurial initiatives, primarily due to the small size of the firm and the limited available financial resources. Following the establishment of the business in 1975, in 1980 the business established a small bakery production, distribution and retail unit in the village of Athienou in Larnaka catering for the needs of a community of around 5,000 inhabitants. During the early years it was owner-manager Andreas Zorbas who was taking all the business decisions, being quite conservative in terms of facilitating developments beyond the core bakery production. Despite this, Andreas was always in pursuit of new ideas that would help create better prospects for the business, such as the ongoing introduction of new bakery products.

However, it took the business almost 20 years to create an initiative that would help grow the business beyond the bakery focus. This was in 1994, when it was decided to establish a new business unit, producing also confectionery products. Following this, in 1996 a sister bakery business 'To Zymoton' was also established. It was primarily due to the active engagement of his sons into the business, during the late 1980s and early 1990s, when Andreas started thinking 'outside the box' and how to grow further his small bakery business. When Andreas's three sons officially joined the business, milestones for the future development of the business were also set, and the management of the firm became a team practice. Father and sons, the company's top management team, were overwhelmed by a feeling of safety to co-operate together, and committed their efforts to expand the business to which they were all emotionally bonded. They felt comfortable working together and taking the necessary steps to grow their business further.

A problem, however, was that the aspirations of the family team could not coincide with the financial capabilities of the business. As Demetris explained: 'We wanted to expand and offer our products Cyprus-wide. It was very difficult, however, because our financial resources were very limited at that time.' It was the clash between aspirations and capabilities that led the family members to start exploring ways that could help the business to make the desired leap. These concerns did not overwhelm the family members for long, as certain changes in the economic environment of Cyprus opened a much-awaited window of opportunity. This was during the mid- to late 1990s, when the Cyprus Stock Exchange surged in popularity for IPOs. At that time, the Zorbas family was making all the necessary arrangements to float the business on the Stock Exchange. This was primarily due to the zeal of family members to secure additional capital to develop the business. 'Going public would mean that we would be able to expand our capital and thus commit more resources in shaping the future of Zorbas's business as we were envisioning it at that time,' said Demetris.

In 2000, the business became a public limited company, listed on the Cyprus Stock Exchange. The company's valuation before the stock market launch was CYP 6 million (€10,200,000), broken down into 30 million common shares of CYP 0.20 (€0.34) each. The owning family relinquished their 49.9 per cent share of the business during the IPO, but remained in control of Zorbas Ltd (through 50.1 per cent ownership). As a result of the IPO, 14,975,000 shares were sold to the public at CYP 0.20 (€0.34) each. This helped the company to raise an additional capital of CYP 2,980,000 (€5,066,000). While the opening stock price of the firm was CYP 0.20 (€0.34), within a period of 11 years this price increased almost fourfold, reaching €1.35 at the end of 2011. The increase in the company's share price reflected the phenomenal growth of the business in the years following the IPO.

The year 2000 shaped a new era for Andreas Zorbas's business. What followed was quite impressive and beyond the vision of the Zorbas family as well. Demetris explained:

> We have invested in growth across markets and products, and introduced new production technologies. We wanted to expand geographically across Cyprus. However, we did not expect that we would reach such a size and be ready to embark on sales internationally.

From the first year of its operations as a public company, the Zorbas family registered a number of significant developments. A key development was the establishment of a new factory in Aradhippou industrial area in Larnaka. Moving from a small-scale unit in the village of Athienou, the company established a new 20,000m² manufacturing plant in one of the largest industrial districts in Cyprus. Through the establishment of this factory the company invested in new, more effective and more efficient production technologies for managing the company's constant growth and increasing consumer demand. The retail chain of the business grew dramatically, expanding the company's retail end at a considerable extent. Within a year, seven new retail bakeries were established in all key districts in the country, magnifying the company's reach and sales potential. A new business was also acquired during that year. This was a successful confectionery business at that time, which allowed Zorbas to become an established player in the confectionery end as well.

These movements reflected the very much anticipated time when the business would have more financial resources to commit to its further growth and development. Following the year when it was listed on the Cyprus Stock Exchange and until today, the business has engaged in a series of notable entrepreneurial initiatives, including the establishment of the largest network of retail bakery stores in Cyprus (51 in total); the introduction of new production innovations and distribution processes that secured constant provision of hot bakery products in bakery stores; the introduction of radically new concepts for the Cyprus market, such as Zorbas's delivery of bakery products to businesses, and the expansion of its product line beyond bakery products (e.g. pizza, sandwiches, ready meals). It has also extended its value-chain operations by introducing businesses in the areas of cooling systems, and trading (see Table 2.2 for the timeline of the company's entrepreneurial performance).

The development of the business is reflected not only in the firm's growth and innovation, but also in the maturity of its ethos and responsibility towards society. In 2009, the second-generation Zorbas family established the MAZI – Together Foundation in honour of their parents, Maria and Andreas Zorbas. The foundation aims to build a scientific centre (the first of its kind) for the recovery and rehabilitation of people with eating disorders and obesity in Cyprus. This is an initiative that the Zorbas business family is promoting as a testimony to their ethos and social responsibility, which is to give back something to the community.

A strategic orientation to the company's entrepreneurial development

The year of flotation (2000) was a turning point for the business, since it had signified a change in the company's entrepreneurial orientation. Within a period of 12 years (2000–2012), the company initiated numerous new ventures within related industries and, to a lesser extent, unrelated market activities. It was during this period that the company felt the need to craft strategic initiatives to strengthen the core business with operational efficiency and excellence, and lay the foundations for the long-term success and prosperity of the owner-managed family business.

The secret behind the company's impressive entrepreneurial development has been the fact that any new movement would be carefully evaluated and measured against the core business. While there is a strong willingness on behalf of the family owners across the generations to expand into new ventures, there is also a

TABLE 2.2 Timeline of the entrepreneurial development of Zorbas Ltd: key developments

Year	Activity
1980	Establishes a production unit in Athienou, Larnaka, and increases its product range
1994	Incorporates Zorbas and Regency Sweets Industry Ltd, a confectionery business
1996	Establishes a new bakery business unit, 'To Zymoton' Ltd
2000	Establishes a new high-tech factory in Aradhippou, Larnaka, with the guidance of specialists from Greece and France
	The company fully acquires 'Charis Gregoriou Workshop', a Cyprus-wide confectionery firm
	Establishes 7 new shops in Nicosia, 4 in Larnaka, 2 in Famagusta, 3 in Limassol and 3 in Paphos
2003	Incorporates Ancopa Cooling Ltd, which offers installation/maintenance of cooling systems
2003	Incorporates Mega Z. Point Trading Ltd (controlling 50 per cent of shares), a chain of kiosks
2004–2005	Operates 12 new shops, increasing to 39 stores all over Cyprus
2007	Operates new-concept production line: ready, semi-cooked, frozen, semi-frozen and pre-cooked bakery products. Production capacity extended by 300 per cent
2009	Establishes the 'Mazi Foundation', focusing on problems with stomach disorders and obesity
2010	A new pioneering service is introduced offering delivery of bakery products: B2B and B2C
2011	The company initiates exports and distribution within the Greek community in Canada
	In the UAE, Zorbas Ltd becomes involved (24 per cent share) in a newly established bakery business
2012	As of October 2012, the company's stock is no longer traded on the Cyprus Stock Exchange. The Zorbas family acquires all remaining shares and transforms the business into a private family enterprise again

strong desire to maintain the bakery business as the core business model. For an opportunity to be materialized into a new venture for the business, a number of issues need to be considered. First, any new development has to relate directly or indirectly to the core bakery business. Second, any expansions need to secure the company's competitive advantage and leading position in the bakery line of work. Thus, new developments can take place only if there is a priority judgement that these can help sustain the company's competitive advantage over the long term. Third, there is also consideration of the company's portfolio of businesses as a whole. The idea is that new ventures should fit into the company's existing portfolio and, in fact, help the company leverage synergies and economies of both scale and scope. Thus, the idea is that any new additions need to help improve the company's operations and cost efficiencies, both in terms of the core business and also in terms of other peripheral ventures, which Zorbas has effectively seized over time.

The firm has been pursuing expansion via both internal and external growth strategies. New ventures that the business considers are presenting themselves both in the form of established businesses that could be acquired or organic developments the company could embark on. About a third of new ventures are coming through acquisitions. New opportunities can come in different forms, and can include new products, new services or processes within the core bakery division. They can also include other entrepreneurial initiatives (e.g. new products, services or businesses) that can link in some way with the core business and the company's portfolio as a whole.

The year 2000 was important not only because the family members secured more resources for growing the business, but because a number of non-family directors were introduced to strengthen the governance of the growing enterprise. This was a notable development since it helped the family to start capitalizing on the knowledge and expertise of other specialists. The family members were still in control, but since 2000 they had the privilege of being consulted by a team of experts and co-operating with them, and together they worked towards setting the right foundations for the entrepreneurial development of the business. Demetris emphasized:

> We needed to establish a board and introduce directors outside the family. We were lucky because we had the privilege to welcome people who were very knowledgeable in relevant fields and could help us grow this business in the successful way.

Prior to 2000, the family members in control were expanding with a view to strengthen the core business, but after that year they started thinking and acting more entrepreneurially and strategically. The partnership of family and non-family stakeholders in the business enhanced the capabilities and professionalization of the top management team and helped in making them appreciate entrepreneurship as a strategic practice. Drawing on the expertise of non-family directors, the Zorbas family evaluated, selected, planned and pursued entrepreneurial strategies in a professional approach that allowed the business to go from strength to strength, and thus achieve sustainable high performance and offer added-value to all stake-holders. The interactions between family and non-family directors in the business soon led to the establishment of a strategic–entrepreneurial orientation, under which new business initiatives would need to be carefully planned to make sure that they strengthened and expanded the core business model. Actions, plans and visions in the past were mainly informal and relatively restricted by the limited financial resources, and also the limited expertise of family members in business. The dual changes that flotation brought about (i.e. the additional capital and the introduction of non-family experts) shaped a new era of formalization, professionalization and strategic forward-thinking. Demetris explained: 'That was a crucial point for us since we started thinking more strategically around the development of the business. Of course, this was done primarily because we started valuing the advice and support of all these non-family directors.'

The winds of change brought about the introduction of a clear long-term strategy for Zorbas Ltd. This is a strategy that can help the core business to secure further growth and development through entrepreneurialism across three pillars. The first pillar involves new activities for the protection and further development of the core business; the second pillar is the establishment of new ventures that can allow the expansion of the business into related markets not currently being served; the third pillar involves innovations that can allow expansion into businesses beyond the food industry, but ones that were still relevant to the company's supply chain. This allowed synergies with and the integration of the existing bakery business. The family members have a clear appreciation of this strategy. Demetris noted:

> Long discussions and the essential support of specialists outside the family helped us to understand that our growth path should be through the establishment of new ventures and innovations that could develop the core business through further efficiencies, integration, and economies.

The first dimension of this long-term strategy represents the company's core business that is providing the greatest profits and cash flow. This is the bakery line of business. Here the aim is to concentrate strategic efforts to extend and defend the core business, and improve performance via economies of scale and scope. Since its establishment, the core company has gone through a series of transformations, converting a network of bakeries into stores, which could source their bakery products from a central production centre. The company has succeeded in its efforts to centralize and standardize production and distribution by investing in a large-scale production plant. This has been done with the aim of securing the best possible efficiencies through economies of scale, utilization of its production and distribution capabilities, and changing from doing business locally to delivering its products and services nationwide.

The second dimension of Zorbas's strategic long-term plan involves the building of new growth opportunities, including emerging entrepreneurial ventures. Over time, the company has managed to diversify its revenue streams beyond bakery products, offering a range of related products such as confectionery, sandwiches, pizzas and ready foods. This has allowed the company to access new related markets that are not served with the initial bakery business. Among others, the company established new ventures for the provision of catering services for very large and small occasions, and the supply of ready foods to large organizations such as airlines and franchise chains. The integrated business that enjoys the market leadership position in Cyprus is currently spreading its wings to pursue international strategies – trading its high value-added products in overseas markets (notably Canada) and aiming to establish an integrated bakery business model in the United Arab Emirates (UAE). While Andreas Zorbas and his sons carry substantial expertise in the bakery line of work, there is much knowledge and expertise that has been transferred into the business by non-family stakeholders. Allowing non-family directors to sit on the company's board as part of the IPO process, the business capitalized on new human capital that was substantially diverse from the one carried by the Zorbas family. This has been critical in terms of nurturing capabilities that could allow the company to expand into new grounds that were virtually unknown and outside of the comfort zone of the controlling family. The Zorbas family played an important role in choosing these specialists very carefully and strategically. The idea was that these people needed to help the business to venture out into new business ends, both locally and internationally.

The third dimension involves the exploration of ventures beyond the food industry that could turn into emerging new business models and subsequently diversify revenue streams. The aim is that these new ventures can still relate to the core business, either vertically or horizontally in its supply chain, and can be ones that can contribute to the further strengthening of the bakery business. As a result, the company has been experimenting with a range of non-food specific ventures, which relate to its value chain, such as cooling systems, publishing–printing and (online) retail trading. Such investments could help strengthen the existing company's supply chain and develop a truly integrated company. A company with a network of kiosks, for example, was acquired for the potential transformation of the kiosks into new Zorbas stores, integrated with the bakery business model. Again, without the expert advice and guidance by non-family directors and consultants the Zorbas family could not have embarked successfully into the establishment and management of a diverse portfolio of ventures that would link to the core business. These people brought a new strategic thinking into the business that set the structures for practising entrepreneurship more professionally, sustainably and responsibly. Demetris elaborated:

> These specialist managers that we have recruited into the business have helped us appreciate and understand that not every attractive opportunity is good for us. They helped us see opportunities as a team, and the need to appreciate the intermarriage between them, and their joint effects on the business as a whole.

In the context of this strategic dimension, Zorbas Ltd embarks also in the divestment of certain ventures that appear to disrupt the overall efforts to establish an integrated enterprise. An example is the Ethos publishing company, which was acquired in 2005 for providing printing and packing support for Zorbas's production processes. Realizing that it would be more profitable and strategically useful to outsource such services instead of maintaining a wholly owned publishing–printing venture, a few years later the decision was taken to sell this part of the business. Mistakes in the context of the company's portfolio management cannot be avoided. Despite the presence of highly capable and diverse managerial capital, certain entrepreneurial initiatives do not perform as expected. This is, in fact, a reflection of the company's strategic thinking and the acknowledgement that not all new entrepreneurial initiatives can eventually fit strategically within the company's scope and direction. Thus, implicitly, there is recognition that in the context of portfolio management, divestments are necessary for securing a viable future for both the core business and the portfolio as a whole. This orientation, coupled with the prolonged experience of the business in new venture establishment and associated failures, have transformed Zorbas Ltd into a learning organization that appreciates the need to manage expansion through proper strategic thinking.

The company's strategy and vision behind entrepreneurial actions have enabled the creation of a successfully integrated business, both horizontally and vertically, coupled with extensive economies of scale and scope. Thinking and acting strategically when exploring and seizing new opportunities has been the core pillar of the company's success over the years. There is much explicit recognition in the business that any new ventures have to fit and contribute to the existing company portfolio that is built around the core bakery business. New cultural norms have been nurtured into the business since the year 2000, which call for a strong pro-active orientation towards entrepreneurship and a full appreciation of the connectedness between entrepreneurship, strategy and sustainability. This strategic orientation, coupled with the stewardship and financial prudence of the family owner-managers, has also protected Zorbas Ltd from the negative influence of a maturing market and the prolonged financial crisis that had affected the Cypriot economy after 2008.

Challenges in the company's entrepreneurial journey

The Zorbas family has gone through many hurdles in order to develop a successful and viable business. In the early days, when Andreas Zorbas was the sole leader of the business, there were many struggles to keep the business going. Demetris said:

> I admire my father in how he managed to sustain this business, especially at the early start. Those were hard times; the economy of the country was recovering following the Turkish invasion. People had no money to spend; doing business at that time was very difficult.

Andreas Zorbas was barely keeping the company alive, worrying endlessly how to sustain and grow the family business. Entrepreneurial activities were not a primary concern of the owner at that time.

A key challenge that the business had to face was the saturation and maturity of the bakery market, which became evident from the mid-1990s onwards. While until the late 1980s and early 1990s the bakery business mainly revolved around neighbourhoods, small districts and villages, in the mid-1990s the bakery business model began to change in Cyprus with many enterprises establishing chains of bakeries, covering wider areas and offering a larger range of products, including confectionery items. The industry was attractive at that time, which led many new businesses to enter the market either with single stores or extended Cyprus-wide chains. Andreas was not a lone leader in the business when these pressures began to surface. He had his three sons next to him and the whole family team felt the pressure to reduce the risk of overdependence on the bakery market that was becoming increasingly fragmented and mature. However, endeavours and aspirations towards this end tended to be obstructed by the lack of the required financial resources and also the expertise that was needed to do so. Demetris explained:

> It took us five years to resolve this complexity. We needed to grow, but we could not do this because the market was becoming more competitive and mature. To expand you need the money but also the people who will help you to do this in the right way. We lacked both at that time.

Both the transition of the family business to the next generation during the early 1990s and the transformation of Zorbas to a public entity in 2000 has transformed the entrepreneurial culture of the family business. While these changes shaped the future of the company, there were many complexities and difficulties in facilitating the transition from the old to the new status quo. When Andreas was the company's sole owner-manager, there was a more paternalistic culture and the business was seen as a source of funding for the family. When his sons joined the business, they brought with them a desire to change certain things and expand further the business through new ventures. There were times when discussions were intense and critical, since Andreas was still conservative and reluctant to agree to change, fearing that new initiatives could disrupt what he had managed to build up to that point. Andreas's sons exerted great efforts to persuade their father to let this thinking go. The three brothers were together in this. In any occurrence that the family members would meet, during business meetings or family gatherings, the three brothers would initiate relevant discussions. They would often talk about new ideas that would help grow the business or discuss the progress of key competitors and the conditions in the market. In this way, they were trying to make their father realize the need for changes and further entrepreneurialism. This was their way to pressurize their father to take more risks, which eventually worked. Demetris explained:

> I understand that my father was a bit reluctant at the start to new ideas that we wanted to implement. It took us time to persuade him that we need to engage in the development of the business if wanted to remain competitive.

Another turning point for the business was the year 2000, when the business became public and had to facilitate a number of corporate governance changes, including the recruitment of independent directors, the presence of a board, and key corporate governance committees led by non-family directors. Along with the three brothers, who were the company's executive directors, three independent directors were recruited at the board. While a board of directors would then have to govern the direction and development of the business, a number of committees (e.g. nominations, remuneration and audit committees) would help secure the transparent functioning and accountability of the firm. That was a major cultural shift for the business, which signified the professionalization of the business and led to the creation of a strategic entrepreneurial mindset in the business. It brought along, though, an initial shock for all the family that was involved in business. 'We needed to start coping with new ways of doing things, including collaboration with non-family directors, and the formality and professionalism in the way we would approach the development of the business,' Demetris added.

A tale of reunion between the Zorbas business and the Zorbas family

While still reflecting on the company's development so far, Demetris remembered the vision and aspirations that family members had when their business was about to be listed on the Stock Exchange. 'Through the flotation we were seeking, as the owning family, to marry traditional values, commitment and independence with strategic innovation, seeking long-term investors that had faith in family entrepreneurialism.'

Since October 2012, Zorbas is no longer traded on the Cyprus Stock Exchange. Twelve years after the company's IPO, the Zorbas family is making the family business private in order to preserve and reinforce further the 'Zorbas miracle'. While the IPO helped the Zorbas business to recapitalize and expand, the family members feel that the company can better preserve its momentum as a private enterprise. Facing a prolonged global crisis and an underperforming Stock Exchange with a lack of investors with an appetite for long-term investment plans, the family decided to acquire all the remaining shares and take full control of the business. By freeing strategic planning from external influences and bureaucratic compliance, family members acknowledge that their initial aspirations and dreams for the business can eventually become a reality. 'After a long journey, the Zorbas business and the Zorbas family values and aspirations, fully reunite,' Demetris Zorbas reflected further.

While becoming a public company has been an interim point for the Zorbas business, there is a broad understanding that this has been a fruitful experiential journey for both the family and the business. It is obvious for the Zorbas family that they will now face a new era and new challenges that they did not come across before the year 2000, when they were a small private family-owned enterprise. The three brothers, Costas, Anastasios and Demetris, appreciate the need to remain strong, proactive and strategically oriented in their firm's entrepreneurial initiatives. They acknowledge that they need to safeguard and reinforce the capabilities, professionalization and entrepreneurial orientation that they have managed to build through years of hard work, commitment towards the business and their common vision to grow the Zorbas bakery enterprise under the values of the Zorbas family.

Towards the end of 2012 the whole orientation of the Zorbas family had changed radically. Starting with efforts to sustain the family through business, family members now see themselves facing the challenge of nurturing and expanding further their growing business through integrated strategies, entrepreneurship and managerial practices. The family grew together with the small corner-store bakery of Andreas Zorbas and became a true business family ready to face the challenges of the future in a professional, timely and judicious manner. While leaning back on his chair and reflecting, Demetris Zorbas, General Manager of the firm, is thinking about the future of the business and the next steps that they need to take to secure both the family legacy in business and the further professionalization and growth of the firm:

> We need to start planning for the structures, processes and schemes that will help us nurture and develop the next generation of management. As a business family we need professional talent —both from the Zorbas family ranks but also from our extended family — our loyal managers and associates; we need to continue to grow and better serve all our clients locally and now beyond our islandic frontiers, with quality products and superior service.

Notes

1 Larnaka is the third largest city in Cyprus with a population of 132,000 (Cyprus Statistical Service, 2009).
2 Cyprus Statistical Service, 2012a.
3 Cyprus Statistical Service, 2011.
4 Cyprus Statistical Service, 2012b.
5 Cyprus Statistical Service, 2007.
6 Poutziouris, 2010.

Bibliography

Cyprus Statistical Service (2007) Census of Establishments 2005, Nicosia, Cyprus: Printing Office of the Republic of Cyprus.

Cyprus Statistical Service (2011) Industrial Statistics 2010, Nicosia, Cyprus: Printing Office of the Republic of Cyprus.

Cyprus Statistical Service (2012a) Population Census 2012. Retrieved from the Cyprus Statistical Service website: www.mof.gov.cy/mof/cystat/statistics.nsf/populationcondition_22main_en/populationcondition_22main_en?OpenForm&sub=2&sel=1.

Cyprus Statistical Service (2012b) National Economic Accounts 2011, Nicosia, Cyprus: Printing Office of the Republic of Cyprus.

Poutziouris, P. (2010) The Entrepreneurial Family Business Economy in Cyprus, CIIM and Cyprus Chambers of Commerce and Industry Monograph, Nicosia, Cyprus.

Zorbas (2012a) Annual reports 2002–2011. Available online at: www.zorbas.com.cy/zorbas/page.php?pageID=62&mpath=/93.

Zorbas (2012b) History. Available online at: www.zorbas.com.cy/zorbas/page.php?page ID=9&mpath=/34.

3

ALUCAST S.R.O. – CZECH REPUBLIC

Martina Rašticová and Vladimír Bartošek

The ALUCAST s.r.o.[1] company was founded in 2001 by specialists in the field of investment precision casting who, in the last decade of the twentieth century, initiated serial production of investment precision aluminium (Al) castings. If during the period of socialism in the Czechoslovak Republic this precise technological production of Al castings was described as the 'rough' casting technology, then, thanks to the founders of the ALUCAST, parts produced by this technology are currently requisite for many world-renowned companies for their products, which can be found in outer space, in the air, on land and under water. The precision Al castings produced by ALUCAST offer designers and users the possibility to produce light, highly durable, complex parts that today successfully meet the requirements of tomorrow's designers, in terms of forms and high-level specifications of utilized castings.

Investment casting

The investment-casting (precision or lost-wax casting) technology is no doubt one of the leading modern foundry technologies. Over the last 50 years, this manufacturing method has developed from a technology thought of as a highly specialized method to one that is widely used today, meeting customers' requirements concerning the shape, size, precision and material consumption of the castings (Horáček, 2009).

In today's foundry, a near-net-shape technique is used increasingly with the initial production of an item being very close to the final (net) shape, reducing the need for surface finishing. Thus, customers are provided with a method enabling direct, efficient and economical manufacture of a final part. The name 'investment casting' applies to the process of creating a ceramic mould known as investment by coating a wax model.

In short, the method consists of first forming a wax pattern (by injecting wax into a mould known as the master die), which is then, along with other patterns, connected to a gating system (also made from wax), with this wax cluster being repeatedly coated with a ceramic. Then, wax is melted out or vaporized from the ceramic investment, which is then annealed. Hot moulds are mostly used for casting. What follows is finishing – that is, removing the shell and jetting the surface of the product, which is cut off from the gating system.

As suggested by the above description of the lost-wax casting (see Exhibit 30.1 and Figure 3.1), this is a highly specialized and constant process, with a specific feature that it cannot be automated, with each step requiring the assistance of an expert.

As pointed out by (Doškář et al., 1976) the lost-wax method has been known for several thousand years. This is evidenced by the works of art of ancient nations and cultures such as at Eufrat, Egypt, Palestine, Spain, Persia, China, Mexico, and other places. The original ancient technology was basically identical with the modern one. The original wax pattern was manually coated with suitable clay to form a mould. Hollow castings were made on the earthen shells. In early modern times, sufficient evidence was found corroborating the existence of a lost-wax method mostly in Renaissance Italy.[2] However, the most interesting and detailed accounts of this technology were written by Cellini, an Italian goldsmith living in Italy in that period (description of deaeration, heading, etc.). Perhaps the most famous work/casting of art by Cellini is a bronze statue of Perseus holding the head of Medusa.

FIGURE 3.1 World production of castings by the lost-wax method in 2009 (Williams and Hirst, 2010)

In the nineteenth century when sectional sand mouldings were generally used, the lost-wax method had almost sunk into oblivion. It was only at the end of the nineteenth century that it began to be used in dentistry for making crowns, tooth prostheses and fashion jewellery.

In the Second World War, industrial use of this technology began. It became clear that, even upgraded sectional sand mouldings could not produce advanced castings with the very narrow size tolerances and surface quality required. According to Doškář *et al.* (1976) – the modern era has only used the technology principle with state-of-the-art science providing new patterns, and forming materials and modern procedures carried out on automated production lines. Precision casting has been improved by numerous significant technological enhancements such as using pattern materials of constant size, strong self-supporting shell moulds preserving size under high temperatures, vacuum melting and casting, and the use of inserted ceramic cores to create sophisticated and precise cavities. Such improvements made it possible to produce larger castings with more precision and sophistication. Today, precision casting is successfully used in mechanical engineering (mostly in power engineering), in aviation, in the arms industry, in electronics, in medicine (artificial joints, dentistry), and in many other fields. Artistic casting, too, has made major advances using this progressive technology. The production of castings by the lost-wax method has been growing steadily worldwide, reaching total sales of about US$5 billion in 2000 (Williams, 2000, cited in Horáček, 2009).

With 38 per cent, North America (more specifically the USA, which produces 95 per cent – Canada 3 per cent, Mexico 2 per cent) participates most in precision casting. The distribution of production in North America by end-users is shown in Figure 3.2. The UK is the biggest European precision-casting producer, with

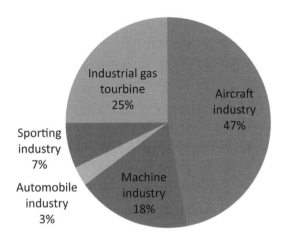

FIGURE 3.2 Customers for precision-casting products in North America (situation in 2000, edited by Horáček, 2009)

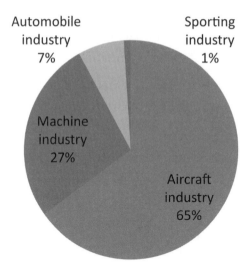

FIGURE 3.3 Precision-casting customers in the United Kingdom

47 investment foundries – the most of all European countries – and almost half (49.2 per cent) of the total European investment casting value (Williams and Hirst, 2010). Aircraft/space, power, automotive, leisure and sporting, and, generally, engineering industries are the most important markets. The end-user distribution is shown in Figure 3.3. Precision-casting annual sales have been growing, with about US$360 million in 1994 and US$545 million in 1999, which is by 50 per cent more over the last five years.

History of the Czech foundry industry

Situated in Central Europe, in the past the Czech Republic always played the role of an advanced industrial country. The Czech lands were used by the Austrian–Hungarian monarchy as an industrial base and, at the time of the birth of an independent Czechoslovakian state in 1918, it was among the European economic superpowers. This is demonstrated by the fact that, by occupying a part of the Czechoslovak territory in 1938, Germany almost doubled its own production potential. Unfortunately, the development after the Second World War caused the Czechoslovak economy to considerably lag behind the advanced Western economies, and it will be some time before its full productive potential is restored and the consequences of central planning are removed. It is clear that the Czech foundry, always accompanying a strong industrial potential in every country, has a long tradition.

In the early 1920s, Czechoslovakia was among the five countries that founded Comité International des Associations Techniques de Fonderie (CIATF), an international committee of foundry technical associations, today renamed as World Foundry Organization (WFO). In the late 1980s, there were about 120 foundry factories in Czechoslovakia (about 20 of them in Slovakia), annually producing about 1.5 million metric tons of castings (today about 450,000 metric tons). The drop in production was caused by the changes after 1989. The collapse of political systems mostly in East European countries brought about significant changes in the markets. Also, the structure of the castings produced underwent an abrupt change towards higher utility values of the castings, increasing their prices. Quality issues became a necessary development trend in the foundry industry, along with the introduction of ISO standards and concerns over environmental problems (Horáček, 2009).

Precision-casting industry in the Czech Republic

On a worldwide scale, the position of the Czech Republic is seemingly insignificant – 0.4 per cent participation in the worldwide production of castings by the lost-wax method. However, the per capita figures can successfully be compared with those of the most advanced countries of Europe. Regarding technology development, it should be remembered that this was retarded strongly by the existence of the Iron Curtain between 1948 and 1989, which prevented the transfer of strategic

TABLE 3.1 SWOT analysis of the precision-casting industry in the Czech Republic (based on Horáček, 2009)

Strengths	Opportunities
– Positive engineering approach to production (capability of fully using the existing equipment and raw materials to produce precision castings) – Low labour cost in precision-casting industry	– Step-by-step transfer to new technologies – Increased labour efficiency – Expected revitalization of the aviation, arms and power industries in the Czech Republic and in the former East European countries
Weaknesses	*Threats*
– Old management concepts and equipment (i.e. injection moulding machines and coating lines that are Czech designs of the 1960s) – Inferior quality, locally sourced raw materials (so-called Montan waxes or soft ones – paraffin/ceresin, quartz as facing material, ethylsilicate as binder, etc.) – Low labour efficiency (income per head only 25–35 per cent as compared with other countries) – Attitudes and motivation reflecting the communist era	– Lack of specialists at all levels – Environmental limits – Lack of raw materials such as for melting

technologies such as precision casting. This resulted in the necessity to stimulate Czechoslovakia's own development in raw materials such as waxes, binders and facing materials, cast alloys, etc., as well as the design and production of the necessary equipment (injection moulding machines, coating lines, etc.).

Although the quality of castings made by this technology was rather high, its further use is limited due to the requirements of an increasingly demanding world market. In the modern market, a larger variety of sizes and materials are required for use by the aviation, power and other industries. Thus, introducing the state-of-the-art raw materials and equipment used in the most advanced countries of the world is a necessity for long-term viability in today's market. Milan Horáček (2009) made an SWOT analysis of the precision-casting industry in the Czech Republic (Table 3.1).

History of ALUCAST s.r.o.

ALUCAST s.r.o. was established in 2000 with three employees and an initial capital of CZK7,500,000 (about €300,000) as a limited company owned by five co-owners (four Czechs, one Swiss) with two of them being employed by the firm. ALUCAST's registered office is at Tupesy, a small village in the south-eastern part of the Czech Republic, a traditionally rural area 15 km away from Uherské Hradiště, a district town, and 75 km from Brno. This choice of location was driven by accessibility of the railway, the cost of building and availability of space for future development.

The firm started to grow and in 2006 began to build its own production facility, completing it in 2007. At first, the construction of the firm's own premises was met with resistance by the local community, which, having had no previous experience of a manufacturing company in the vicinity of their village, were afraid of possible environmental pollution caused by the production. The protests complicated and prolonged the construction of a new production facility. However, an open, communicative and educational approach by the firm's management to village representatives eased the initial problems and the production facility was completed in time. After five years of its existence, cooperation with the local community is very good (see below). Moreover, ALUCAST has created over 40 new jobs for the locals. Co-financed by the European Union, the construction of a new production facility was started in 2010 and opened in May 2011.

Management

The company's Chief Executive Officer (CEO) graduated at Brno University of Technology, Department of Foundry Engineering, in 1973. He started his career as an engineer in the national enterprise MESIT Uherské Hradiště. From 1978 he worked as chief metallurgist in the same enterprise. In 1992 he became the head of the FIMES a.s. foundry (at that time the foundry had 15 employees). After nine years he left FIMES a.s. (at that time the foundry had more than 100 employees) and, together with the current Chief Technology Officer (CTO), he founded ALUCAST. The CEO received the ZLATÁ PÁNEV Award at the FONDEX foundry exhibition for the best display of investment aluminium castings. During the years 1997–2002 he served as the President of the Casting Association of Czech Investment Casting Association.

Products and services

ALUCAST produces lightweight, high-strength, complex components, which are today successfully meeting tomorrow's requirements of designers and users in terms of their shapes and of the high-quality technological features of the castings. The cooperation between ALUCAST and the customer even during the preparation period enhances functionality and technical excellence as well as product aesthetics.

In the last three years ALUCAST has introduced eight completely new or innovative processes that represent a substantial advance in the quality of castings with a total cost of €1 million. Some examples of the firm's technologies are:

- The JF casting technology allows the production of castings with fine structure and high-quality mechanical values (in respect of this technology an application has been submitted to the Office of Industrial Property for the utility model No. 22155).
- Pressure water jetting. This technology enables the production of castings with very sharp contours.
- Constructing a unique method for the heat treatment of Al castings that meets the NADCAP (National Aerospace and Defense Contractors Accreditation Program, now known as Nadcap) requirements.
- Evaluation of mechanical values on microsticks that are sampled from critical parts of the castings.
- Checking homogeneity using X-rays with the possibility of either recording them on film or utilizing digital imaging.

Objectives

ALUCAST's objective is to become a reliable and stable business partner specializing in the production of precision Al castings for highly sophisticated fields such as aviation and the medical industry. ALUCAST is based on the ability to predict and respond to the requirements of the market and customers' needs. Its production capacity, productivity, quality, labour organization and investment policy ensure ALUCAST a strong and competitive position in the European marketplace of precision Al castings.

The mission statement up to 2020 is defined as follows: 'ALUCAST s.r.o. is the EU's leading provider of premium precise Al castings and premium services for customers and business partners.'

The firm is built on the following five pillars:

- Quality – that is, customer satisfaction.
- Loyal employees.
- Environment-friendly production and support of/by the local community.
- Research and development.
- Profitability.

Quality

An emphasis on quality was the firm's credo in 2000 when it entered the market. Only high-quality products could enlarge the portfolio of industries in which the firm offers its products. A reputation for high-quality products, deadlines met and correct customer relations is the best reference for new customers. In 2004, the firm was EN ISO 9001 certified; in 2007 a new production facility was built with a size of 1,100 square metres; in 2010 it was certified according to AS 9100 revision B, EN 9100:2300 and ISO 9001:2008. In 2009–2010, a major inspection and technology investment was made. The firm took out a patent on a new JF casting technology to enable it to manufacture high-homogeneity castings with the best mechanical parameters, which is required especially in aviation.

At present, ALUCAST's products are used in production fields requiring high quality such as aviation, arms, automotive and textile industries, in electrical engineering, healthcare and optics, etc. (see Figure 3.4). Services offered by ALUCAST are unique as they are capable of meeting customers' specific requests:

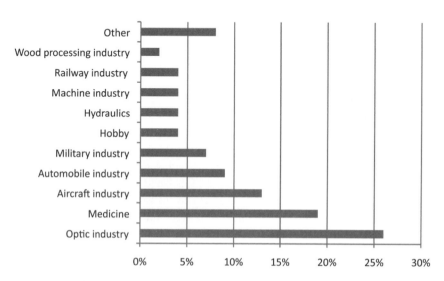

FIGURE 3.4 Industries in which ALUCAST's products find their applications (in per cent)

- Very short time-frames (4–6 weeks).
- Small series (100–1000 pc).
- Design changes after pilot series.
- High-precision requirements.
- Demanding mechanical parameters (strength over 330 MPa, minimum elongation of 5 per cent).
- High-quality surfacing (1.6–3.2).
- Complicated, difficult to machine parts.

Systematically, ALUCAST has extended its exports and it has major customers in Slovakia, Austria, Germany, Switzerland, England, France, South Africa, USA, Iceland, India and Israel, in addition to its domestic customers.

Loyal employees

From the outset, ALUCAST has adopted a qualified and loyal employee policy. Since 2000, when the firm had three employees, the number of people working for it has multiplied almost thirty times. At present, the firm has 82 employees. The organizational hierarchy is formed by the top management, senior workers in individual workshops, technicians and clerical staff, and workers.

The top management team of three women and five men consists of a manager, deputy manager, production manager, technical manager, trade manager, business manager, inspection manager and development manager. In general, there are almost the same number of men as women, with men, however, prevailing in management positions while women line workers being more numerous.

The firm's workers receive wages ranging between CZK16,000 and CZK25,000 (between €600 and €1,000) with the management's salaries depending on the

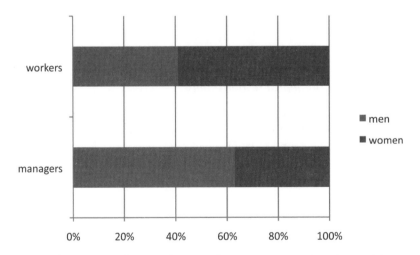

FIGURE 3.5 Percentages of men and women in management and worker positions

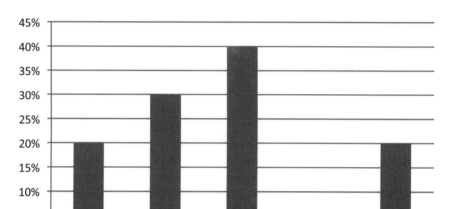

FIGURE 3.6 Age structure of the firm's top management (by age bracket)

company's profits. Turnover of staff at top-management positions is very low, but is somewhat higher among line workers. It is caused either by the short-term and periodic reduction in production (in the summer months), such as worldwide economic depression, and occasionally by the employment of individuals in positions for which they are poorly qualified or lack motivation.

Compared with other production firms in the region of a similar size, the employees' fringe benefits and working conditions are above average. Employees are offered lunch by the firm at a reduced price, mineral water is available on site, showers are available and workshops are air-conditioned. The company pays a contribution to each employee's holiday, offers an interest-free loan of up to €5,000 for emergency cases, supplementary pension insurance (€10–€100 for each employee) and on-site massage by a professional masseur.

Social and environmental responsibility

ALUCAST places a significant value on environment-friendly production. In accordance with the current Czech regulations, a set of in-house rules has been instituted concerning continual training and waste removal. The quantities of all substances leaking from production are monitored on a regular basis, even though they are well below the prescribed limits.

More than 40 jobs are undertaken by local employees. The firm cooperates with other small businesses and companies in the neighbourhood (machining, transport, surface finishing, manufacture of patterns, etc.). It also promotes local sporting and cultural events, the local school and football team. Land was donated to the community to build a cycle path.

Research and development

ALUCAST cooperates with Brno University of Technology on the development and research of new technologies. At present, the firm has successfully finished a project supported by the Ministry of Trade and Industry as part of the Business and Innovation cooperative programme. This involved ALUCAST investing in production facilities, inspection devices, building additional facilities for inspection processes and meeting the cooperation conditions with the aviation industry. At present ALUCAST owns state-of-the-art production equipment and inspection processes such as X-ray inspection for digital and film recording, and launches the production of precision castings for highly sophisticated fields.

Profitability

Every year, ALUCAST increases its turnover (see Figure 3.7) and profitability, although a drop in 2009 was caused by the worldwide economic recession. The 2011 turnover refers to the first six months. In 2011, ALUCAST planned to produce €4.5 millions' worth of castings.

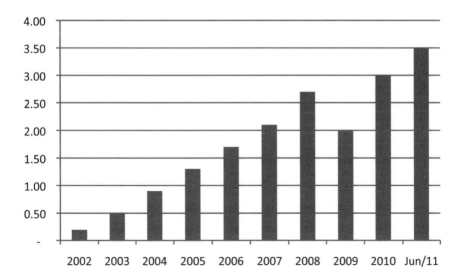

FIGURE 3.7 Turnover in million euros

Challenges of the twenty-first century

The company faced a number of challenges at the beginning of the twenty-first century:

• Although based in the Czech Republic, a country of long industrial history in terms of the precision-casting industry, the business has been impacted by the negative consequences of its geopolitical context – for example, being geographically linked with the raw-materials suppliers from Central and Eastern Europe. This has limited ALUCAST's capacity to face the current global economy challenges.

- The low efficiency of the casting technology used to process the essential raw materials, as well as the need to meet the high-quality requirements of customers from different industries, create challenges for conforming to ISO quality standards (such as aviation AS9100, NADCAP, etc.).
- Significant technical and technological innovation waves have also touched the use of aluminium and its alloys, resulting in a lower demand for these materials by industries. The only exception is artistic and creative casting where demand seems to be constant. In other industries, however, the need for precision casting and use of aluminium has started to dwindle.
- The general attribute of shorter times and earlier delivery dates also create challenges. In the case of aluminium casting, this general property can be identified in the way of management but, above all, in the possibility of shortening the preparatory phase of casting and linking to the state-of-the-art

TABLE 3.2 SWOT analysis of ALUCAST s.r.o.

Strengths	*Opportunities*
– Positive engineering approach to production (capability of fully using the existing equipment and raw materials to produce precision castings) – Low labour cost – State-of-the-art inspection equipment – Use of quality raw materials – Application of new technologies for high metallurgic quality production – Continual development of new technologies in cooperation with Brno University of Technology – Work on research projects supported by the Czech Ministry of Industry and Trade – Low job-switching of experts	– Step-by-step transfer to new technologies – Expected revitalization of the aviation, arms and power industries in the Czech Republic and in the former East European countries – Finding new customers – Expansion to East European markets
Weaknesses	*Threats*
– Wax patterns manufactured with domestic equipment – Large number of wasters in some sophisticated castings	– Decreasing demand for Al castings all over the world – Lack of specialists at all levels – Environmental limits – Lack of raw materials such as for melting – Protracted economic recession

methods of communication, data management and transfer, and customer–manufacturer cooperation, including rapid prototyping and others.

- The waning appeal of this industry and the severe lack of professional and technically qualified personnel and college graduates capable of managing the tasks and activities related to all production phases of precision aluminium casting are additional negative aspects of the foundry industry and, virtually, of the entire processing industry in the Czech Republic.
- In the case of lost-wax precision aluminium casting, each phase of the economic and social crisis takes effect with a certain time lag (for instance, the company market share for aviation, an industry with long-term contracts and orders, is 25 per cent), necessitating the need to effectively forecast risk.

In contrast, analysis of ALUCAST has identified the following internal challenges:

- Having two owners, the company has been built from scratch. Even with a successful period of dynamic sales increases and diversified customers from many industries and countries, precision aluminium casting requires extremely large capital, which makes financing and investing in new technologies such as non-destructive material testing immensely difficult.
- Despite some very good economic figures (e. g. the number of employees has risen seven times; there has been a €1 million investment in production technologies and innovations over the last three years; the production moved to the company's own premises and the production hall extended by another 1,100 square metres, etc.), the company faces the problem of having to appoint a successor and new manager after the present owners retire. There are also numerous questions concerning the succession plan for the present company secretary. Considering his expertise and personal contacts with business partners, it is not clear how all this could be passed on to the new manager when the owner moves into retirement.

Summary

The position of ALUCAST s.r.o. in the marketplace is stable and promising. After the first ten years of the firm's existence, its policy centred around high quality, and customer satisfaction has proved to be right along with the building of a stable and motivated team of managers. The firm also pursues the principles of corporate social responsibility[3] by voluntarily integrating the social and environmental issues in its business activities and everyday interactions with the firm's stakeholders. Among the main threats that could destabilize the firm in the near future are the lack of experts in precision casting and environmental restrictions that could dramatically raise the price of raw materials or production, as well as the protracted economic recession that hit ALUCAST in 2009.

However, maintaining or increasing the quality of its products, maintaining high-quality customer relationships, continuing development and innovation in production methods, and the continual training of young experts seems to be the right way of overcoming difficulties and increasing the firm's strengths. ALUCAST has all the conditions to defend its firm place in the European marketplace and successfully expand into other areas.

EXHIBIT 3.1 **The lost-wax method technological procedure**

Making a wax pattern

The quality of the wax pattern is decisive for the quality of the finished product. A wax pattern may be made by gravity casting (above the wax liquidity temperature), by injecting under increased pressure (0.5–1 MPa) – immediately below the temperature of liquid from foamed wax – or by injecting under a higher pressure (2.5–5 MPa) – below the temperature of liquid from a pasty state. Master dies used to produce moulds are usually made from metal. They are manufactured by machining, casting, galvanoplastically or by metallizing.

Assembling wax clusters

This is done after a wax pattern is hardened (stabilized) – for a minimum of 24 hours – with smaller models being assembled to form clusters or trees by soldering or pasting. The tree shape is affected by the way the patterns are connected, the techniques used for coating, melting out, casting and separating the castings from the gating system. The gating system is often made from regenerated (not new) wax.

Coating the patterns

Coating is made by repeatedly dipping the pattern (tree) into a slurry of fine refractory material. This consists of a binder (alkosols or hydrosols) and a filler (mostly quartz powder). After the cluster is taken out of the refractory material and any excess optimally drained off, it is stuccoed with coarse ceramic particle by dipping it into a fluidised bed, placing it in a rainfall-sander.

Drying the investments

The investments are dried in the air (controlled temperature, humidity and flow) or using a gas agent (ammonia).

Melting out the wax

Melting out the wax is done as follows:

- At a high temperature – in a furnace at a minimum temperature of 750 °C with subsequent annealing to 900–1000°C.
- At a low temperature:
  - in boiling water;
  - in an autoclave in overheated steam (0.3–0.6 MPa, t = 135–165°C);
  - by dielectric heating (a moistened shell is placed in a high-frequency oscillation field);
  - in a hot-air stream (aimed at the wax pattern centre).

When melting out the wax, it is important that an expansion gap should be formed (in other words, a layer of liquid wax at the investment-material/wax pattern boundary) to allow for the pattern dilating freely without breaking the investment shell. The reason is that a ceramic shell dilates substantially less and slower than the wax pattern.

Burning out the shell

The shell is burnt out to transform the amorphous form of a binding SiO_2 layer into a crystalline form while removing all the volatile substances. The burning out temperature ranges between 900 and 1,000°C (for SiO_2) and between 1,200 and 1,400°C for molochit, corundum and others.

Casting

Casting is done either in the air (open casting) or in a vacuum (vacuum casting). During casting, the ceramic shells are kept at a temperature of 700–800°C (immediately after being taken out of the furnace – called hot mould casting) or at the ambient temperature (cold mould casting, which cannot be used for quartz moulds as there is a danger of these cracking when cooled off because quartz is transformed at 572°C).

Notes

1　ALUCAST – the name of the company s.r.o. (společnost s ručením omezeným) – means limited liability company. I will use ALUCAST when writing about ALUCAST s.r.o.
2　For a detailed history of this technology, see also Baker (1997) who published his paper called Five Thousand Years of Precision Casting in the journal *Slévárenství*.
3　Corporate social responsibility (CSR) can be defined as the 'economic, legal, ethical, and discretionary expectations that society has of organizations at a given point in time' (Carroll and Buchholtz, 2003, p. 36). The concept of corporate social responsibility means that organizations have moral, ethical and philanthropic responsibilities in addition to their responsibilities to earn a fair return for investors and comply with the law (Putnová, 2007).

Bibliography

Carroll, A.B. and Buchholtz, A.K 2003. *Business and Society: Ethics and Stakeholder Management.* 5th edn. Australia: Thomson South-Western.

Cileček, J. and Mikulka, V. 2011. Přesnéodlitky proletech průmysl vyráběné metodou vytavitelného modelu. Investment casting for aircraft industry made by the investment pattern method. *Slévárenství.* 3–4, pp. 85–86.

Doškář, J. 1955. *New Ways of Metal Casting.* Prague.

Doškář, J., Gabriel, J., Houšt', M. and Pavelka, M. 1976. *Výroba přesných odlitků.* SNTL Prague.

Horáček, M. 2009. *Rozměrová přesnost odlitků vyráběných metodou vytavitelného modelu.* Brno: Vysoké učení technické, Fakulta strojního inženýrství.

Horáček, M. January/February 1997. *Investment Casting in Czech Republic.* INCAST.

Horáček, M. and Rous, S. 1997. *Investment Casting in Czech Republic.* 23rd BICTA conference, Cambridge.

Horáček, M. 2000. *Central and Eastern Europe*. 10th World Conference on Investment Casting, Monte Carlo.

Horáček, M. 1999. *Technologie vytavitelného modelu v České republice*. Bulletin: Czech Investment Casting Association.

Putnová, A. a kol. 2007. *Etickéřízení ve firmě*. Prague: Grada Publishing.

Williams, R. May 2000. *Investment Casting Markets 2000*. 10th World Conference on Investment Casting, Monte Carlo.

Williams, R. and Hirst, R. 2010. *Review of World Investment Casting Markets*. The Blayson Group Ltd, EICF 27th International Conference & Exposition, Krakow, Poland, 17 May.

4
NOMA – DENMARK

Søren Henning Jensen

Entrepreneurship literature is ripe with stories of companies built on an idea written down on a napkin. This story is slightly different but it has much in common with the traditional napkin tale. In Copenhagen the restaurant Noma was chosen in 2010 as the best restaurant in the world – a status it maintained in 2011 and 2012. In 2013 it fell back one place but regained the prestigious title of the best restaurant in the world in 2014. This was a major achievement not only for the restaurant but also for a movement that started with a manifesto in 2004, less than half a year after it opened its doors in 2003. The manifesto contained 10 rules outlining the New Nordic food paradigm. It was signed by 12 top chefs from the Nordic region. Claus Meyer was the architect behind the symposium where the manifesto and movement came into being and was one of the two co-writers of the draft manifesto. He is also one of the founders of Noma and is considered the "Father of the new Nordic kitchen". Another was Rene Redzepi, the intense and highly dedicated head chef of Noma. This case will describe how the restaurant Noma has achieved immense success in a relatively short time. It is also about how the love of food combined with a keen sense of business and authenticity has created something as unlikely as a top-class restaurant based on Danish and Nordic food. The restaurant has had a major impact on the national as well as the international restaurant scene.

The core of the case will show how the dedication to and respect for the restaurant trade, combined with an innovative approach and good old business understanding can create remarkable and sustainable success, even in the most unlikely setting. It is about how two people combined their competencies and used the concept of authenticity taken to the extreme to revitalize an entire regional kitchen by opening a groundbreaking restaurant. The case is about Claus Meyer and Rene Redzepi, and about the culinary, cultural and economic footprint they have left on the Danish food industry. The footprint they have left is not just local but global, and it shows us what it means to be entrepreneurial and to succeed in industry in a region where success of this magnitude seemed beyond reach. As such, the key phrase used to capture this case would be evangelistic entrepreneurship with a pragmatic touch.

The name "Noma" is an abbreviation of "Nordisk mad", which translates into "Nordic food", and the Noma dogma is that all dishes are made entirely from ingredients found in the Scandinavian region, including the North Atlantic islands, Iceland and Greenland. Throughout this case the word "kitchen" will be used in lieu of the word "cuisine" since this is the word the founders use. The rustic nature also lends itself better to the word kitchen than cuisine. The Danish or Nordic kitchen is therefore where we will start.

The traditional Danish and Nordic kitchen

The Danish kitchen is traditionally seen as rather heavy and maybe even bland. Sausage, pork roast, meatballs, pickled herring, liver pâté, bacon, potatoes and cabbage are traditional Danish dishes. For decades the only traditional Danish food was "smørrebrød" (open sandwiches), a dish that has been developed extensively over the last century. There are several smørrebrøds restaurants in Copenhagen that are well known and excel in good quality. However, they are not on the international culinary radar and there is not much going on in terms of entrepreneurship. A recent survey showed that Danes and Scandinavians in general have the lowest self-confidence when it comes to the value of the local Nordic kitchen.

Denmark has had Michelin star restaurants and innovative restaurants but they were always based on the Italian, French or Spanish kitchen. As an example of a high-profile restaurant with an innovative kitchen is Era Ora, an Italian restaurant with one star in the Michelin Guide. The Danish kitchen was not to be found in any of the Michelin restaurants. The restaurants serving traditional Danish food both smørrebrød and warm dishes did so honoring the old traditions, never breaking the mold, never questioning the approach to Danish food. Also, they never made any kind of impact on the restaurant scene.

The general trend in foods was to move away from the Danish kitchen in order to show dynamism and culinary craftsmanship. For decades foreign food has influenced Denmark and young people turned towards the Italian, French, Spanish, Asiatic or ethnic kitchen for inspiration. Traditional Danish food was old school – something you ate around Christmas and Easter, or when visiting your grandparents.

What Claus Meyer saw when he envisioned Noma and the rise of the new Nordic kitchen was to cut through the blandness and start over by being curious about the richness of ingredients around us. Refusing to accept that Denmark had nothing to offer except "smørrebrød" and meatballs, he endeavored to deliver his vision and did so by being very entrepreneurial in an area where groundbreaking entrepreneurship is hardly ever seen and even more rarely successful.

The Danish restaurant industry in numbers

In Denmark there is a total of 4,351 restaurants as of 2011, a slight decrease from 4,443 in 2010. The restaurant industry had a turnover of DKK13,839 million, equaling US$2.5 billion in 2011, an increase of 7.2 per cent compared to 2010. The industry employed 70,588 people – this number is up by 2.9 per cent compared to 2010, a positive trend after the industry saw its first decline in employment in a decade in 2009.

Danes dined out in restaurants roughly 50 million times in 2011, making the average price per visit DKK276, or US$50. As a comparison, a trip to Noma is almost 10 times the average price per visit and Noma has a long waiting list to admit guests. The restaurant industry as a whole is slowly recovering from the recession as the service and hospitality industry are always among the most affected industries when the economy slows down. Yet Noma with its tight dogma of only using ingredients from the Nordic region and high prices is more than thriving and has been doing so throughout the economic downturn. However, in addition to the numbers for the restaurant industry, we must also look at how entrepreneurship unfolds in Denmark.

Entrepreneurship in Denmark

The entrepreneurial climate in Denmark is somewhat complex but deserves attention in order to better understand the case of Noma. The Gem (Global Entrepreneurship Monitoring) report classifies the entrepreneurship drive or regime in Denmark as innovation driven – usually driven by technology or knowledge-based innovation due to the country's high standard of education. The Gem report measures entrepreneurship on a wide range of characteristics. This includes attitudes (perception of opportunity and capacity for entrepreneurship), activity (measuring startups, persistence and exits) and aspirations (growth potential, innovation and social value creation). In the 2010 report Denmark is ranked rather low on most of the parameters compared to other countries in the same entrepreneurship regime. Reasons for this can be the high taxation and strict bankruptcy laws making the risk/reward ratio inherently tied to entrepreneurship less attractive. This has led to the characterization of Danes as non-risk takers and a nation of working stiffs rather than entrepreneurs. However, in a report from the Danish Enterprise and Construction Authority lists Denmark as medium to high, comparing Denmark with other OECD countries, using data from 2007.

In terms of startups, Denmark is listed among the best in the EU with comparable data, and in terms of high-growth startups Denmark scores in the middle. This shows that there is some discrepancy and variation when it comes to measuring entrepreneurial activity as the measure is multifaceted. A fact that is not debatable is that the Danish government has ambitious goals to make Denmark the most entrepreneurial country in OECD by 2020. A report also from Gem using numbers from 2011 concludes that while low on necessity-driven entrepreneurship,

Denmark shows an overall high level of entrepreneurial work among employees across industries.

The national pattern for entrepreneurship has typically been that in the greater Copenhagen region and around other large cities entrepreneurship has been technology and knowledge based fueled by the proximity to universities. On the other hand, among ethnic minorities there has been a tradition for entrepreneurship in the service industries, corner shops, greengrocers and ethnic restaurants. In the peripheral and rural parts of Denmark focus has also been on manufacturing companies and from recent statistics we can see that the peripheral parts of Denmark have been quite successful as concerns entrepreneurship. Possibly, this stems from the otherwise disheartening fact that jobs are vanishing from these parts of Denmark, so entrepreneurs have to create new jobs and opportunities.

While there have been many startups in the restaurant business, these are usually either short-lived, high-profile but locally oriented ventures. Another variation is local restaurants catering for neighbourhood clients offering various ethnic food and inns in picturesque locations serving traditional Danish food. In other words, it has been very low key – often taking advantage of the relatively low-entry barriers of the restaurant industry and often short lived.

All of the above does not point towards a high-profile restaurant focusing solely on Nordic food as the obvious choice for success, yet in 2003 that was exactly what happened, which leads us directly back to the two entrepreneurs who made this possible. In order to understand the success of Noma, it is crucial to understand the founders and their motivation. The above description of the Danish kitchen, the Danish restaurant industry and the general entrepreneurial climate is the backdrop against which we have to understand Noma.

Noma: the background and the paradigm

The Nordic kitchen has until recently not been held in high esteem in the culinary world. The idea that a restaurant based on this kitchen would until a few years ago have sounded like a joke. Nevertheless, in 2010 Noma, a restaurant developed by two Danish chefs and culinary entrepreneurs, received the award as the best restaurant in the world. Two years previously they had received their second Michelin star.

Noma is the direct result of a unique cooperation between a young energetic chef and a more seasoned chef, cooking-show host, author of several cookbooks and culinary entrepreneur. Their cooperation shows what can happen when an uncompromised love for craftsmanship and authentic food is coupled with a keen sense for business. However, in a larger picture it is also the result of a new phase in Denmark and the Nordic region concerning culture in general. In the late 1990s the dogma film concept was developed by a group of Danish directors and screenwriters. The idea was to go back to basics and tell good stories with little or no artificial lighting and handheld cameras. Filmmakers wanting to adhere to this approach to filmmaking had to sign a dogma document in which they pledged themselves to uphold these rules. This created an immense energy in Danish film-making and a string of masterpieces resulted, winning both critical acclaim and audience approval. Suddenly Denmark was more than Danish design when it came to aesthetics. This seems to have had a positive effect on the culinary scene – an effect very much driven by the success of Noma. However, before venturing into the restaurant, we will look at the Danish restaurant scene – an unlikely stage for entrepreneurship of this sort.

Start of Noma: the founding of success

While Noma opened its doors in 2003, the two minds behind the enterprise met in 2002 when Claus Meyer contacted Rene to discuss the project as he knew that the young chef shared his passion for authenticity and had the skills needed to head the kitchen. From the first meetings it was obvious that the two made a great team and that Rene shared Claus's enthusiasm for the project and could see the potential. It is the relationship between the two founders and their unique combination of skills that explains the success of the restaurant. Both share an immense interest in food and cooking and both share a love for authenticity – this is the core of the restaurant. In addition, Rene has the drive to excel as a proud and flamboyant head chef and Claus has the business flair. This combination of skills with a common aim has turned an apparent recipe for disaster or fad into a world-class success. It has also ensured that Noma has been able to balance between the culinary and the commercial, ensuring that the business has thrived while never moving away from the dogma of only using Scandinavian ingredients in the food. This means that a sauce will not contain wine but beer, ale or fruit juice instead. This approach is very different from the restaurant scene in Denmark before 2003, since when much has changed.

Looking at how the place became so successful, it is a clear case of word of mouth – no big advertising campaigns were launched. The restaurant did get some media attention due to the fame of Claus Meyer and the uniqueness of the concept, but had the place not delivered it would have turned out to be a fad, a quirky experiment and nothing more. Nor did the founders' rising fame cause them to sell out in any way. Nothing changed in their concept in order to accommodate the rising demand. Their strategy was to remain authentic and stay true to the dogma. So who are the two people behind Noma?

The founders of Noma

Claus Meyer was originally trained as an economist and in 1991 he received his Master's degree in business administration and international affairs at Copenhagen Business School. However, since his childhood he has loved cooking. His Master's thesis was on startups and business development. He started his first catering service in 1983, cooking in his one-bedroom apartment. In 1989 putting theory into practice he used the surplus generated to start up "Meyer's kitchen", a company catering to private parties and events. The company is still operating.

In 1991, the same year as he graduated, Meyer starred in a television cooking show, which was his first launch into the public domain. It was also the first time that he showed his ability for making the ordinary interesting and shaking off the dust of Danish cooking and making Danes interested in food. Previously, cooking shows in Denmark had been very elitist, demonstrating fancy French cooking – showing what chefs could cook in their restaurants but not what the general population could cook at home. There have also been examples of the opposite, where very traditional Danish chefs heralded the traditional Danish kitchen with little if any inspiration outside Denmark. Neither approach did anything to promote an interest in the Danish or Nordic kitchen.

Claus Meyer was a different breed altogether, combining his enthusiasm and curiosity about introducing new ingredients or reinventing old ones with a pragmatic approach to cooking. He showed how everybody could experiment with new dishes and was not afraid to mix old with new, foreign with domestic. The show ran for almost a decade and propelled him to become a household name in Denmark. Simultaneously, he opened new restaurants, always with an experimental touch. One such example is "Meyer's Spisehus", which he opened in an up-and-coming neighbourhood where the guests also cooked with the assistance of professional chefs. The restaurant is still in operation.

In 2007 Meyer was back on TV with a show called "Cooking in Scandinavia". This was three years after Noma had opened its doors and the show focused on rediscovering the Danish and Scandinavian kitchen.

Claus Meyer has showed a gift for combining an enthusiasm for food, for cooking and for an authentic kitchen – for going back to basics – with a flair for business. He has never exploited his name or sold out, nor has he gone bankrupt with a restaurant as so many other chefs have done due to lack of business flair. Noma is a shining example of this ability. However, without Rene Redzepi, Noma would not have been the success that it has been. Claus Meyer first had the idea to start up Noma when facilities in an over 200-year-old former warehouse right by the waterfront in central Copenhagen opened up. In order to employ someone to run the place as head chef he contacted a few very accomplished chefs, one of whom was Rene Redzepi.

Redzepi trained as a chef at the restaurant Pierre Andre in Copenhagen. He had already worked in the Michelin-awarded Danish restaurant "Kong Hans Kælder", the esteemed restaurant "El Bulli" in Barcelona and the "French Laundry" in America before he initially discussed opening Noma with Claus Meyer in 2002. He is well known for his uncompromising approach to cooking and his skills as a top chef. He is the head chef at Noma and as such is the face of Noma to the public. As a testament to his thoroughness and dedication, Rene Redzepi and Claus Meyer spent a month travelling around the Nordic region. They wanted to see for themselves if there were indeed enough high-quality and interesting ingredients – meat, poultry, game, fish, shellfish, vegetables, fruits and herbs – to sustain the restaurant. Upon their return they were convinced that the region could well sustain Redzepi's demand for authenticity and that it was as rich in taste as any region.

Redzepi argued in an interview with the magazine *World Chef* that the blandness of the Scandinavian kitchen is perceived rather than real. When it comes to self-confidence in regional cooking, Scandinavians have scored the lowest for a long time, looking to exotic kitchens for inspiration rather than looking at what is right in front of them.

As his career shows, Redzepi has always been attracted to the international scene. In an interview he remembers how some of his friends laughed when he told them about his and Claus Meyers's plans to start up a restaurant serving only food based on Nordic ingredients – no caviar, no foie gras – joking that he would ruin his brilliant career. Today, Rene has proved that this was not the case.

What does the future hold for Noma?

Currently, Noma is at the very pinnacle of success, after regaining the title as the world's best restaurant in 2014 and one of the few restaurants in Denmark with two stars in the Michelin guide. It was expected that it would receive the third star upon being granted the status of "Best restaurant in the world" in 2010, but this did not happen and Noma remained a two-star restaurant, receiving its first Michelin star in 2005, just one year after opening its doors, and the second star in 2007. Despite the disappointment of not getting the third star the restaurant has achieved a level of success that was not in any way anticipated when it opened. This raises the question – What now? Is the third star the final goal? What more can the future bring for the restaurant? Several scenarios are possible: is it feasible to expand the Noma concept and dogma to other countries? London, Paris and New York are possible places for such venues in order to boost the restaurant's financial aspects and the concept could be kept intact since it is within the dogma to fly in products as long as they are from the Scandinavian region. According to Claus Meyer, the fact that the restaurant is a two- and not a three-star restaurant is not a hindrance to taking the Noma concept abroad. Two-star restaurants are worth taking a detour to experience, while three stars means that they are worth traveling to, and this opens the question as to whether the two-star status could mean that success abroad would cannibalize the domestic success.

To some extent the future is already here when it comes to expanding the success of Noma. Claus Meyer has gone to Bolivia to start up another entrepreneurial culinary project. The idea is to reinvent and rediscover the Bolivian kitchen and to revitalize it in some way – a distillation of the totality of the Claus Meyers company and his 25 years of experience as an entrepreneur – not by creating a big fancy restaurant but by opening a school teaching young people to cook. The intention is to implement the Noma concept of authenticity, using only local or regional ingredients, getting to the core of local cooking and rediscovering the local kitchen. In a country where 60 per cent of the population is living below the poverty line this is a significant challenge. It could also be the start of another spin-off from Noma. If the team behind Noma can create the best restaurant in the world in a region where self-confidence in the qualities of the local kitchen was at the lowest by going back to basics, clearly Redzepi and Meyers have important insights to share with any region or country.

In an age where there is a strong focus on sustainability, especially in developing countries, such programs could have a great impact by helping local populations to become better educated and better able to survive on limited resources and become self-sufficient. To this end Redzepi and Meyer have created a foundation "the melting pot", which, in cooperation with other NGOs, is starting up initiatives to help boost local interest in cooking and start a local food revolution – another concrete example or examples of how the success of Noma has fuelled other projects. In the fall of 2011, Claus Meyer opened a restaurant called "Radio", near the old Radiohouse in Copenhagen. The idea was to create a restaurant where the authentic Nordic kitchen can be experienced at a lower price than at Noma and where the dogma of Noma has been loosened slightly. As the head chef puts it, "Here it is OK to use lemon to add taste." The restaurant focuses on creating good authentic food, taking the point of departure in the rediscovered Nordic kitchen and sourcing their ingredients locally from farms, small dairies and local hunters in the game season. The restaurant has a more urban interpretation of the Nordic kitchen. As Claus Meyer explains, "the idea was never to create a uniform regional kitchen", so Radio is very much inspired by Noma but is developing in a different direction.

Yet another challenge looming in the near future is that Rene Redzepi stated when Noma opened that he would stay there for a decade. Currently he is still head chef. However, this raises the question of what will happen if he leaves – has Noma reached the point where the reputation it carries and Claus Meyers's continuous involvement is enough to keep it successful in the absence of the charismatic chef Rene Redzepi? Or will its chef leave along with the drive that has been pivotal in the success story? It could simply be that Rene Redzepi's drive comes partly from his pledge of staying for a decade to build up the restaurant and that this momentum is now self-sustaining and he can move on to even more challenging projects. The economic and culinary success of Noma ensures that the place could attract other international top chefs.

Looking at Claus Meyer's entrepreneurial track record it has not been a history of opening up places and firms only to close them down later. Rather, they have kept going and most are still around even if they have been redefined over time. Noma could well serve as a platform for other projects for the entrepreneurial chef. The same goes for Rene Redzepi. So even if he does leave the restaurant in a few years true to his pledge, he is not necessarily totally out of the picture and could even use some of the time he has at present tied up in Noma (he usually works 80–100 hours a week) to further his role as ambassador for the Nordic kitchen or to propel other promising restaurants to success.

Possibly this brings us closer to the core of the success of Noma as well as the future. Noma has succeeded in all possible ways both on the culinary, the cultural, the financial and the personal level. Redzepi and Meyer have put Copenhagen and the Nordic region on the culinary map and showed what love for food and cooking coupled with curiosity and authenticity as well as good business sense can achieve. As such, Noma will for a long time be a beacon on the Danish and Scandinavian restaurant scene, both as a stellar restaurant but also as a visible sign of the transformation we have witnessed, particularly in Denmark with regard to restaurants and the general population's interest in the Danish local kitchen. Perhaps this is the future for Noma – to act as a platform for future entrepreneurial ventures from the two founders, Claus Meyer and Rene Redzepi, and for the Danish culinary scene in general. Using the power of example Noma can serve as a platform for innovative restaurants.

The impact of Noma on the Danish restaurant scene – and beyond

It is not possible to state directly how big the influence of Noma has been on the Danish restaurant scene since the restaurant was not the only factor in the revival of the Nordic kitchen, even if it has been the most significant. However, there are several indications of how influential the restaurant has been. In Copenhagen there are currently 11 restaurants with Michelin guide stars; of these, 6 serve food inspired by the Nordic kitchen – this was not the case when Noma opened its doors. Rene Redzepi has just published the first cookbook based on the food served in Noma and on the very strict dogma of how to cook and what to cook with. Claus Meyer has launched several cookbooks inspired by the new Nordic kitchen and his latest restaurant Radio is, as mentioned above, heavily inspired by Noma. Looking at restaurants outside the Michelin stars we see the same pattern. Many new restaurants have either taken up the trend of serving food based on an interpretation of the Nordic kitchen or have been inspired by the "back- to-basics" approach to cooking. Others have stayed true to their original concepts be it French, Italian, Spanish or Japanese, but have started putting old ingredients back on the menu.

One such example is the herb sea-buckthorn, a plant found along the coastline. A few years ago it was all but unknown, but now, thanks to Claus Meyer, it has been rediscovered and is used by the new Nordic restaurants, traditional restaurants and even sushi restaurants. It has even found its way into dairy products such as yoghurt and is a good example of how the tight dogmatic approach to the new Nordic kitchen exemplified by Noma has affected the Danish food culture as a whole.

In a 2011 article in *Wall Street Journal* a journalist identified six potential candidates as the next big thing on the restaurant scene, the next El Bulli or Noma. It is in itself interesting that Noma is seen to be in the same league as El Bulli as an innovative restaurant. It is equally interesting that three of the new candidates were operating along the same lines as Noma, except that they were using only local, sometimes very local ingredients in their cooking. One example is the restaurant "The Willow Inn" located on the small island of Lummi, just south of the Canadian border. The place is run by the young chef Blaine Wetzel who worked as chef de partie (section chef) at Noma. The concept is that they cook only what they can source locally from a small farm or get directly from the rich flora and fish from two fishing-boats. Clearly, this shows that the impact of Noma is not only on the local scene but has also spread to the international restaurant scene and has created a new type of highly authentic restaurants emphasizing the importance of using local ingredients.

In early 2016 Claus Meyer will be opening a 1,200 square metre restaurant and food court in Vanderbilt Hall, Grand Central Station in New York, based on the new Nordic Kitchen, using local produce. This new project truly shows that the concept on which Noma is based is international and that the idea on which the restaurant is based continues to carry it forward.

On Noma's website there is a category called "Noma alumni" showing a list of former Noma employees and the culinary projects and restaurants they work at now – Blaine Wetzel is one of them. The list is impressive and the use of the word "alumni" shows that Noma is more than a restaurant – even if it is the best restaurant in the world. It is also a place of learning and the chefs graduating from Noma venture out and use their knowledge in new and exciting projects.

It is obvious that Noma is an unlikely success in itself. However, it is also much more than that – it is the symbol of a new way of thinking about food worldwide and the renaissance of the Nordic kitchen. So, in short, no matter what will happen with Noma in the long run, the success it has already achieved and the impact it has made will remain. What began as a brand new idea for a restaurant has become the world's best restaurant. This, despite the fact that it did not look promising from the start both from a business point of view and from a culinary perspective. The case of Noma spurs the following questions to all businesses and industries: How well do you really know your industry? What is the core of your business? How do you infuse your business with authenticity?

Case study questions

1   Will it be possible to export the concept of Noma abroad to other big cities and what are the major challenges?
2   How can the entrepreneurial potential of the new Nordic kitchen be harnessed?
3   What will happen to Noma after Rene Redzepi leaves as the head chef?

5

AML – HONG KONG

Kevin Au and Jeremy Cheng

John Mok had just finished his guest speech on "Nurturing Entrepreneurship in the Next Generation" at the Chinese University of Hong Kong. Being a renowned entrepreneur in the manufacturing industry,[1] he had enjoyed a successful entrepreneurial career and intended to step down from daily business operations. Succession was no easy task, let alone laying a foundation for entrepreneurship across generations. Scores of questions were asked by the participants regarding the innovativeness of Automatic Manufacturing Limited (AML) and his elaborate scheme to develop the entrepreneurial spirit across generations.

Participants were impressed by his scheme but split as to whether the entrepreneurial spirit and practice could truly be transferred to the incoming generation. Some were even skeptical as to whether AML and the Moks had realized the best potential in accumulating wealth and bringing the best out of the company for society and the family. "With your early success," asked the audience, "why didn't you grow AML more quickly, list the company, and raise more funds for development?" There are no straight answers to these questions. After developing a reputable company, John and AML faced serious decisions in dealing with succession challenges.

The AML story

After graduating with a physics degree in the late 1960s, John began to work in a semi-conductor company. Two years later, he joined a computer manufacturer and was promoted to manufacturing manager. During that time, John's eldest brother, Peter Mok, worked in a large multinational company for sales and business development. Peter predicted a large demand for advanced machine tools and engineering plastics[2] from his international exposure. He proposed that John and his wife Meg should open a factory together to address the demand. This gave birth to AML in 1976 (Exhibit 5.1).

John recalled that AML "was founded on the opportunistic vision and quick payback calculations". The founders worked hard together with a small group of loyal staff to grow the company. AML started with a plastic parts and molds factory. The three founders, however, quickly found that the market for advanced products was small in Hong Kong. Instead, AML spotted a large market for low-tech non-engineering plastics widely used in plastic flowers, which was one of Hong Kong's major exports. AML reacted to market changes quickly and, more importantly, at low costs. Meanwhile, AML also gained a foothold in manufacturing remote-controlled toys and electrical appliances. Like many other new companies at that time, it established itself as an original equipment manufacturer (OEM). The market was simple in technology, low in margin, but large in volume.

From low-tech to high-tech

Expanding quickly, AML was incorporated as a limited company in 1979. However, John smelled the danger of "swimming in the red ocean" with hundreds of other OEMs in Hong Kong. He believed that AML should stay ahead in technology, enjoy a higher margin, and refrain from fierce price competition. Following this path, he directed AML to produce products with more technology, such as advanced office electronics and industrial control systems. In addition, he also focused on reducing defects and raising production quality. In 1984, AML obtained GMP certification, a compliance standard for producing medical equipment, enabling the company to manufacture medical and surgical products. Since then, the Moks manufactured products with ever higher technology and quality. The stress on quality was reflected in the motto of one of the divisions, "No quality, no business". Gaining progress in these new areas, AML actually sold their low-tech, low-quality mechanical manufacturing and the toy production one-by-one in the early 1980s. As John put it, "One factory cannot have two different systems of quality". The uniqueness and achievement of AML would best be appreciated as most Hong Kong manufacturers continued to struggle in keen competition (Exhibit 5.2).

Towards internationalization

Following China's Open Door Policy, AML had expanded its production capacities in Shenzhen to benefit from lower production costs and abundance of engineers. The plants were later relocated to Dongguan and Baoshan, two manufacturing hubs in Southern China, taking advantage of policy change and encouragement by local governments. AML invested increasingly more in R&D and product design. Meanwhile, promoting self-learning and self-experiment, the founders gradually trained up a few department heads to assist divisional growth and to produce innovative products. For example, AML cooperated with Imperial College London to develop a three-dimension (3D) stem cell bio-reactor. Different from a traditional

2D machine, this 3D incubation machine mimicked the microenvironment of the living tissues, and the 3D skin was thus good not only for beauty treatments but also for biology. Another example of AML's innovation effort was a joint venture, called SGAI, with Sagentia. Sagentia of the UK was one of the world's pre-eminent technology management and product development companies. In 2002, lacking an understanding of Chinese culture, Sagentia decided to form a joint venture with AML to reduce R&D costs owing to cultural mismatches. AML benefited from Sagentia's Cambridge base, which employed over 150 Ph.D. qualified personnel.

Management during expansion

As AML continued to grow, the founders nurtured a Top Management Team (TMT) and started a multidivisional structure in 1996 (Table 5.1). Following the philosophy of the founders, the TMT of each division were assigned to guard each of the three "gates": market development and sales (the front gate), R&D and product design (the middle gate), and production and quality control (the end gate). Each General Manager (GM) would require different qualities, experiences, and skill sets. The founders gave autonomy to the divisional TMTs and stepped back from their day-to-day operations. The TMTs spent time on their own divisions and received advice from headquarters. Furthermore, the TMTs also acted as mentors for the second generation of the Mok family when they were learning the ropes in AML (Table 5.2).

The founders continued to own AML collectively. John represented AML in various business and community events, but decision-making was based on liaison and consensus. The founders aside, the TMT also included a few professional managers such as K.M. Chow and James Li. As a divisional general manager, James started working in AML in 1983. He left AML for two years but rejoined the company as a result of John's quest for quality. K.M. worked in a number of listed companies before serving as John's right-hand man. K.M. commented on his career choice:

> AML enjoyed a stable income from stable clients and a handsome margin. It was large enough to be listed many years ago if it so decided . . . In AML, we are encouraged to find the best solution while pursuing financial return. Not many companies would approve that.

Governance and growth

AML's Board of Directors consisted of three categories of members: non-executive directors, independent non-executive directors, and executive directors. The non-executive directors comprised the chairman and the vice-chairman, responsible for high-level corporate value architecture and strategic development. Independent non-executive directors were the corporate management coaches and internal

TABLE 5.1 Overview of the group's Top Management Team

Member	Post	Year of joining AML	Year of becoming TMT	Responsibilities
John Mok	Chairman of BoD*	1976	1976	General management and strategic decision
Peter Mok	Vice Chairman of BoD*	1976	1976	Mechanical technology, global marketing, strategic alliance and joint venture
Meg Mok	Director of BoD*	1976	1976	Finance, purchasing, personnel and administrative functions
4 nephews of Moks	NED**	2000– 2010	Executive Director of 4 spin-offs of AML; NED** of AML	Finance and business networking
K.M. Chow	Corporate General Manager	2003	2003 as Corporate General Manager	Developing growth strategies, heading the corporate university, coaching startups and importing technology for product development
James Li	Division General Manager	1983	1992 as Divisional General Manager	Office and telecom equipment
Asso Lee	Division General Manager	N.A.	2001 as Divisional General Manager	Home automation and industrial controls

* BoD: Board of Directors ** NED: Non-executive Director

Source: Au *et al.* (2012)

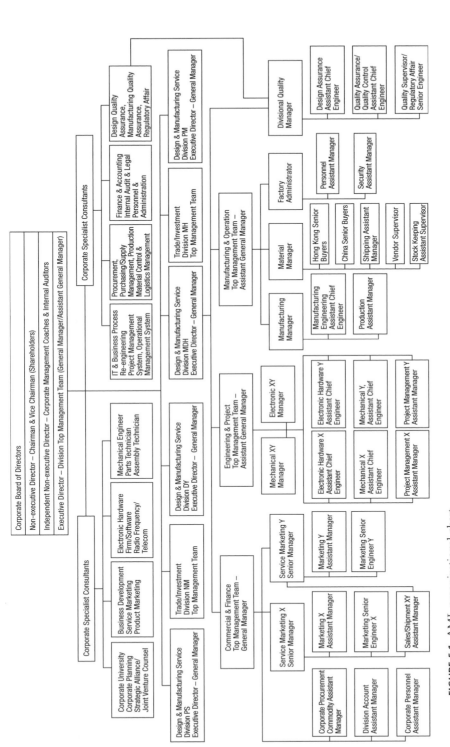

FIGURE 5.1 AML organizational chart

auditors. Executive directors were the divisional TMTs who took most functional strategies and implementation on hand. A corporate audit committee was also formed to audit, monitor, and guide strategic business units according to the board's decisions.

Despite a clear understanding of management-ownership separation, the AML board comprised only the founders and William Mok, Matt's son. John commented:

> When a company is still mid-sized, the board has only a few non-executive directors – only those investors not participating in management. Most of the executive directors are shareholders or TMT. They have stock options exercisable upon IPO. Before the company goes public, it is difficult to convince the existing internal auditor and management consultant to carry the legal obligation of an independent non-executive director. The financial rewards may not be attractive enough to outside professionals . . . The board planned to list AML to get a market valuation and to facilitate the use of other corporate devices (such as stock options) to govern the firm. The economic environment and the situation of the stock market would determine the timing and success of this plan . . . Listing the company is not for the benefits of the incoming generation but for those who created the glory of AML with me. The incoming generations are well off because of their professional education. It is my responsibility to look after those who realized my dream.

A learning organization

Driven by John's aspiration, AML developed a strong learning culture (Figure 5.2). Such an emphasis is best reflected in a story by Michelle Lum, a divisional TMT member. She recalled a troublesome business trip in the United Kingdom, but "when John found that an exam was coming up in my EMBA study, he urged me to take the first flight back while he stayed behind to solve the problem."

Another case in point was the setup of the "Automatic Manufacturing University" (AMU) in 2003. Headed by K.M. Chow, the AMU covered different specialties such as corporate strategy and planning, marketing and sales, engineering and project management, and R&D. Each specialty had a specialist consultant (a "professor"), a researcher, and a research assistant. The primary responsibility of the AMU was to introduce "modernization" or new advancements into AML. The AMU also searched for and customized new knowledge, and provided training and coaching of the new knowledge to the employees. The employees took exams and underwent auditing and benchmarking exercises. Awards were given to those who outperformed other groups. The AMU served all AML members and nurtured the incoming generations of the Mok family. Sometimes, the AMU would send specialists to help the AML startup customers or partners to solve their specific problems.

Team creativity, group consensus and joint commitments

團策邀群論，眾識堅承諾

Harmonious collaboration using complimentary skills

群力先親和，樂助不囂功

Award team excellence and share group rewards

共榮互贊謝，共利賞忠義

Quality for leadership, effectiveness for growth

質量求優勝，效益求發展

FIGURE 5.2 AML company belief

Source: Company file

The Mok family and the second generation

Society changes as institutions develop and people become independent. The Moks had a small extended family like most others in Hong Kong (Figure 5.3). The father of Peter and John was in the shipping business. Peter (the eldest son) and John (the youngest son) had two other brothers, Matt (the elder son) and Phil (the younger son), and two sisters. Matt and Phil started their own garment businesses in the early years. John and Meg did not have any children. Peter had three sons – Rob, Bill, and Alex; Matt also had two children, Salina and William.

The history of the Mok family was relatively young, and the AML business involved only two generations. The founders expressed their wish to step down from being executive directors to gradually become non-executive directors. All the male second-generation members worked several years in AML after college. Peter's sons started and ran their own spin-off companies as owner-managers in a joint venture with American and European partners. William, on the other hand, worked for AML as executive director, taking care of legal and intellectual property matters, corporate finance, and angel investment. William admired his cousins' success and dreamt of spinning off a company one day. His first job was with AML as a management trainee in 2000. After nine months, William left AML and joined his father's toy-trading company. William helped expand the company. In October 2007, William returned to AML as Matt retired from the business and transformed it into a consulting firm instead.

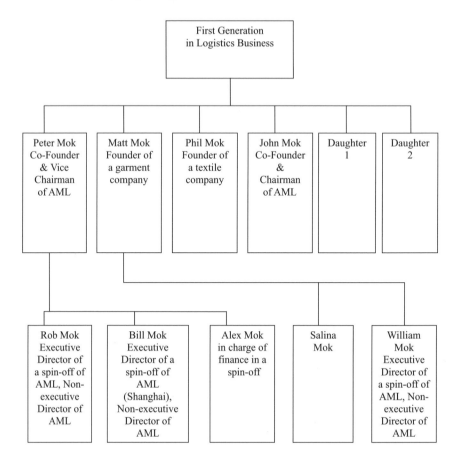

FIGURE 5.3 The Mok family

The intrapreneurship scheme

John was aware that the two generations of the Mok family had a gap of 30 years. To continue the family entrepreneurship, he designed an intrapreneurship program that combined an angel investment scheme and a family education curriculum. The program was also open to committed TMTs and their offspring. John expected the succession to occur when the second generation succeeded in their spin-offs and merged with AML. By that time each of the succeeding generations could act as executive directors of their spin-offs in the merger, and the TMTs could run and grow their divisions profitably without seeking continual advice from the founders.

Early career development

Instead of working in AML immediately after college, the incoming generation worked as executives in other large firms to learn best practices in at least two complementary disciplines. John explained the idea behind this approach:

> The second generation does not have the necessary operational skills. If the second generation is to work in AML shortly after college, they are most vulnerable to making wrong decisions. Other staff and indeed their mentors may laugh at them. They might either feel intimidated to take risks at work or lose authority for future governance.

The Mok family financially supported the second generation in their pursuit of specialist masters in engineering technology. Between the ages of 30 and 35, the second generation was encouraged to return to AML and worked as supervisors, receiving "incubation nursery" from the divisional TMTs and the AMU professors, and attending a master's degree in marketing. The major learning "goals" of the incoming generation at this stage were people and marketing skills.

The pre-spin-off stage

In their mid-30s, the second generation completed their EMBA and finance education, and formulated a business idea in a related but non-competitive area and wrote a startup plan for the patriarchs. Headquarters could introduce customers and complementary partners to co-write the business plan with the second generation. With financial management skills, the incoming generation could found or acquire a small company as a TMT or a business division under the corporate parent. With this, John wished to accelerate the revenue growth to secure angel investment before a spin-off. The startup team might consist of the incoming generation and, if necessary, existing AML employees. While John encouraged "open recruitment" of people, this did not always guarantee that the most experienced people would go with and "escort" the second generation in their new venture. John commented:

> The TMTs are older and very experienced, and they have a very deep understanding of the company. They prefer staying in the headquarters and in the old divisions. This is because of the generation gap. Those TMTs with a five-year gap with the second generation may be fine; but those with a ten-year gap will not spin off with the second generation.

For example, the non-family divisional general manager James coached Rob Mok for about two years before he spun off this company. James thought that the relatively stable internal environment of AML allowed the second generation to pick things up gradually and to learn better. In his words, "A person may be asked to sign a cheque without knowing well what is accounting." AML provided the exact environment for the person to learn why. Michelle also mentored Rob before his spin-off. She taught him people management skills such as fairness and people development. She reckoned that Peter could teach business skills much better than she did. Both James and Michelle said they treated their mentees like other employees.

No one knew the exact feelings of the mentors when the mentees actually received a higher position or even if they headed their mentors later on. The mentors knew that this might happen one day following the business succession (or even before that). Rob was promoted as executive director in his own spin-off. Michelle was happy for Rob, and she said she saw it coming and did not mind it. John expressed his view:

> The TMTs became the "masters" or mentors of the second-generation trainees. It would be hard psychologically for the second generation to control what their masters did. The masters would, anyway, not listen to them. The generation gap exists. In Western cultures, capable people take a higher post. Even though a person used to be the subordinate, he will be able to lead his former boss with confidence. This does not happen in Chinese culture. People have a strong memory of how the old days looked like. And the master–apprentice relationships are often strongly imprinted in the mind.

Spin-off in action

Approved plans first received seed money from the family. If the concept was proven with the seed money, AML or the family would provide a more substantial "loan" for the second generation to spin off a "joint venture". John was specific about the size of the funding:

> The new venture must be large enough to challenge the skills of the second generation and make their time and risk worthwhile. The substantial size of the venture, normally of several millions Hong Kong, also made the second generation concerned about their company's survival, driving them to look for clients themselves.

John expected that the risk-reduced path would speed up the growth of the spin-off. At the ages of 40 and 45, the incoming generation could serve as general manager in the spin-off and as non-executive director in the headquarters.

As the venture was mature and became profitable, the incoming generation could merge the spin-off with AML in an exchange of shares. In other words, the second generation bought back or even took over the corporate parent. After the merger, the second generation could operate their own division as executive directors, serve on the board of the group, and coach new startups. John believed that this arrangement had a good deal of advantage in integrating and developing the incoming generation in the family business.

TABLE 5.2 AML second generation: education and working experience

	Rob Mok	Bill Mok	Alex Mok	William Mok
College education	Bachelor of Engineering in Manufacturing, Engineering and Management	BBA in Marketing	BBA in Accounting and Finance	Bachelor in Economics
Continuing education	Executive Diploma in Corporate Governance	M.Sc. in Engineering Business Management and EMBA	Executive Diploma in Corporate Governance	MBA and Executive Diploma in Corporate Governance
Work experience in AML	5 years in Marketing and Business Development	3 years in Engineering and Manufacturing	4 years in Headquarters	8 years in Accounting and Finance, Purchasing and Trading, IT and Legal
Spin-off	In 2008 spun off an international joint venture in an OBM self-brand Advanced Electronics	3 years ago spun off an international joint venture in an OBM self-brand Power Tools	In 2010 served as Executive Director of an international joint venture group	In 2010 served as Executive Director of a spin-off of AML; in 2013 founded his own company

Continuing family entrepreneurship

John knew his priorities and those of his family. At the startup stage, wealth creation was the most important goal of a family enterprise. Founding family members could hold controlling stakes and participate in the board as directors and in the routine management of the business. To John, it was natural for founders to step down from management and ownership after years of work, and perhaps try to contribute to the family and the business through other ways.

The challenge to incubate transgenerational entrepreneurship was common among family businesses like AML. John truly appreciated the difficulty. His scheme for the incoming generation was elaborate but it would not be perfect. While several of the incoming generation had followed this scheme to develop their career (Table 5.2), a critical point was expressed by one of them: "The different strengths of the second generation cannot be cultivated by the first generation. This has more to do with our individual choice of college education." One of the TMT members also raised another concern:

> The second generation may no longer need our "escort" when they return to the corporate parent. They might even bring their own professional team back. The dynamics are not foreseeable when all spin-offs return and merge with the corporate parent. The whole AML may be changed completely.

As the founders developed AML into a reputable company (see Table 5.3 for company statistics), the succession plan was gradually implemented. The second generation, all well educated, expressed their interest to build a business career. Would the scheme work to maintain the family legacy? Looking back, could they have pursued entrepreneurship differently? What might John and the Moks do further to increase the chance of success in continuing the family entrepreneurial spirit?

TABLE 5.3 Growth of AML since 2007

Year	2011	2009	2007
No. of total employees (HK and PRC)	3,000	2,800	4,000
No. of new ventures/partners	2	2	2
Annual sales in HKD (million)			
(i) Medical and healthcare devices	425	140	86
(ii) Office equipment and telecom products	285	224	358
(iii) Industrial controls and home automation	344	235	416
(v) Others	14	1	–
Total	1,068	600	860

Source: File provided by AML in November 2012

Case study questions

1 Is AML a successful company in entrepreneurial, financial, or social terms? What are the key success factors of AML?

2 What are the major challenges for the Mok family and for AML to maintain entrepreneurship across generations?

3 Evaluate the AML intrapreneurship scheme. Is the scheme useful in nurturing transgenerational entrepreneurship?

4 What may John and the Moks do further to increase the chance of success in continuing the family entrepreneurial spirit?

EXHIBIT 5.1 Profiles and milestones of AML

AML provides integrated design and manufacturing services for a range of electronic products. These include medical and healthcare devices, automotive electronics, office equipment, telecom products, industrial controls, and home automation products. In 2008, AML employed over 3,000 employees, 260 of whom were engineers. Headquartered in Hong Kong, AML had several manufacturing facilities of around 330,000 square feet in Dongguan, and a trading and liaison office in Shanghai. Also, a spin-off of AML was setting up a plant in the Czech Republic to support final assembly and distribution services in Europe.

AML company history

Year	Corporate Events
1976	Established in Hong Kong with plastic injection and mould-making plants.
1978	Expanded Hong Kong plant into mechanical manufacturing and product assembly.
1979	Incorporated as a limited company and expanded Hong Kong plant into electronic manufacturing and product assembly.
1985	Expanded Hong Kong plant into medical devices manufacturing with GMP.
1987	Established manufacturing plant at Shenzhen, China.
1990	Moved the design and production to Dongguan, China.
1998	AML factories were certified ISO 9001.
	Voice Announce Caller ID (VA-059) won Product Innovation Award in Consumer Electronics Show 1998.

1999   Voice Announce Caller ID (VA-073) won Product Innovation Award in Consumer Electronics Show 1999.

2000   Voice Announce Caller ID (VA-082) won Product Innovation Award in Consumer Electronics Show 2000.

        Internet Call Alert (ICA-100) awarded Winner of the Best Innovation at Show Award, UK.

2001   Medical devices factory in Dongguan obtained ISO 13485.

2002   Opened branch office in Shanghai for trading and liaison.

2003   AML factories were certified QS 9000.

        AML has registered in China SFDA.

2004   Established a joint venture with Science Generics Ltd, Cambridge, UK to form SGAI Tech Ltd in Hong Kong.

        Won 2004 Quality Grand Award in the Hong Kong Awards for Industry.

        Medical device factory in Dongguan, China, obtained ISO 13485 (Version 2003).

2006   Won 2005 Product and Quality Award in the Hong Kong Awards for Industry.

2007   AML factories were certified TS 16949.

        AML won the Operation Excellence Award by the Mould and Die Council.

        AML factories were certified ISO 14001.

2008   AML factories (Po Shan and Da Ke Shan) were certified ISO 14001.

2009   Won 2008 Machinery and Machine Tools Design Grand Award in the Hong Kong Awards for Industry.

2010   Expanded one more medical device manufacturing plant at Dongguan.

2011   Worldlight Engineering Ltd (R&D Division of AML) was certified ISO 9001 and ISO 13485.

        Awarded Outstanding Enterprise in Year 2011/12 Partner Employer Award.

2012   Awarded Corporate Social Responsibility Award – SME group organized by *Mirror Post*.

        Won the Innovative Technology Achievement Award 2012 by the Hong Kong Federation of Innovative Technologies and Manufacturing Industries.

Source: Automatic Manufacturing Ltd. (2014). *History.* Retrieved April 25, 2014 at: www.automatic.com.hk/history.htm

EXHIBIT 5.2 **Background note: history of industrial development in Hong Kong**

From its colonial beginnings, Hong Kong advocated a laissez-faire approach to governance for over 150 years. The essential features of this approach in Hong Kong include free trade, no import or currency restrictions, low taxes, negligible state borrowing, regular budget surpluses, minimal interference with market forces, and no long-term state planning. The government relied heavily on market forces to pave the way for economic development. From the mid-nineteenth century to the 1980s, Hong Kong has gone through different stages of economic development, evolving from a fishing village to an entrepôt, an export manufacturing center, and a business service center.

Hong Kong had a variety of industries, including ship-building, textiles, and plastic products after World War II. The civil war in China drove many industrialists from Shanghai and other places in China to Hong Kong and accelerated its industrial development. Subsequent embargoes due to the Korean War forced Hong Kong to complement trading with more manufacturing. Exports grew dramatically as most developed countries rebounded from war-ridden destruction and as trade barriers started to drop in the 1950s.

Small and medium enterprises (SMEs) in Hong Kong were born in the manufacturing sector. The laissez-faire policy nurtured a business environment that encouraged refugees to open their own firms. Most firms were original equipment manufacturers that took orders for labor-intensive goods from overseas buyers, using their design and technology. Relying on their social networks, small firms were competitive and were able to obtain and use information, technology, and capital in an efficient way.

Despite their success, SME owners were not completely satisfied with the non-interventionist policy. As early as the 1950s, they lobbied the government to provide industrial land and set up an industrial bank to provide cheap loans. The 1973 oil crisis and overseas competition were shocking, so much so that the government decided to assist the industries to upgrade themselves. Various public agencies and organizations were set up to supply land, trading support, training, new technology and products, and quality assurance. In addition, infrastructure such as roads and container ports were built to connect Hong Kong and China. The Convention and Exhibition Centre was also built to promote tourism and exhibition businesses.

These measures, together with China's Open Door Policy, transformed the SMEs and Hong Kong's economy in the 1980s and 90s. Many manufacturers enjoyed huge growth as they took advantage of cheap labor and land in China. They, in turn, spurred new SMEs that provided services for trade, marketing and design, financing, insurance, logistics, and wealth management. These services replaced the labor-intensive manufacturing, which was no longer competitive in Hong Kong. In the process, SMEs split the valued-added activities into a so-called "front shop, back factory" manner, using services in Hong Kong and producing in the Pearl River Delta. The wealth created in the Delta was plowed back to Hong Kong, and domestic services, real estates, and the stock market all enjoyed a boom.

The Asian crisis in 1997 put an abrupt stop to the boom. Many SMEs were hard hit. Because of collapsed property prices, SMEs no longer had collateral to borrow from banks to keep their businesses running. Money was injected to buoy collapsing firms. After the situation stabilized, the government implemented policies to boost funding and training for SMEs, and established the Closer Economic Partnership Arrangement (CEPA) with China so that Hong Kong products and services could enter China's expanding market.

Source: Au, K., Chiang, F. F. T., Birtch, T. A., and Ding, Z. (2012). Incubating the next generation to venture: the case of a family business in Hong Kong. *Asia Pacific Journal of Management*, 30(3): 749–767.

Notes

1   John Mok was a fellow member of the Hong Kong Institute of Engineers. He was active in the society, serving as the founding Chairman of the Hong Kong Medical and Healthcare Devices Industry Association, Chairman of the Biomedical Division of the Hong Kong Institution of Engineers (HKIE), and advisor to some universities. Apart from his achievements in engineering, he was awarded the "Directors of the Year" due to his outstanding corporate governance by the Hong Kong Institute of Directors in 2005. He was also recognized as an Outstanding Entrepreneur in 2009.

2   Engineering plastics refer to plastics with superior thermal and mechanical properties. It is easier to handle and can save time and money compared to traditional materials.

6

TERUMO-PENPOL – INDIA

*Mathew J. Manimala, Kishinchand P. Wasdani
and Clare Kurian*

A pioneer Indian enterprise in the biomedical device industry for producing blood bags, Terumo-Penpol (a joint venture of Peninsula Polymers Private Ltd with the Japanese company Terumo Corporation) is currently a leading player in blood-bag manufacturing in the world with a capacity of 20 million blood bags and a turnover of INR1,500 million. Its products are exported to 82 countries around the world (see Figure 6.1 for the geographical spread of TPL's operations as of 2012). This case study explores the entrepreneurial journey of C. Balagopal, Founding Managing Director of Peninsula Polymers Private Ltd, popularly known by its short name Penpol, with a view to understanding the special issues and problems faced by R&D based enterprises in India. Penpol is India's first blood-bag manufacturing company and is located in Thiruvananthapuram, capital of Kerala (India), a state that is particularly notorious for its hyperactive trade unionism and labor militancy. That, however, is not the cause of the myriad problems faced by Penpol in its initial years, which led to the near collapse of the enterprise. Creating a new venture based on a "half-baked" idea from an R&D lab in a developing country like India would naturally have all the ingredients for failure. The company not only managed to overcome all these initial problems through a phoenix-like resurgence, but also forged ahead to create a joint venture with a Japanese multi-national company and become a globally recognized blood–bag manufacturer.

Background: a nation's need and an enthusiastic bureaucrat

In the early 1980s, the blood transfusion services in India were not following the state-of-the-art technology and were a cause of quality and hygiene problems, which arose mainly from the reusable glass bottles. In a bid to improve the blood transfusion services in the country, the government of India proposed to create a National

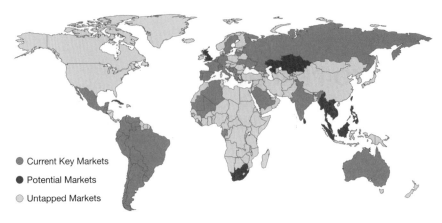

● Current Key Markets
● Potential Markets
○ Untapped Markets

FIGURE 6.1 The geographical spread of TPL's operations (2012)

Blood Transfusion Service (NBTS), modeled on a similar service in the UK. For this, a consultant was invited from NBTS (UK) who suggested that the country should replace the reusable glass bottles with disposable plastic blood bags with a view to enhancing the safety of the transfusion process. For a large country like India, the changeover to the new system would necessitate the import of the entire requirements, resulting in a huge drain on its limited foreign exchange reserves. The alternative was to develop and manufacture blood bags in the country.

While searching for an R&D institution that could develop an indigenous blood bag, it was observed that the Sree Chitra Tirunal Institute for Medical Sciences and Technology (SCTIMST), a government-funded medical research institution in Thiruvananthapuram under the Department of Science and Technology, had the capabilities to develop blood bags. SCTIMST (founded in 1974) had already successfully developed an indigenous blood oxygenator and cardiotomy reservoir for coronary artery bypass graft procedures. Since the materials employed in these devices had similar biocompatibility criteria and performance as blood-bag systems, SCTIMST was entrusted with the task. The blood bag developed by SCTIMST was successful in all in-vitro trials, experimental use in a few hospitals and scrutiny by the Ethics Committee, and was deemed ready to be transferred for commercial use. The opportunity for heralding this pioneering venture into the country was 'grabbed' (rather surprisingly) by a bureaucrat with a difference – C. Balagopal.

Balagopal, who had the opportunity to study at some of the best schools and educational institutions in India, had a distinguished academic career. Having graduated with a gold medal in economics from Loyola College, Madras (now Chennai), Balagopal enrolled at the Centre for Development Studies (CDS), Thiruvananthapuram, to pursue a doctoral program in Agricultural Economics. Due to strong differences of opinion with his research guide, he decided to end his research aspirations and pursue a career in the civil service, which included the prestigious Indian Administrative Services (IAS). After clearing the examination and gaining entry into the IAS, he went on to hold all the key administrative positions in the central and state governments in India.

Contrary to his expectations, Balagopal did not find his IAS career very exciting. There was no way that one could do focused work in the government – one had to keep shifting gears according to the whims and fancies of the political bosses. While Balagopal was starting to have doubts on his choice of career in the civil service, he stumbled on an announcement in a local newspaper that the National Research Development Corporation (NRDC) was on the lookout for entrepreneurs to transfer workable indigenously developed technologies for creating new business ventures. The technology of manufacturing blood bags developed by SCTIMST was mentioned in the advertisement.

Balagopal was particularly enthused about pioneering the manufacture of a life-saving device because of its potential for making a social contribution. Even though he lacked prior experience in technology or entrepreneurship and came from a family with no entrepreneurial background, SCTIMST scientists were impressed by the young man's enthusiasm, freshness of approach, social vision and entre-preneurial zeal and decided to partner with Balagopal to manufacture this hi-tech product. Beckoned by the challenges of this 'untested' new technology and a new product, Balagopal ended his career with the IAS and plunged head on into the uncertain world of high technology.

The startup – and problems galore

Based on the technology transferred to him by SCTIMST, Balagopal started a venture called Peninsula Polymers (Private) Ltd, which was incorporated in 1983 with its registered office in Hyderabad. They were to be the sole manufacturer of blood-transfusion bags in India, at least for the time being. In February 1984, after signing the technology know-how transfer agreement with the National Research Development Corporation (NRDC), Penpol was shifted to Thiruvananthapuram, presumably to facilitate collaboration with SCTIMST to develop the commercial product as well as to set up the manufacturing plant.

Locational (dis)advantage

In 1985 Penpol was converted to a public limited company, after which they purchased 3 acres of land with an abandoned film studio building in the Vilappil Panchayat of Thiruvananthapuram district. The first challenge faced by the company was the lack of proper roads and other transportation facilities, which made it difficult to transport the machinery and equipment required for the plant. Vilappil, though close to the capital of Kerala, was an isolated village, where the only "important" institution in those days was a primary school. Although the factory was commissioned in March 1987, within two years of starting the project, the transport and infrastructure problems pushed the costs of construction from the original estimate of INR18.6 million to INR21.4 million.

While the disadvantages of the remote location were acutely felt at the construction stage, the expectation was that it would not be a problem at the production stage when the requirements for the interface with the external agencies would be restricted to the supply of raw material and the transporting of the finished products, which were expected to be of small quantities at infrequent intervals, as the company was planned to be a small-scale venture. Furthermore, there were high expectations of deriving many technology-related benefits from being close to SCTIMST. However, later events showed that both these expectations were rather unrealistic.

Finance

The preceding period of construction really gave some rude shocks to the aspiring entrepreneur. To begin with, no one was prepared to fund his venture because of the "untested" nature of the technology involved. Since the technology was new, financial institutions insisted on getting a Process Guarantee Certificate from the supplier of the technology as a precondition to investing in the new venture. Balagopal spent the better part of 1984 (almost ten months) putting together a techno-economic feasibility report and requested both SCTIMST and NRDC for the process guarantee certificate. Unfortunately, neither of them was prepared to provide any process guarantees – the former (SCTIMST) refused because they had not developed the "production prototype", and the latter (NRDC) because they were only the mediators and not the suppliers of the technology. This was a major setback for the fledgling enterprise, but in a truly entrepreneurial manner Balagopal found a solution to it – using his contacts in the bureaucracy, he discovered that there was a provision for NRDC to invest up to INR2.5 million in "new technology-based ventures" (NTBVs), and persuaded them to do so for his venture, which they readily agreed to. He could then convince the financial institutions that the process is feasible, as the investment in the venture by NRDC was a testimony to their confidence in the process.

With the newly generated confidence of having secured investment support from NRDC, Balagopal resumed his talks with financial institutions. In November 1984, he had a chance meeting with S. Padmakumar, Chairman of Kerala State Industrial Development Corporation (KSIDC), where he presented his project proposal. Convinced by the social usefulness of the venture, KSIDC invested equity capital to the extent of 38 per cent. Further investment support came from different schemes/sources, such as the seed capital scheme of Industrial Development Bank of India (IDBI), central investment subsidy funds from Kerala Financial Corporation (KFC) and working capital from the State Bank of Travancore (SBT). Thus, after he procured the funds for the initial investment of INR18.4 million in his project, he started the construction work in 1985.

Technology know-how

One of the biggest challenges for a new technology-based venture is to master the technical know-how involved in the manufacture and servicing of the product. Penpol too faced this problem, as there were no ready-made documented procedures available for the manufacture of blood bags. Of course, there were a few companies internationally that manufactured blood bags, but their technology was proprietary, and there were hardly any literature or consultancy services available on the process. In effect, therefore, many of the problems faced by Penpol were unique, especially because there was no support of any kind available from any external sources.

Hoping to find solutions to their technology problems from the technology providers themselves, Balagopal approached SCTIMST, but they were unable to help, as the project team that developed the indigenous blood-bag technology had been disbanded and its members were reassigned to other projects. In the process, their capability to develop biocompatible materials and products had also perished through disuse. Thus, Penpol had to do independent "research" and master each step in the manufacturing process on its own.

In hindsight, Balagopal felt that it was a huge mistake to jump into the venture without having a pilot plant in operation. Many of the technological problems experienced by Penpol arose from an initial perception that the product they were to make was a fairly simple one. In its unused state, the blood bag looked like a thin transparent deflated vacuum suction bag, with a tube sticking out of the top. It was a deceptively simple product that belies its highly sophisticated manufacturing process. In reality, blood bags are quite complex, as they are specially designed high-quality devices consisting of plastic bags, connecting tubes, outlet ports, special flow-regulating valves, filters, safety features, sampling ports, and so on. They enable the safe collection, separation (into components like red blood cells, plasma, platelets, and so on), preservation and transfusion of blood. The manufacture of these components was itself an arduous procedure, especially when there was limited knowledge available about them within the company.

One of the first things that Balagopal did at the start of the project, therefore, was to assemble a good team of technologically competent professionals (some of whom are still with the company today). By creating a dedicated team, which worked extensively on researching these components taking a fresh look at them, they were able to develop the manufacturing process for the products on their own. By this process, Penpol was able not only to resolve most of the technology issues, but also to create new technical know-how and fresh procedures. Thus, during the course of setting up the manufacturing process, Penpol ended up developing new processes and obtaining ten industrial patents.

Raw materials

Although Penpol was equipped with an annual installed capacity of 2 million blood-bags, its initial production (in July 1987) was on a very small scale. The main constraint against large-scale (or any scale) production was that there were no suppliers of medical grade plastic granules in India. The special additive for making the non-toxic PVC compound was being imported at that time, which was not viable for Penpol due to the high import duties being levied on that product. The only workable alternative was to make the material in-house, which would also ensure quality. Penpol took this option and succeeded in making high-quality plastic granules in sufficient quantities to meet its own manufacturing requirements.

Quality issues

Having solved the raw material problem, the company started the production and marketing of blood bags. However, there were still some quality problems. Customers reported discoloration of labels on the blood bags from some batches. Even though the problem was affecting only the labels, the company took it as a serious problem and recalled all those bags and destroyed them. The problem was traced to some deficiencies in the sterilization system, which was corrected. In the process, they not only achieved the specified quality standards but also came up with some other innovations in packaging and post-sterilization treatment. The strict adherence to a customer-centered quality policy and standards has held Penpol in good stead even when the domestic competition increased later, with Hindustan Latex Ltd (a public sector company) entering the market with the same SCIMST-NRDC technology. On the process front the company has created a system that fully complies with the Good Manufacturing Practice (GMP) of the pharmaceutical industry.

Government policies

While the credit for the startup of Penpol should partly go to the government initiative of National Blood Transfusion Service (NBTS), the subsequent support from NBTS or the government in general was woefully missing. Blood bags could be imported paying 40 percent import duty, while its accessory components such as needles, polymeric materials and other such items attracted import duties in excess of 150 percent. Thus, the import duties, which were supposed to be playing a facilitative role for the development of indigenous manufacturers, were themselves creating major impediments in the way of this enterprise – first, this policy makes the components prohibitively expensive, and second, it makes the competition tough in a market flooded with foreign products.

Penpol did consider getting the components from indigenous sources. However, another government policy came in the way of this. These products were reserved for the small-scale sector, and to reduce competition for their products, high import duties were imposed on foreign products. Thus it was prohibitively expensive for Penpol to import these components. Neither could they buy locally because of the poor quality of the domestic products induced by limited competition. The only way to overcome this crisis was to work with the government to effect a change in the import duty structure, which would act as a double-edged sword and solve the raw material as well as the marketing problem. Surely, this was not an easy task, but was eventually accomplished, as we will see in the next section on marketing.

It was only after the production issues were sorted out through dedicated R&D work that Penpol made a serious attempt at marketing its products. Naturally, they tried the open market first, but the response was disappointing. The Indian medical profession was too cost-conscious to replace the reusable glass bottles with the costlier alternative of blood bags. Besides, there was the general perception that medical devices manufactured in India are substandard.

The setbacks in the open market made the company turn to the government for help, recalling the promise made under the NBTS project that they would be the single-point purchaser of the product. When Balagopal contacted the Department of Health regarding this, he was shocked to realize that NBTS was confined to a file, whose contents were the only two letters written by him during the initial discussions on the project. There was nothing in the files on how to carry the project forward, not to speak of any promise of purchasing the blood bags produced by his company.

Having lost the hope of getting the sales organized through the NBTS project of the government, Balagopal started to look for alternative marketing strategies. Finally, a marketing and equity tie-up arrangement was entered into with TTK Pharma, Madras (now Chennai), in June 1987. TTK picked up a 20 percent stake in Penpol's raised equity and undertook the task of marketing the product. Penpol found TTK to be a competent, reasonable and supportive partner. This partnership produced very good synergies and significantly reduced the financial insecurity for the company.

As the new marketing tie-up started showing results, there was a new threat, this time from foreign competitors, who started to dump blood bags in the Indian market at artificially low prices. Such dumping was made easier by the government policy of classifying blood bags as a "life-saving" health device and including it under the Open General License (OGL) scheme for importing without any duties. As a result of such dumping, Penpol's sales drastically declined and the plant was operating only at 40 percent capacity, and, in spite of the reduced production, unsold blood bags started piling up. Under these circumstances, Penpol could no longer withstand the foreign onslaught and decided to commit "commercial suicide" by offering huge discounts and thereby incurring huge losses, hoping to retain its hold at least on the Indian market.

Discount sales did clear the inventories, but it was only a short-term relief. The long-term solution lay in changing the adverse duty structure, and Balagopal started campaigning for it. Soon he realized that the importers too had their people lobbying hard with the government for maintaining the status quo. The sustained campaign by Balagopal against unfair foreign competition finally bore fruit, when in 1988 the Board of Customs and Excise imposed an import duty of 40 percent on blood bags and reduced the import duty on raw materials and intermediaries for blood bags from 150 to 100 percent. With this change and with the marketing support from TTK, Penpol was ready to be launched on the road to recovery by globalizing its operations with products made to international standards.

The road to recovery

The recovery of Penpol was based on the policy and practice of technology development (R&D) and trouble-shooting by competent and empowered employees. This policy has helped the company to maintain (and in some cases improve) quality standards, enhance customer satisfaction, diversify into related products (mostly based on in-house R&D) and globalize its operations with products made to international standards.

R&D initiative

The commitment of Penpol to R&D-based innovation and trouble-shooting is evident from the fact that they set up an R & D centre in 1989 (within two years of commissioning the manufacturing facility) at an investment of INR 10 million (at a time when the company was making losses). Research output of the Centre has led to several patents and publications, which have earned a respectable place for the company among world leaders in the medical device industry. Part of the credit for this goes to Balagopal's policy of hiring the services of eminent scientists as top managers and advisors as well as giving a free hand to his research scientists.

Employee engagement

Right from its inception, Penpol believed in engaging its employees by enlisting their participation in the affairs of the company. It is perhaps the only company in Kerala (an Indian state notorious for labour militancy), where the management took the initiative of forming a labour union with the intention of creating a forum for workers to exercise their rights and learn about their responsibilities. Penpol's solidarity with the workers was strengthened by encouraging collective participation in company affairs and concern for their welfare allowed a strong sense of loyalty to develop among workers, which remained one of its greatest strengths through thick and thin.

Community development and corporate social responsibility (CSR)

In recruiting employees for Penpol, Balagopal adopted a deliberate policy of giving preference to local people, which he believed would be his contribution to the welfare of the local community and the development of the local economy. Another CSR initiative of Penpol was developing the infrastructural facilities such as classrooms, ceiling fans, toilets, tennis courts, etc. for Vilappil Lower Primary School and other neighboring schools. Moreover, in line with the major business of the company, it has initiated a Blood Donation Campaign among its own employees, who were encouraged to register themselves at the Regional Cancer Centre (RCC), Thiruvananthapuram, to donate blood.

Quality through and with people

The quality management systems developed by Penpol finally got the international recognition in 1995, when the company received ISO-9001 certification for its quality management process. The Penpol factory maintains the highest standards of fire and safety compliance. Similarly, their pollution control standards are also of the highest (green category) standards, in recognition of which the company was chosen in 1995 for the Kerala State Pollution Control Board award. Another environment-friendly system of the company is the harvesting of rainwater and the treatment and recycling of wastewater for gardening purposes.

Diversification into allied products

R&D and customer-responsiveness is a powerful combination that could produce innovative products and thereby help the company to diversify and grow. Taking clues from the market and using their R&D capabilities, Penpol started production of urine bags and blood-transfusion sets in 1992, and by 1994 they developed platelet storage bags, which had higher permeability to O_2 and CO_2 and were free from DOP (the plasticizer used in blood bags) as per the norms of international quality standards. In 1995 they developed continuous ambulatory peritoneal dialysis bags and accessories. By the end of that year, they set up the Medical Systems Group (the medical equipment division of Penpol), with a small group of about 20 staff, which added many more products to its portfolio, such as plasma expressors, blood-collection monitor, platelet agitators with incubators, electronic blood scales, blood-bank refrigerators, and tube sealers. The first orders for medical equipment were received in 1997. As the number of products increased, Penpol set up a Service Support Group, which provides world-class customer service and support. Today, it is a differentiator in the market because a major problem with imported products was the inability of the agents to provide spares and after-sales service. All these customer-friendly policies have helped the company to remain the market leader in India, despite tough competition from within the country and outside (see Figure 6.2 for the Indian market share of the company as well as competitors as of 2012).

Export/global reach initiatives

In spite of maintaining high standards of quality and customer orientation, the domestic sales of Penpol products were stagnating because of Indian customers' tendency to accept lower quality at low prices. As it was almost impossible to increase domestic sales for the reasons mentioned above, Penpol decided to explore the

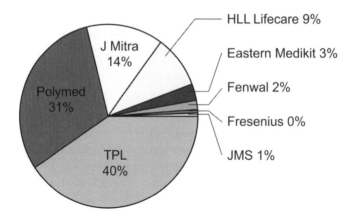

FIGURE 6.2 The Indian market share of TPL (after the merger of Penpol with Terumo Corporation, Japan) as well as its competitors (2012)

international markets. Needless to say, going international was a tough task for a company that did not have adequate selling experience even in its domestic market. Fortunately for Penpol, help came from an agency of the Dutch government, which provided training and consultancy assistance regarding various issues involved in international marketing, such as packaging, technical literature, and quality standards.

Equipped with the knowledge and skills thus developed, Penpol made its first exports of 40,000 blood bags to the Philippines in 1989. The next export was to the Union of Soviet Socialist Republics (USSR), whose health ministry approved the quality of Penpol's blood bags. Soon there were business partnerships established in the Middle East, the UK, Italy, Germany, and Greece. In some countries like the UK and Germany, Penpol's trading partners and third-party vendors were selling Penpol products under their own brand names. This was an easy way of quickly establishing the credibility of the product with the customers of those countries. Other global reach initiatives, such as a turnkey project to transfer the technology to Indonesia, received support and encouragement from the Indian government.

The series of successes in foreign markets gave the confidence to Penpol to take up a consultancy assignment for establishing a blood-bank project in Egypt in 1992, and in 1993 they registered their blood bags for sale in Brazil and Colombia. All these achievements of Penpol in foreign markets were also recognized in the home country, when the Indian government chose this small company in 1995 for the Top Exporters Award and the National R&D Award. The lessons learned in the foreign markets also helped the company to come back more vigorously to India and substantially increase the domestic sales of blood bags as well as the indigenously developed medical equipment. When the accumulated loss of INR20.4 million was wiped out, the company was able to persuade the Industrial Development Bank of India (IDBI) to invest INR6 million towards capacity expansion.

Joint venture with Terumo Corporation of Japan

The successes of Penpol in foreign markets have brought some recognition, sales increase and investment support from India. However, the improvement in the domestic sales was temporary. Just as the company was able to wipe out the accumulated losses and make decent profits from its operations by the mid-1990s, trouble started brewing in the form of foreign competition in the domestic market. The economic liberalization policies implemented by the Indian government since the early 1990s turned out to be a boon as well as a bane for Penpol. On one hand, it facilitated the foreign operations of the company; on the other hand, it not only brought direct competition from international healthcare giants like Baxter and Terumo, but also helped other domestic players to obtain the technology from foreign sources (as well as NRDC) and compete with Penpol. Although the competition from domestic players could be managed with Penpol's reputation of being the most reliable supplier of the best quality among the local brands, the competition from international giants was not easy to fight because of the latter's scale of operations, R&D capabilities and financial resources. Under such circumstances, Penpol decided to follow the dictum: "If you can't compete with them, collaborate." This strategy was deemed to be particularly appropriate, as the 10-year-old plant of Penpol was due for modernization or preferably replacement.

The partnership

After two years of negotiations with various foreign companies with a view to identifying a partner who could bring in capital as well as new technology, Penpol entered into a joint venture agreement in 1999 with the $3.5 billion Terumo Corporation of Japan. Under this agreement, Terumo was to acquire 74 percent of Penpol shares (which were then held by the financial institutions), leaving 26 percent for its promoters. After the merger, the firm was renamed as TERUMO PENPOL LIMITED (TPL). Even though Terumo Corporation had a majority stake in the joint venture, the promoters of Penpol were given complete freedom for the day-to-day management of the new entity. The larger partner's inputs were received every year, in terms of the targets, during the annual business planning exercise. TPL has always been able to achieve the agreed targets and is rated as performing better than Terumo's manufacturing facility in China. Currently, the turnover of TPL is INR1,500 million (see Figure 6.3 and Figure 6.4 for the trends in TPL's output and sales respectively).

Terumo Penpol's exports gradually increased to INR102.48 million in 2001, to INR263.19 million in 2004, INR298.84 million in 2005, and INR500.19 million in 2008. Currently, about 60 percent of TPL products are exported to more than 80 countries, making TPL one of the most important subsidiaries of Terumo Corporation.

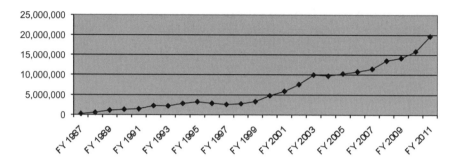

FIGURE 6.3 Production of TPL in units (1987–2011)

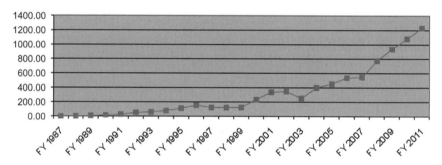

FIGURE 6.4 Sales of TPL in INR millions (1987–2011)

Conclusion

TPL is a hugely successful company now and is India's largest manufacturer of blood bags, with an annual capacity of 20 million. It is an associate company of Terumo BCT, a world leader in blood management. The company pioneered the manufacture of blood bags in India and then successfully launched a range of medical electronic products required for blood transfusion. Driven by its strong customer focus and innovative spirit, the company has been the market leader ever since it introduced blood bags in India. Today, it is more than double the size of any other blood-bag manufacturer in India. Being a part of the multibillion dollar Terumo Corporation – which has 20 factories around the world, generates annual sales of about US$4 billion, employs 14,000 people worldwide and pioneers products of the future like implantable left-ventricular assist systems, artificial vessels, minimally invasive surgery devices, nano-capsules, etc. TPL definitely has a bright future ahead. "If you have the strength to keep focused on your aim without being discouraged by bad experiences, then you can be an entrepreneur," says Balagopal.

Case study questions

1 For a hi-tech startup based on R&D, how would you rate the relative importance of the following factors in facilitating new venture success?:

   (a) entrepreneur's technical background;
   (b) entrepreneur's vision and enthusiasm;
   (c) support from the R&D institution;
   (d) support from government and other public agencies;
   (e) availability of human resources;
   (f) availability of financial resources;
   (g) availability of infrastructural facilities.

2 Discuss the "five Cs of opportunity identification" – namely, circumstance, context, constraints, compensating behavior, and criteria (as proposed in the HBR blog of the same title by Scott Anthony dated 26 October 2012) and its appilicability to technology-based new ventures.

3 Critically analyze the strategies adopted by Balagopal in different phases of the development of his entrepreneurial venture.

4 Can you think of alternative ways in which this business could have been started and managed with similar or better success under the environmental conditions prevailing in India during the 1980s?

5 Based on the post-liberalization changes that have happened in India since 1991 (do an Internet-search on this), discuss what kind of issues would be faced by an entrepreneur starting a similar venture now. What kind of strategies would you recommend for him/her?

Note

This case has been prepared using primary (interviews with the promoter and examination of company documents) as well as secondary sources. The latter include: "Drawing first blood", *Business India*, 10–23 December 1990; "Successful Transfusion", *Business India*, 6–19 September 2010; C. Balagopal (2000), Inventions and Innovations: Enterprises – Key actors in the commercialization of inventions and innovations: "Arrow in the blue or technology development as (un)guided missile", Report prepared for the World Intellectual Property Organization Conference (WIPO/IP/HEL/00/9), Helsinki, 5–7 October 2000; Terumo Penpol website (accessed 10 September 2011). The authors thank the promoter and the other officials of the company for the information provided for preparing this case study and Padmashree Vijayakumar for her contribution to an earlier draft.

7

THE SOCIAL CONSEQUENCES OF CORPORATE ENTREPRENEURIAL PRACTICES

Evidence from global initiatives of an Italian family firm[1]

Tommaso Minola and Alfredo De Massis

Italcementi is a well-known family business in Northern Italy, with a long story in the cement industry and has now reached the fifth generation; it is well recognized for having strongly invested in building social capital and leveraged on this to create socially innovative corporate initiatives. This case study provides an insightful example of an entrepreneurial family controlling a profit-oriented enterprise, with a strong social attention, especially towards the environment and the community, which, instead of conflicting, is found to sustain the global operations of the business itself.

This virtuous circle between business and social sustainability is a unique representation of an archetypal Italian understanding of the nature of entrepreneurship. Welter and Lasch (2008) broadly discuss the importance of adopting an approach to entrepreneurship research in Europe that allows it to capture its richness and diversity, crossing thematic and disciplinary boundaries; by recalling some example of specific approaches, such as the British, the German, the French, and the Nordic ones, the authors suggest that this diversity is where the study of European entrepreneurship might add value. These approaches show a strong consideration of the context and environment in which entrepreneurship takes place, justifying the statement that "the societal dimension of entrepreneurship research has been initiated by European researchers, who are implicitly drawing on a European tradition" (Welter and Lasch, 2008: 245). However, an explicit reference of what this contextual dimension of entrepreneurship means for the Italian case is missing; therefore, a contribution from the present case consists in showing, based on evidence from an Italian family firm, that entrepreneurship can be straightforward, an antecedent of social innovation and welfare, at both corporate and family level. Starting from middle age and the renaissance (Toninelli and Vasta, 2009), Italy has always been characterized by a strong participation to communities as trigger of socio-economical activities. This has allowed Italian entrepreneurs to exploit networks and gain legitimacy (Toninelli and Vasta, 2009), and to utilize unique localized resources (e.g. artisan and hand-crafted items – see Rusk et al., 2011). Italian entrepreneurs are therefore found to be prone to build on their community to create value, and highly committed to invest in social capital. In Italy this is particularly true when considering family firms that have unarguably a predominant role in the national economic scenario, accounting for the majority (92 percent) of firms (CERIF 2008; Osservatorio AUB 2010), employing 52 percent of the national workforce and contributing to 70 percent of GDP (CERIF 2008).

Based on those figures, a holistic view of entrepreneurship cannot disregard the social value that it creates and the social consequences that it produces. From the activities performed by Italcementi it clearly emerges with a commitment to *sustainability* that is meant to satisfy the current generation's needs without putting at risk the ability of the next generation to meet their challenges to find the answer for their demands and aspirations. It should be noted that the issue of sustainability as a principal paradigm of any social and economical activity is becoming a great concern in the Italian and European landscape, also due to the difficulties of public finance, the recent financial crisis and the threats that are now challenging the Italian social and institutional environment. The strategic orientation towards sustainability is a major societal concern and, as shown by this family business, is pervasive to any sector of society, well-respected business, enterprise and entrepreneurs.

An example of how this concern towards sustainability deploys in strategy and innovative corporate efforts is represented by corporate social responsibility (CSR) initiatives; these are defined as the "integration on a voluntary basis from the companies of the social and environmental issues in their commercial operations and in the relationship with their stakeholders" (European Commission, 2001). A survey has been conducted in Italy on a group of family businesses, trying to formulate a picture of the extent and the characteristic of CSR adoption in those types of firms (Zocchi, 2005). The survey focused on four main areas: the awareness about the existence and the potential of CSR; the specific focus of CSR with respect to the improvement of the relationships with local stakeholders in the community; the implication of CSR in improving the relationship with the environment; awareness of the potential of CSR as a specific way to improve the quality of the global supply chain mechanism. The results from the survey show that a growing commitment to the issue of sustainability is leading to several new typologies of CSR initiatives, and this is positively moderated by factors like the size of firm, the local legal and institutional system, the intention to improve the relationship with the local community, and the quality of the human capital on which the company is based.

First, all these aspects are affected by family influence; in particular there is a widespread acknowledgment in the scientific community that family firms are particularly prone to commit resources to sustainability (Danes et al., 2009; Stafford et al., 1999), mainly because of the relevance that social capital and social wealth have for these types of firms. Therefore we aim to shed light on the role of family influence to the perception and the promotion of sustainability as a critical corporate-level strategy. Second, by extending the focus on sustainability to a broader set of socially relevant initiatives and by looking in depth at an Italian family firm, we aim to analyze such practices as inherent consequences of entrepreneurship.

The chapter is structured as follows: in the next sections, after a short description of the firm, we explain the motivation for the relevance of moving a step forward in social entrepreneurship by looking at the social consequences of entrepreneurship; we then present social innovation as a means to generate positive social consequences. In the following sections we discuss the entrepreneurial family and its commitment towards sustainability. Finally, we revise some specific family entrepreneurship practices in the field of social innovation, and conclude by discussing the findings and commenting on the challenges the firm is facing.

History of the firm

Italcementi Group is one of the largest cement producers in the world – namely, the fifth. Its turnover is over €5 billion and it employs more than 20,000 workers in more than 20 countries. This huge group originated as a family business at the beginning of the twentieth century, in the province of Bergamo, based on the smart technical capabilities of two entrepreneurs, Giuseppe Piccinelli and Antonio Pesenti. Italcementi is one of the largest Italian companies and is well known and renowned nationally. The story of the firm is strictly intertwined with the story of the country, surviving two world wars, experiencing the Italian economic miracle, the reconstruction and industrial consolidation, and concluding with the recent industrial and financial turmoil. During World War I a strong expansion characterized the company at the international level. An extensive recourse to merger and acquisition and the construction of a new plant allowed the company to become a leader in the domestic market. As early as the mid-1920s it emerged as an important international player.

After World War II, Italy was characterized by the "economic miracle". The growth of the social and economic system was strongly enabled and supported by the development of the infrastructure. The company grew dramatically and followed a twofold strategy to foster such a growth: on one hand, the company consolidated technical assets and production capabilities in the cement industry with growth in technological expertise and industrial collaboration; at the same time, during the 1950s, the company started a process of transformation to become a diversified industrial group. Besides the traditional cement sector the company started new industrial firms – corporate ventures initiatives – mainly through acquisitions in very different fields such as banking and finance, or other industrial sectors. This gave the company a central position in the Italian economic system and in the industrial network. During the last part of the twentieth century instability and recession have challenged the operations of Italcementi on a global scale. The firm was able to inject resources for new acquisitions that consolidated its international presence and allowed the company to be properly designed and managed as a multinational company. Nowadays Italcementi is among the world's most important enterprises in the field of infrastructures, and in cement in particular.

FIGURE 7.1 Cement factory of Alzano Lombardo (Bergamo, Italy)

Social consequences of entrepreneurship

As an academic field, the social consequences of entrepreneurial behavior have not been systematically examined, either at individual or corporate level. To better capture the contributions of entrepreneurship, both for the purpose of advancing scientific discipline and to provide relevant insights and suggestions, we need to pay attention to social outcomes as the key elements of a sustainable society. As suggested by Zahra (2011), it is interesting to study the social consequences of entrepreneurship, and particularly the negative side effects and dysfunctions, which are largely underinvestigated. Sometimes entrepreneurs are said to be a delaying factor for social and political change, especially when systematically adopting corruption as a mechanism for generating competitive advantage, or to abuse power and cause the misallocation of resources. While striving for new technologies and innovations, sometimes entrepreneurs, in the race for their creative destruction, simply delay or suppress technological changes by killing rival projects or threatening disruptive technological innovation.

On the other hand, evidence can be provided that the underinvestigated effects of entrepreneurship at a social level are largely positive and can trigger a virtuous circle. Zahra (2011) refers to a "social multiplier effect" by suggesting that entrepreneurs create infrastructure, relationship and social capital, which promote the generation of wealth, and in particular social wealth, which in turn creates new material wealth through investment, resources and new ventures.

This case connects entrepreneurship, social entrepreneurship and social innovation by providing evidence of the fact that one of the positive effects of entrepreneurship is the creation of socially innovative initiatives. These types of initiatives are first at an individual level where entrepreneurs or family entrepreneurs generate social value by creating a new social venture by sustaining social causes (they can act by making a charitable contribution and supporting the cause) and introducing social innovation in the way they conceive workplaces, company organization and their relationship with society. The second level of impact is at the corporate level, where family enterprises can generate a charitable contribution in most cases to the creation of foundations, implement CSR programs with the broad spectrum of approaches described above, and found new ventures with a social focus or with a social mission. Family business can support and select the social initiative, and, most importantly, promote social innovative practices in the way their business operates.

There are three main domains in which the social implication of entrepreneurship can fruitfully act. The first is the enhancement of the quality of the human capital by supporting its qualification, education and skill creation, and by providing a positive role model for the company, in particular the workers and society. The second is the network: through physical systems and infrastructure entrepreneurs create the conditions for human capital to circulate, diffuse and generate value. The third level is related to relationships and social capital. By creating incentives and motives for qualified human capital to use the infrastructures, entrepreneurs can support the creation of a value and the generation of social wealth. At those three levels entrepreneurs promote social innovation, defined as "new concepts and measures that are accepted by impacted social groups and are applied to overcome social challenges" (Hochgerner, 2009: 38).

Social innovation can include three distinct domains (Zahra, 2011). The first is the way entrepreneurs and enterprise newly conceive the global market and their relationship with the business environment. As described below, the positioning on global markets and a global approach to sustainability can be the first trigger for social innovation practices. The second level is management: the way a business organizes its supply chain, the production systems and the accounting principles can be highly pervaded by socially innovative tools and approaches. The third and last level is the cooperation domain: by creating coalitions and new models of partnership (such as public and private ones), business can help governments and public administrations tackle the lack of resources, and on the other hand can gain the legitimacy and visibility necessary to promote such innovation with a broader scope.

Starting from the awareness that it is not enough to simply *feel* good for social causes, firms and entrepreneurs want to support initiatives to *do* real good and have the potential to generate long-lasting solutions. Employment creation, social innovation, community support and global engagement towards sustainability are examples of an approach centered on valorizing the positive social effects of entrepreneurship. Based on this perspective, entrepreneurs are enabled to grow their business with greater vision, to support development and enrich the world.

The entrepreneurial family and the commitment towards sustainability

The history of Italcementi as a firm, and in particular as a family firm, is characterized by a commitment towards excellence, with a rare abundance of talented human capital that is strongly tied to the close-knit family comprising five generations (see Figure 7.2).

The family involvement started with Carlo Antonio who took over a company after a merger of two small businesses at the end of nineteenth century. The company was named Italcementi, the name that made it famous, in the early 1930s. The first process of industrial consolidation was led by Cesare, a member of the third generation, and his nephew Antonio. It was indeed Antonio who was the first family member to conceive the idea of the necessity to grow in order to gain a leading role in the cement industry. He fostered a strong national relationship and became Chairman of the National Federation of Cement Manufactures, a coalition of manufacturers that he had been promoting since its inception in 1918. Later, Carlo became another crucial figure in the development of the firm. He was Cesare's nephew and cousin of Antonio, and he was strongly persuaded that the company

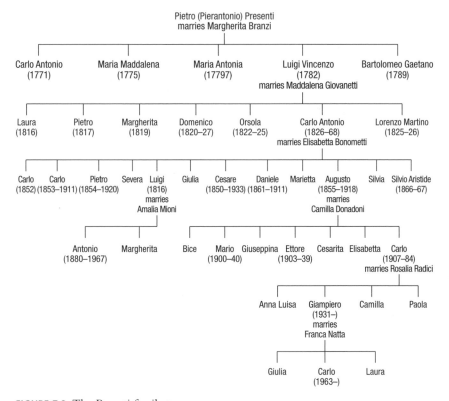

FIGURE 7.2 The Pesenti family tree

could become at the center of a vast network of a growing industrial milieu in Italy, a network that included other famous companies like Falk, Bastogi and Montedison; with them Italcementi contributed to the creation of a successful national industrial ecosystem. In the 1980s, after the national and international growth occurred following World War II, Carlo's son Giampiero, a fifth-generation member of the Pesenti family, became head of the firm. Giampiero was successful in reshaping the internal and external focus of the company by providing it with a solid operation and production at an international level, and retrieving resources to sustain growth; the company was consolidated among large corporations in a national scenario that was culturally and historically driven by the fragmentation of companies, a shrinking of size and the dominance of small business. Giampiero pursued the willingness to create a European-based corporation with a global presence. He succeeded in guaranteeing business competitiveness, while approaching the global markets; at the same time he introduced an awareness within the

FIGURE 7.3 Carlo Pesenti (1959), third-generation leader of the firm

FIGURE 7.4 *i.lab*, the new global R&D center (Bergamo, Italy), opened in April 2012

whole company towards the social issues relating to the company and the implication of its presence around the world.

There is a widespread belief in the Italian academic and practitioner community that Italcementi, although maintaining a founding family in the top management position, is a strongly managerial and professionalized company. Italcementi has always been distinguished by a predominance of qualified and talented people, especially at the technical and managerial levels. The company has significantly invested in the development of culture and knowledge, and has always had a relationship with universities and research centers, aiming at promoting innovation, research and exploitation at an industrial and societal level. For example, *i.lab*, recently inaugurated within the area of Kilometro Rosso (one of the major privately owned technological parks in Italy), is Italcementi Group's new global center for research and innovation. It occupies around 10,000 square meters with research labs. Besides confirming its commitment to research and innovation for the economic growth and sociocultural development of the whole group, the company has explicitly launched *i.lab* with the goal of pursuing its expansion under the principle of sustainable development, in particular sustainable architecture. *i.lab* engineers are designing industrial processes that will allow for innovative products with a high environmental compatibility and high energy efficiency. The whole center will promote the use of renewable energy sources (such as photovoltaic and solar panels) and further efficiencies in energy consumption will be granted by a geothermal system.

Another aspect that is worth mentioning is the top managers' life-long commitment to the company, both family and non-family members. Most of the top managers have several decades of experience within the company, having started their working lives there. This is due to the company's constant effort to foster and nurture the loyalty of its workers, mainly through a permanent interest in the human capital qualification, education and training. This is a model of

FIGURE 7.5 Ait Baha cement factory (Morocco, North Africa)

so-called "company as a family" and this life-long employment produces a strong identification and strong ties of the workers and the local community as well as the communities where the company is engaged, based on trust, transparency and social cohesion. Throughout the company's history, the personal development of the family entrepreneurs at both professional and human level has always been strongly intertwined with the area where the company was acting and operating, in particular Lombardy and the province of Bergamo. Entrepreneurs' lives and culture were strongly rooted in the beliefs, culture and tradition of their territory, and affected the characteristics of the company, especially the human and social capital, as we have mentioned before, seen as the driver of value for long-term success: "The goal of the company is not just seen from the economic point of view, but is more and more evolving to a wider concept of economic, environment and social mission, centred on the concept of sustainability" (Carlo Pesenti, CEO).[2] The company is seen as a system that promotes a new welfare in its social and economic system, and, as mentioned above, being a family strongly enhances these aspects, because families are acknowledged to have higher social capital, but also because family businesses are found to be more prone than non-family businesses to pursue and sustain non-economic goals.

The sustainability focus of the company originates from its deep root in the territory and culture where it was started, but has strongly increased and has been perceived as necessary throughout the whole process of growth and globalization. Operating across economies worldwide raises a consciousness that any entrepreneurial action has a relevant and potentially positive implication in any context, from North Africa to Eastern Asia.

Family entrepreneurship and social innovation practices

This section provides evidence of some practices of social innovation pursued by the family firm. At firm level, a focus on sustainability is strongly pervasive, due to the family's attention to this topic and this therefore is straightforward set in the agenda of the top management team. A Director of Sustainable Development was appointed and the top managers are expressly requested and willing to discuss the sustainable development of the company every quarter collectively. This confirms the importance of sustainability as embedded in the company strategy, which is meant to further increase the company's growth and the workers' awareness about how well integrated sustainable development and strategic decision-making should be. It is particularly interesting, therefore, to observe how it is from the global engagement of the company that an overall focus on sustainability and practices emerged at all levels of the company. Carlo Pesenti, the CEO of the group, explains:

> The worldwide downturn has highlighted the need for a new financial ethic. Human rights, equal opportunities, easier access to resources and information, public health and meeting basic social needs: all these ingredients are necessary to build more sustainable business relationships with our suppliers and customers.

The first effort in this direction was made in the 1990s, when the company was one of the first in Italy to adopt a so-called "Code of Ethics". Furthermore, a series of other initiatives was introduced to affect the day-to-day activities with sensitivity towards sustainability. For this reason, in 2000 the enterprise joined the World Business Council for Sustainable Development. It is a global consortium of industrial companies that was created to help company share approaches and practices at the crossroad between business and societal sustainable development.

A Group of Environmental Affairs was a structural function created in the company in 2001. The following year the company subscribed an agenda for action, made by the Cement Sustainability Initiative. This is the first commitment that puts together a large group of leaders in the cement industry worldwide and calls for an action plan that complies with the present needs of the companies and industry, by pursuing the safeguarding of the environment for future generations, with an emphasis on sustainability.

In the Cement Sustainability Initiatives (CSI), Italcementi played an important leadership role since it took over the co-chairmanship of the consortium for two years, in 2006 and 2007. In 2003 the Sustainable Development Steering Committee was created to manage the operations and activities derived by a focus on sustainability in developing the company, and its first report was published the next year. In 2006 a Charter of Values was issued, highlighting the commitment of the family owners to several principles. These can be grouped around five main areas:

- Honesty and fairness of the behaviour, transparency and respect in managing the company internally and externally, particularly in its relationship with stakeholders.

- A culture of dialogue and listening to the community needs in any new and existent operating context where the company acts.
- The protection of individuals by appreciating diversity and respecting cultural identity and dignity at work.
- A safeguarding of the environment by promoting an harmonious integration of the industrial plant, and the landscape and territories where they were installed; also through the recourse to innovative technologies to save resources and to promote renewable energies (a field where Italcementi is excelling at the international level as mentioned above).
- The promotion of overall innovation at technological, organizational and societal level for the growth and development of the local areas where the world company is engaged.

These principles originate from, as we have said, the cultural and historical background of the family, as asserted by Carlo: "The group's sustainable development roadmap to date is the natural consequence of a mindset that has been deeply rooted in Italcementi's DNA right from its early industrial history". All these values are explicit in the charter and derive from the strong conviction of the company that it is an harmonious development of human resources embedded in the territories that can promote a coordinated excellent pattern oriented towards growth and consolidation.

In 2007 Italcementi earned the "Best in Class" status from Storebrand Social Responsible Investments, a research department from the Storebrand Asset Management, which aims at highlighting companies that have excelled in environmental and social screening; it entered the Dow Jones Sustainability Index and created the Sustainable Development Department (SDD). Finally, in 2009, Italcementi took part in the World Business Council for Sustainable Development's regional network, which is an alliance driven by the CEO of 60 organizations that share a commitment to provide the leadership of global business with the sustainable development agenda, with evidence and tools deriving from their own experiences to be spread in their respective countries and regions of operation. Italcementi has been included in "The Sustainability Yearbook 2010", released by the Sustainable Asset Management, which is an independent company in asset management. They focus exclusively on the sustainability issue. The company has achieved for the first time the "SAM Silver Class" distinction and bronze in 2010. In the same year Italcementi joined the United Nations Global Compact, which is an international network that promotes social and environmental sustainability of the economic processes related to growth.

A very important initiative made by the family was the creation of a foundation named after Carlo Pesenti that was established in June 2004 in his honor, as he was one of Italy's most prominent industrial entrepreneurs in the post-war period and contributed to the growth of business in Europe and Italy. The foundation promotes education and scientific research, collaborating with and supporting the activities of several centers at international level, with a special emphasis on the sustainable and social economic development of enterprises enabled by the efficient use of resources, and the ethical approach to foster societal and cultural growth of communities involved with Italcementi. Moreover, the foundation supports and fosters international humanitarian projects for people who have been affected by natural disasters by providing support for their needs in emergencies. The foundation also conducts studies and research as well as promotions and activities aimed at spreading awareness and creating a cultural background so that the importance of sustainability can be perceived.

A final important initiative led by the company is the creation of their CSR division. Until the end of 2007 there was not a dedicated structure within the company. It appeared in 2008, when Italcementi created an organization that was explicitly devoted to handle sustainable development, to provide indications and monitor the operations of the company at every functional division. The unit is in charge of four particular strategies and strategic levers: safety and quality of the workplace; environment and hygiene; climate compliance and climate protection; and social initiatives. It is very important to highlight which type of organizational effort is put in place by the company by establishing a strong relationship between the divisions of the company and the CSR division. The Italcementi Group's top management structure is depicted in Figure 7.6.

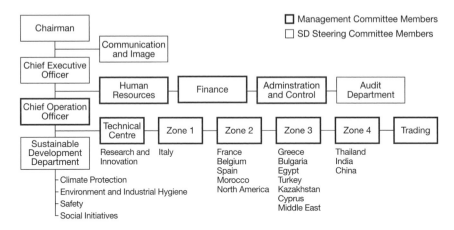

FIGURE 7.6 Members of Italcementi Group's Sustainable Development Steering Committee

Challenges and future developments

The company proves its entrepreneurial imprinting by always being innovative and proactive in its strategic and organizational decisions. Several future challenges are being addressed and studied by the company in the field of sustainable development. This occurs mainly around seven areas:

- Climate protection.
- Responsible use of fuels and raw materials, with special attention to water depletion.
- Employees' health and safety.
- Emission reduction.
- Impact on territory and local communities.
- Reporting and communication.
- Continuous engagement with stakeholders.

According to Carlo, particular relevance has been given recently to climate protection:

> Current environmental protection requirements compel us to face a number of key issues: a more effective alignment with the long-term international agenda for the reduction of direct and indirect greenhouse gas emissions; a strong standardization of environmental performances across all the countries where we operate; and finally a renewed attention towards major global and social issues such as the responsible use of resources, particularly water and biodiversity.

As we have said, the company always perceived the social and human capital to be the most precious resource for its development, both at the global and local level. Carlo expresses this focus and commitment towards the qualification of the employees as follows:

> Health and safety are the pillars of our approach to social responsibility. This is put into practice through the application of equal standards and strict industrial hygiene rules across all locations reinforced by a renewed commitment to human rights within the wider community surrounding the "Italcementi system".

Italcementi is committing numerous resources to promote the safety of workplaces and has launched an initiative called "Zero Infortuni" ("Zero Accidents") whose main goal is a real and new pervasive culture in the companies to prevent accidents. The "Zero Infortuni" policy also defines common standards to take care of the workers in the whole group and by avoiding materials and behaviors that prove dangerous, especially in some countries.

Italcementi is investing conspicuously to promote the safety of human rights for both its employees and all the other individual incorporate stakeholders, such as contractors, suppliers and customers who are engaged with the company. Compliance with this aspect is becoming more and more important among the indicators adopted by the company to monitor its overall performance. For instance, the percentage and total amount of industrial investment, partnership and deals that include clauses about human rights is being monitored as a performance indicator of the company, as well as the number of suppliers or contractors who have accepted to undergo screening on the human rights compliance.

Finally, Italcementi signed an agreement with Building and Wood Workers' International, the world organization for workers' rights, and at the end of 2009 the group celebrated Human Rights Day, with an amount of local initiatives or events to support this concept in all the countries of operation. Italcementi is also increasing its investment in the development of the communities as stated by Carlo: "Over the years our group has extended its relationship with key stakeholders, leading to several joint initiatives with governments and NGOs for the development of local communities." For instance, several initiatives aimed at solving the problem of poverty are being undertaken in developing countries where the company is engaged. These projects include poverty alleviation or education for children, and the diffusion of literacy and culture. In some other countries new services and projects are being put into place to support a meal delivery service to the people where the company is active.

Discussion and conclusion

The evidence provided here is a comprehensive example of the implications of "entrepreneurship as a multiplier of social innovation" (Zahra, 2011). It shows that for-profit family firms can reach extraordinary performance in terms of innovation, organization renewal and global presence, by being aware of the importance of sustainability issues; this comes from the ability to take into consideration economic as well as non-economic goals. The sustainability dimension and the tools that are generated affect the quality of the company as a workplace and the relationships with the stakeholders, as suggested by Tencati and Perrini (2006), which are based on strong ties, trust and transparency. This has been reached through a constant commitment to common values that were shared, conveyed and explicitly stated. Having an entrepreneurial family still leading the company enhances the pursuit of this approach as suggested by Fukuyama (1995) and Tagiuri and Davis (1992). The family, normally, is more proactive and demonstrates the advantages of nurturing social capital (see, for example, Tsui-Auch, 2004; Gomez-Meja et al., 2001). It is capable of sustaining long-term oriented relationships across the generations and therefore stakeholders are more likely to develop a strong commitment to the family firm. This "humus" has enabled the company to take care of sustainability issues at both local and global level, where its operations are undertaken. The entrepreneurial spirit that has driven the company and the family seems far from being extinguished, as can be seen from the words of the family CEO and the new projects undertaken.

Case study questions

1 Examine the duality of the entrepreneurial outcome: which are the positive and the dysfunctional or negative effects? How may they change over time or vary across generations? This is meant to provide a more fine-grained discussion about entrepreneurship and its role.

2 Adopt a multilevel of analysis and suggest how different social innovations can be promoted by a family enterprise at individual, business and societal level.

3 Discuss the dynamic interplay between financial and societal wealth: how does the multiplier role of entrepreneurship occur in fostering social innovation?

4 What is the role of state and government in promoting the positive consequences and the social innovative practices of entrepreneurial firms?

5 What are the implications of being a family business in pursuing sustainability policies and adopting practices that are socially innovative?

Notes

1 While the company has provided valuable support and permitted the use of pictures, the evidence used here is based on publicly available data sources. The chapter therefore does not necessarily reflect the company's view. It should be noted that, as the case was developed in 2011, any information reported in this chapter should be contextualized to that year.

2 The source for Carlo Pesenti's quote is: www.italcementigroup.com/ENG/Sustainable+Development/CEO+statement/ (accessed 24 April 2011).

References

CERIF (Centro di Ricerca sulle Imprese di Famiglia) 2008. Le imprese di famiglia: Imprenditori è il momento di lasciare il testimone?, CERIF Workshop, November 21.

Danes, S.M., Stafford, K., Haynes, G. and Amarapurkar, S.S. 2009. Family Capital of Family Firms: Bridging Human, Social, and Financial Capital, *Family Business Review*, 22(3), 199–215.

European Commission 2001. Green Paper. Promoting a European Framework for Corporate Social Responsibility. Brussels, COM, 366.

Fukuyama, F. 1995. *Trust*. New York: Free Press.

Gomez-Mejia, L.R., Nuñez-Nickel, M. and Gutierrez, I. 2001. The role of family ties in agency contracts, *Academy of Management Journal*, 44(1), 81–95.

Hochgerner, J. 2009. Approaching a Viable Comprehension of the Knowledge Society, *Theory of Science*, 31(3–4), 37–44.

Osservatorio AIdAF-Unicredit-Bocconi (AUB) sulle aziende familiari italiane di medie e grandi dimensioni, II° Rapporto, 2010.

Rusk, M., Poncini, G.M. and McGowan, P. 2011. Using Design, Innovation and Entrepreneurship in Community Building and Regeneration, *Design Principles and Practices: An International Journal*, 5(5), 117–128.

Stafford, K., Duncan, K.A., Dane, S. and Winter, M. 1999. A Research Model of Sustainable Family Businesses, *Family Business Review*, 12(3), 197–208.

Tagiuri, R. and Davis, J.A. 1992. On the Goals of Successful Family Companies, *Family Business Review*, 5(1), 43–62.

Tencati, A. and Perrini, F. 2006. The Sustainability Perspective: A New Governance Model. In: Kakabadse, A. and Morsing, M. (eds). *Corporate Social Responsibility*. New York: Palgrave Macmillan. 94–111.

Toninelli, P.M. and Vasta, M. 2009. Italian Entrepreneurship: Conjectures And Evidence From a Historical Perspective, Working Paper, Department of Economics at the University of Milan Bicocca.

Tsui-Auch, L.S. 2004. The Professionally Managed Family-ruled Enterprise: Ethnic Chinese Business in Singapore, *Journal of Management Studies*, 41(4), 693–723.

Welter, F. and Lasch, F. 2008. Entrepreneurship Research in Europe: Taking Stock and Looking Forward, *Entrepreneurship Theory and Practice*, 32(2), 241–248.

Zahra, S. 2011. Entrepreneurship, Business and Society, Keynote Speech at RENT Conference, Bodø, Norway, November 18. Available at: www.serialive.com/watch.php?id=42152 (accessed March 20, 2012).

Zamagni, V. 2006. Italcementi: Dalla leadership nazionale all'internazionalizzazione. Bologna: Il Mulino.

Zocchi, W. 2005. Le imprese familiari di fronte alla responsabilità sociale. Centro Studi Family Business Office (images.no.camcom.gov.it/f/Economia/in/intervento_Zocchi.pdf, accessed 9 March 2011).

8

FURNITURA LTD – LATVIA

Arnis Sauka and Friederike Welter

Context

Furnitura Ltd[1] was established in 2004, in Latvia – a country located in Northern Europe on the coastline of the Baltic Sea. Extending over an area of 64,589 sq km, and bordered by Estonia, Lithuania, Russia and Belarus, Latvia has approximately 2 million inhabitants. The country is dominated by the service sector (approximately 70 per cent of 2010 GDP), whereas manufacturing comprises only approximately 10 per cent of 2010 GDP.[2] After joining the European Union and NATO in 2004, Latvia experienced the fastest growth rates in the European Union, reaching GDP growth of +12.2 per cent in 2006.[3] This was, however, followed by a sharp slowdown, starting in early 2008 – a consequence of the world financial crisis, with Latvia's GDP falling to approximately −18 per cent in 2009.[4]

The depth of the crisis in Latvia was fostered by greatly increased consumption, resulting from the easy access to cheap bank loans[5] that occurred during the years of rapid economic growth in Latvia. After the 'credit bubble' collapsed in early 2008, to stabilize the financial sector Latvia had to borrow some €7.5 billion from the European Commission and the World Bank as well as other organizations and governments.[6] The downturn of the Latvian economy, of course, influenced the climate for entrepreneurship in the country, with many businesses being unable to survive the 2008 crisis. This was also the case of Furnitura Ltd. What started as a success story in 2004, turned out as a bankruptcy by the end of 2008.

Yet, former owner and CEO of Furnitura Ltd, Edgars Berzins, who has agreed to share his recent business failure experience, certainly looks nothing at all like someone who has failed. Edgars has three degrees: one in physics, a master's degree in public administration, and executive master of business administration degree from the Stockholm School of Economics in Riga. He started his career in a physics laboratory and then moved on to a commercial bank. After working for the bank, Edgars was head of a telecommunications company – currently one of the leading mobile phone operators in Latvia – and later became a divisional head of the big international telecommunications chain. Edgars's entrepreneurship career, however, was influenced by his friends who kept asking whether he was going to open his own company, considering his achievements as a top manager.

Looking for the knowledge to start his own business as well as for a business opportunity, while still working for the international telecommunications company, Edgars attended a number of executive education programmes. One of those programs offered Professor Michael Porter's lectures in Riga, where students analysed Porter's (1998) 'diamond' model of the competitive advantage of nations. Being a physicist, and a person who is very much interested in various creative things, Edgars was indeed inspired by this model and started to look for possible fields and industries where a similar model could be implemented in Latvia. After exploring a number of options, Edgars reached a seemingly obvious conclusion: Latvia is a land of forests, full of this natural resource. So he decided to do something in this area – at that time having no understanding of this industry or what he would end up doing.

There was one thing that was clear to Edgars: that there are only a few furniture companies in Latvia and the other two Baltic states, Lithuania and Estonia. Furthermore, Edgars had a friend, an active person with an education in forestry and experience working for a number of furniture companies in Latvia, which made this choice much easier. The deal was that Edgars would invest his own money – startup capital that had been generated by having a good income stream from previous management positions. Edgars's friend, however, was responsible for finding a promising niche market in the furniture business where they could invest. Still, and mostly since the business idea was relatively vague at that stage – i.e. they simply could not figure out the value proposition that company might offer – nothing serious happened for about a year, by which time Edgars had already started to give up on the furniture business idea.

Development of the business idea

Together with his friend, Edgars continued to develop his business idea. One of the factors that contributed to this process was Edgars's EMBA studies at the Stockholm School of Economics in Riga. In fact, the main reason why he entered the business school was to gain additional knowledge to start his own company. As Edgars explains:

> With all the things I could do, also considering my previous experience in management, I felt like there were certain gaps in my knowledge. So I was partly studying, partly developing my business idea, also receiving useful feedback from my course mates.

The idea for the value-added furniture business eventually came. Namely, Edgars was building his family house at that time and something that was driving him mad constantly was that almost every shelf, even every plank that suited his plans had to be ordered from a particular joiner or designer – that is, Edgars simply could not find one company that would offer him complete, good quality furniture that would suit his expectations. As a result, Edgars had to approach various different suppliers, and thus the process of furnishing his house promised to be both long and very expensive.

Luckily for Edgars, together with his friend they came across a German company that offered a technical solution that could help to solve this particular problem. The solution, which eventually became the business idea, was to build on existing software, and create an Internet platform, an integrated IT solution, where on their own, users would be able to put their home-furnishing wishes and needs on the computer screen. Edgars explains:

> When it is done, all the users will need to do is press the button and the computer calculates all the costs of furnishing a house or the particular parts of a house. The integrity of the system would lie in further steps, that is, the program would send all contents produced by the user directly to the factory, where production could start. Fast, easy and efficient!

Apart from having a value-added product, they also seemed to have picked a good time to implement the idea. More specifically, favourable economic conditions are important as they might help to generate sufficient demand, at least during the startup phase. In 2004, when Edgars was about to start his business, the situation in the Latvian economy indeed seemed rather promising – namely, Latvia was about to join the European Union, which implied some economic development with investments coming in. And during economic development one industry that certainly develops is construction: one could easily predict that houses and offices would be built and they would all need furniture.

To have sufficient time for developing his own company, in 2004 Edgars decided to leave the telecommunications company where he worked as the head of the telecommunications department being responsible for an annual turnover of some €40 million. Yet, both Edgars and his friend soon realized that applying technical solutions to add value to the product would not be as easy as they had initially thought. In particular, they understood that users – i.e. their customers – would simply not be able to put their home-furnishing wishes and needs on the computer screen so that the manufacturers would be able to produce from this content. Overall, the conclusion was that if one wants to offer something that is very friendly for the manufacturing side, it will most certainly not be user-friendly and vice versa. What could solve this is a professional mediator between customer needs and the production process: someone who helps the customer.

At the end of the day, the main product – i.e. the value that Furnitura offered to the customers – consisted of a number of items. First, Edgars bought software from a company in Germany: a program in CD format. This software allowed creating a space in a digital format, with doors, windows, angles, height, width and other parameters, exactly like a customer's house or office. Once the space was created, the customer could choose various furniture elements from an electronic catalogue and furnish the virtual space according to their needs and wishes. Furthermore, to make the processes easier for the customer, both the creation of the space and the arrangement of the furniture elements were carried out by professionals, who usually worked in pairs: one talked to the customer to find out his or her needs, another one put these ideas on the screen.

The real competitive advantage of the product, however, that was different from what was available on the market at that time was the integration of the system with its bookkeeping and manufacturing departments. Such a solution saved lots of time and actually allowed closing the deal much more easily, and that was far from common in the industry. Usually, once the needs of customer are clear, the sales process is followed by preparing and sending a financial offer to the customer. But, as explained by Edgars, customers' needs almost always change – for instance, they may want to adjust colours, some parts, materials – and all this influences the price and delivery time. Thus, once the needs are clarified, a new price offer has to be prepared, then usually also a third, fourth or fifth as customers' tastes and wishes tend to change quickly when it comes to furnishing their houses. At the end, the whole process to close the deal could sometimes last weeks and even months, and during this time customers might also change their minds about making an order at all. With an IT-supported integrated system in place, the process of making the deal became much easier and faster, and both Edgars and his customers appreciated that.

2004 to early 2007: key expansion strategies of Furnitura Ltd, leading to a success story

When the technical solution was clear and while building the factory, it also became clear to Edgars that the commercial sector was developing very rapidly in Latvia. Office houses were being built, banks were expanding, almost everyone needed new offices and all offices had to be furnished. Edgars looked at the current offer in the office furniture market and realized that locally only two Latvian companies – two companies from Lithuania and one firm from Estonia – were producing office furniture. The rest of the office furniture at that time was brought in from other countries, which involved transportation costs, making products more expensive. Furthermore, most of the companies that operated from a distance could not work individually with their customers. Considering the market gap and expanding commercial sector, the focus of Furnitura became obvious: to concentrate on producing office furniture. An argument from Edgars's friend, who helped with the management of the company, that office furniture is simpler to produce, was also convincing.

Even though at later stages Furnitura borrowed some money from the bank to make expansion faster, Edgars had sufficient financial capital in the first years of the startup. This money was invested both in the production process and other activities primarily targeted at increasing the market share of Furnitura in the office furniture business. Namely, even though there were only a few competitors in the market at that time, these were all comparably big companies, with some 10–15 years' experience in the market. Thus Edgars's intention from the very beginning was to show potential customers that Furnitura could be better than those companies – not only better in quality but also at least as big. This, however, meant that Furnitura had to grow quickly, and the way Edgars intended to achieve the growth was not to focus on making profits, but rather to invest all the startup money and income into expansion to increase turnover and thus also their market share.

The key market expansion strategies of Furnitura were closely linked with the sales service and customer support, which increased the value added to the product the company offered. Edgars believed that sales are the crucial element for the success of any business, considering that they came with some innovation in the sales approach. Namely, Furnitura was the first one to sell furniture in Latvia using a direct sales approach and, according to Edgars, this strategy was behind most of the success the company achieved in the first years.

As Edgars explained, most, if not all the furniture companies in Latvia at that time were simply waiting for their customers to arrive in their shops and tried to increase the likelihood that customers would come by placing advertisements in the media. Edgars's previous experience from the time when he was responsible for developing sales staff for other companies suggested, however, that when it comes to sales, it is not so much about "advertisement tricks in the media", but much more about direct contact with the customer. That is why Furnitura actively looked for potential customers who were building houses and offices, getting to know what they might need and when they would need it. In addition, by establishing contact with the potential customer early in the decision-making phase, Furnitura ensured that customers thought about the environment they were creating first and only then started building it. That is, Edgars had observed a rather strange trend in the construction area: people were building houses first and only then thinking about what this environment, where they were supposed to work and live, would look like. As a result, they were often unsatisfied when they found that many things they wanted could not be achieved once the house was built.

When it came to customer support, a focus on high-quality products helped Furnitura to establish a good reputation in the market. Namely, Furnitura always construct their furniture so that it fits all the customer's requirements. This means that no small gaps from the wall are tolerated even if the wall surface is angled, for instance, and the customer can be sure that the colour of all the furniture parts will be exactly as on the screen when the decision to buy the product was made. If there are any complaints from the customers, direct sales staff are always there to solve the problems.

Apart from sales and customer support, the initial success of Furnitura was also built on their diversified customer portfolio and diversified product range. The customer portfolio in Latvia, a market that Furnitura concentrated on initially, was good in terms of size and also well diversified. Furnitura served many banks, car dealerships and companies of all sizes – basically, everyone who needed office furniture – in their customer portfolio. Furthermore, following the development of the household market, Furnitura also made a decision to expand the product range and started to offer kitchens not only to offices, but also to households. With this move, Furnitura initiated another innovation in sales that the company intended to use in order to penetrate the market also outside Latvia.

The household market appeared to be different from the office market. The main difference was that Furnitura could allow much more freedom and internal competition among the salespeople involved in selling the products, not having to fear that, for instance, two sales agents would knock on the same door to sell Furnitura kitchens. Bearing this in mind, Edgars started to develop a network of sales agents to sell kitchens for the household market: anyone could become a Furnitura sales agent. The caveat was the requirement by Furnitura management that most of their salespeople should be woodworkers who could not only explain the features of the product they were selling but also set it up in homes and offices. So Furnitura trained these people to work with their software, gave them the access code, allowed them to build their own customer portfolio, and the like. What salespeople received in return was, being either self-employed or micro companies, they charged the customers direct for setting up kitchens. This turned out to be a win–win situation for the company, sales people and customers as the company gained more customers, salespeople earned extra money, and customers received a full, customer-oriented service for a reasonable price.

As a result, Furnitura's intentions to serve their customers as well as possible were rewarded by a growth in turnover and a rapidly increasing market share during the first three years. By the end of 2007, only three years after Furnitura was launched, the company won the "Sales Tiger": a competition that is run by *Dienas bizness*, a leading business newspaper in Latvia that distinguishes the most successful, fastest developing companies in the country. This award was given to Furnitura since in the space of only three years, the company was able to catch up with all its competitors – companies that had been market leaders for the previous 10–15 years. Furnitura's annual sales amount were more than €2 million and growing. The company employed 40 full-time employees in-house plus another 40 sales agents working on behalf of the company. All in all, it seemed like the only way for the company was up. Unfortunately, it was not.

Economic downturn in late 2007–2008

After stricter regulations for taking loans were introduced in Latvia in 2007 and capital was no longer as easily available, demand for many products, including office furniture, decreased sharply. Another consequence of the credit squeeze was that real-estate prices also started to go down. As Edgars remembers: "Yet prices for the real estate were indeed too high back in 2007 and many knew that. So my guess was that prices would fall, say, by about half . . . it is just that neither I nor many others anticipated what that meant for the economy." As a result, regardless of the signs from the economy, Furnitura was simply continuing its expansion strategy.

Indeed, it looked as if Furnitura had all the prerequisites and reasons for expansion. Even though the economy in Latvia and other parts of the world was contracting, the company was not yet anticipating any trouble: customers were still building offices, needing furniture and producing orders. The turnover of Furnitura was still increasing in 2007, competitors were trying to copy it, and it all looked as if the company would continue to be a success story.

Furnitura also *acted* like a success story – for instance, moving production from 900 to 3,000 square metres in mid-2007. This production site and sales salon was designed as a big showroom where the company's products could be presented to customers, and where agents could come together with customers, sit and plan together with them. When asked by bank representatives in mid-2007 whether everything was fine with Furnitura and whether the company felt any consequences of the economic crisis, Edgars's answer was that the crisis was actually over! By this, he meant that labour costs, which had been rising dramatically over the previous three years, finally had some inclination to stabilize, or at least were not growing so quickly. Yet, if the crisis had already happened, only a few people had noticed it.

There are many reasons why Furnitura did not notice the crisis. First of all, Furnitura, like many other companies, had simply become used to fast growth over the past three years. As emphasized by Edgars: "What happens during economic growth is that you inevitably lose some rigour and do not pay attention to things that are very important." What Edgars meant by this is that at some point Furnitura simply lost control of the real state of their business, and the main reason for that was that they analyzed the situation based on the profit-and-loss statement, which for various reasons can be evaluated after a full year, as the situation per quarter, with all the investments in expansion, etc., might not provide a clear picture of what is actually going on. In other words, the company simply did not pay enough attention to its cash flow, and this was a big mistake.

Looking at the profit-and-loss statement showing the big losses of Furnitura at the end of 2007, Edgars realized for the first time that one should *always* monitor cash flow in order to understand the real situation in the company and if something goes wrong there, take immediate action. The profit-and-loss statement of Furnitura in 2007 indeed looked shocking and Edgars remembers asking his partner:

> How come? We are the best, strongest, and biggest in the market, have everything we need for development, are not spending where it is not necessary, and have not done anything stupid. So where are all these losses coming from?

Looking at things in more depth, Furnitura's management soon realized where the key problems were, leading to considerable losses at the end of 2007. First and foremost it was all about the increase in costs. Namely, almost all fixed and variable costs were increasing in 2007, some of them afterwards as well, and without constantly monitoring their cash flow, Furnitura simply did not anticipate the consequences. The rise in costs came together with a sharp decrease in income, not in the form of a decrease in demand, which came later, but a constant decrease in products' prices. This was a consequence of previous economic growth, in particular the huge competition that it fostered – that is, when Furnitura started in 2004, there were almost no furniture manufacturers in the market, whereas at the end of 2007, following a sharp increase in demand, one could find a furniture manufacturer or distributor on almost every corner of the street. So the only sales argument was price and few paid attention to the value-added advanced technology that Furnitura was offering. Indeed, prices went down, whereas almost every day one or two employees would come into the office asking for a salary rise, threatening to leave the company and work for one of its competitors.

In addition, the construction business – the main stakeholders creating the demand for the furniture business – was starting to slow down. Increasingly, Furnitura faced situations where completed products remained in stock as customers could not pay for their order, or due to a lack of funding, or because construction work on a particular office building took more time than initially planned. As a consequence, the company did not receive the final payment from customers, which negatively impacted cash flow. What made the situation even more difficult was that in furniture manufacturing and the manufacturing business in general, it is not that easy to have complete control over the incoming and outgoing funds. Without advanced accounting programs and professionals on board, it is very difficult to follow the exact costs of the business, especially during 2005–2007, when prices of raw materials were changing rapidly and constantly.

An example will illustrate this problem. Furnitura acquired stock, say, at the end of 2006 and started to use it in mid-2007, then additional stock was bought at different prices – sometimes higher, sometimes lower later on. Different parts of the stock went to different customers' orders, all for different selling prices and some with delayed payments – in other words, the final result was far from clear with all the changes unless it was seriously monitored. However, it was not. Since the company was growing in terms of turnover, Furnitura invested money and time in development – expanding market shares – and did so by drawing on the same strategy that brought success in previous years, rather than adjusting its strategies and introducing control mechanisms for monitoring cash flow.

Bankruptcy

Even with big losses at the end of 2007, Furnitura had no intention of stopping. Edgars explained: "We understood the problem: we had overslept in 2007. But we also thought that not everything was lost and were looking for the solution." The company's strategy was to keep information about the internal problems inside the firm and move forward. First, Edgars took on the cash flow issue and hired a professional financial director to constantly monitor the inflow and outflow. Since some additional finance was required to get out of trouble, Furnitura also took out a bank loan to recover and continue to grow.

Edgars likens the situation at the end of 2007 to sitting in an air balloon and trying to get rid of unnecessary ballast in order to make it fly. He understood the seriousness of the problem and really tried to cut everything where possible, adjusted management structures, changed suppliers to increase efficiency and lower costs, identified many inefficiencies within the operation of the company, and even undertook a restructuring. On the other hand, as Edgars remembers, in the peak of growth it is very difficult to tell anyone – management or employees – that a company should slow down. According to Edgars, not only would this be perceived as a very silly idea, but many employees might interpret such a signal as being a problem of Furnitura only, and thus might consider being "on the safe side" by leaving to work for their competitors. The problems within Furnitura were perceived as being of a short-term nature both by many employees and industry.

All in all, getting rid of some "unnecessary ballast" was simply not possible. The largest problem turned out to be a five-year contract for the rental of 3,000 square metres of production premises, signed in mid-2007. "For various reasons, the owner of the premises simply did not get involved in any negotiation with us, mainly because of their own financial problems," says Edgars, explaining that they started to regularly cut off electricity and one day there was a big chain with a lock on the door, "so we could not even get equipment, and then it was clear that the business was over." In December 2008, Furnitura Ltd officially closed down its business. As Edgars put it: "Simply after all the effort we invested to penetrate the market and establish ourselves as a reputable brand, we never reached profitability, and after all the problems we faced during 2008, I thought it was enough!" This was also the point when Edgars realized that not only Furnitura Ltd, but the entire Latvian economy, were in the waterfall already, and the feeling was that this would be for a long time.

Turning bankruptcy into sustainable bankruptcy

One of the lessons that Edgars has learned from his bankruptcy experience is that when getting rid of ballast to make a balloon fly, one should be cautious not to throw away too many assets. And this seems exactly what Edgars did. Namely, when asked what he does for a living today, in particular whether he is working in some good management position for a big company, as he has done earlier very successfully, Edgars shakes his head emphatically: "When you enter entrepreneurship, I do not think that there is a way back. At least for me, as I am still in business!"

What Edgars implies by this is that the knowledge he acquired during his EMBA studies at the Stockholm School of Economics in Riga suggested that he should be smart enough to diversify his business activities so that the company failure did not automatically mean his personal failure. Edgars, in fact, had businesses other than Furnitura – more than one, in reality – and this worked as a cushion, making his landing much softer. Already in 2005 he was involved in a business selling food supplements and he then acquired 100 per cent of this business. In October 2008, however, a couple months before Furnitura went bankrupt, Edgars launched another business dealing in beverage machines. In addition, Edgars owns a female gym studio, a business that partly developed from the food supplements business and it was also started in October 2008.

Was it a good idea to start new companies at that time? We should keep in mind that Edgars had already started to work on launching those businesses some time before. Beverage machines had been ordered at least half a year before and were on their way, and construction repair work at the female gym studio was also almost finished, so to stop was simply not an option. Thus, in December 2008, Edgars had no choice but to look at all the businesses he had, then he looked into his wallet, and decided to lose the furniture business and concentrate on others. In comparison to many other entrepreneurs whose businesses failed during that time, he may have been fortunate to have such an option: to continue entrepreneurship even after the failure of one of his companies.

Case study questions

1   What are the key factors contributing to the firm's failure, especially during the economic recession?
2   Which strategies would you advise for Furnitura Ltd to avoid bankruptcy at the end of 2008?
3   What are the benefits and potential weaknesses of products/ companies' diversification strategies as implemented by Edgars Berzins?

Notes

1   The company name and names of all the persons in this case are changed.
2   Available at: http://balticexport.com/?article=latvijas-ekonomika&lang=lv
3   Available at: http://balticexport.com/?article=latvijas-ekonomika&lang=lv
4   Available at: www.csb.gov.lv
5   . . . and overoptimistic forecasts with regard to the future growth of the Latvian economy that influenced consumption behaviour.
6   Available at: http://balticexport.com/?article=latvijas-ekonomika&lang=lv

Reference

Porter, M. (1998) *The Competitive Advantage of Nations*, Macmillan 1990; 2nd edn, Macmillan Business.

9

THE LIECHTENSTEIN BREWING CO. – LIECHTENSTEIN

Christine Vallaster, Sascha Kraus and Urs Baldegger

The start

With a size of 160 km², the principality of Liechtenstein (which is not a member of the European Union) is the fourth smallest country within Europe (after the Vatican City, Monaco, and San Marino). In the fall of 2007, the long wait of 100 years came to an end for the population of 36,000 inhabitants: for the first time in nearly 100 years, a brewery on home soil was up and running.

In spite of the decrease in beer consumption, and the dominance of large beer brands, regional beer-makers had still been able to make inroads into the highly competitive market using target group-oriented strategies. But private brands, cheap beer, and the rising popularity of international brand-name beers were just a few of the challenges facing the traditional breweries. For years, the Swiss and Liechtenstein beer markets had been losing ground.

The Liechtenstein Brewing Co. was established in 2007 by Bruno Güntensperger, only one year after he and some of his friends had the idea of opening a brewery in the late hours of a wedding party in Liechtenstein. Güntensperger still remembers the context in which this decision was made – and is nevertheless optimistic when he looks to the future. Together with Leone Ming, owner of a Liechtenstein creative agency, he developed his ideas about how to reach the minds of the Liechtenstein population with his company and product. Güntensperger knew the market and aimed to establish his product and company as a brand name in Liechtenstein, position them long term within the region, and achieve a share of the market.

First, the beer needed to become known and accepted as a local specialty and a part of the culture, as well as a brand name for the region. It needed the brand values of being true, authentic, honest, and fresh. The company's communication strategy was based on the simple slogan *Ein Land. Ein Bier* ("One country. One beer."). The beer's German name is *Liechtensteiner Brauhaus* (Liechtenstein Brewery) along with the name of exactly what kind of beer it is (e.g. Pilsner, Weizen, etc.).

The Liechtenstein Brewing Co. has been a success story since its market entry. Sales are constantly on the rise, and even the large competitors from Switzerland who supply the bars, pubs, and clubs in Liechtenstein with their beers are becoming increasingly worried about their loss of market share in the principality. Although the 10 largest breweries worldwide (the top four being Anheuser-Bush, SAB Miller, Heineken, and Carlsberg respectively) share more than 62 percent of the worldwide market share with their different brands, the demand for local beer is rising again. With this being the case, Güntensperger uses a high(er) price strategy with his different products.

A vision emerges

What started with Quaderer beer . . .

The last brewery in Liechtenstein closed its gates in 1917 due to shortages in raw materials caused by the First World War. This was the Quaderer Brewery, located in Schaan, a municipality of Liechtenstein. The building itself remained in use as a pub or, as the locals called it, the *Bierhüusle*,[1] which was well known throughout the region.

. . . became Liechtenstein Brewing Co. beer

The Liechtenstein Brewing Co. was founded in 2007 by Bruno Güntensperger. The idea had already budded in his head in 1992, during which time he was doing doctorate work at the Swiss Federal Institute of Technology Zurich's Institute of Food, Nutrition and Health. Here, he had the project idea to start his own brewery in Liechtenstein. His passion for brewing beer had come from the internship he had done at a brewery, along with his attempts to make homemade beer with fellow students in his free time. This dream of his own brewery would slumber for 15 years until it became reality; in August, 2006 at a wedding *Apéro*[2] in the city of Triesenberg, the idea was kicked around by friends. Things started to happen quickly after that. A little more than a year later, on October 23, 2007, the first batch of beer was brewed. Well-known Liechtenstein politicians attended the grand opening on December 1, 2007.

"Our major goal is to brew a *Volksbier* for everyone and to vitalize the domestic market with a local beer that is not a standardized industry beer, but rather a distinctive beverage with its own character," says Güntensperger. This means that it's a beer for a wide span of the Liechtenstein population, "and not just the 'wine and cheese crowd' who are the only ones able to afford it. It needs to make its mark with the locals at the town pub, and be known as a beer that's enjoyed among good company and friends," he explains. What Güntensperger has in mind is a one-of-a-kind beer with its own character, and which is distinct from the standardized industry beers currently dominating the Liechtenstein market.

The market

The local Liechtenstein market

The principality of Liechtenstein, the world's fourth smallest country, is geographically embedded between Austria and Switzerland in the Alps, around 70 km away from the German border. In other words, Liechtenstein is encapsulated among three strong beer countries. Although the official language of Liechtenstein is German, the spoken language is Alemannic, a dialect that is very divergent from standard or "High German", and closely related to Swiss German. Liechtenstein has the second-highest GDP per person in the world, and is part of a monetary and trade/customs union with Switzerland. It uses the Swiss franc (CHF) as its currency, and can therefore be regarded in terms of trade as a part of the Swiss market.

Liechtenstein's only large international player is HILTI and its nearly 1,900 employees in Liechtenstein (and 20,000 worldwide). Along with this, Liechtenstein is perhaps most famous for its banks and for being a tax haven. The local industry consists almost entirely of small and medium-sized enterprises (SMEs). The country has 33,000 jobs among its 36,000 inhabitants (of these, around 16,000 commute in from the neighboring countries). Its one state university – the University of Liechtenstein – has a strong concentration on Entrepreneurship, SME and Family Firm Management (the M.Sc. in Entrepreneurship program founded by Professor Urs Baldegger in 2009 holds second place in a cross-country ranking of all the universities in Switzerland, Austria, and Liechtenstein, being exceeded only by the elite university ETH Zürich, 15 times its size). The university's KMU Zentrum (Center for SMEs) is the leading facilitator for new venture foundation and consulting in the country.

Overall market situation

Swiss breweries produced a total of 3.53 million hectoliters of beer in 2007. In the same year, a total of 4.37 million hectoliters of beer were consumed, amounting to a per-capita consumption of 57.1 liters. Table 9.1 shows the overall downturn of nearly 20 percent in per-capita consumption that has occurred since 1990/91.[3]

In 2007, the Swiss market imported 838,094 hectoliters of beer from a total of 74 countries on all continents, while exporting 52,647 hectoliters to 33 countries. In that year, beer sales in Switzerland increased by an average of 1.9 percent compared to the previous year, amounting to a difference of 81,900 hectoliters. Almost all of this increase was attributed to imported beers (which comprised 19.1 percent of the overall beer sales), mostly cheaper varieties for the retail market. "Those suffering the most from the growing market share of imported beers are the medium-sized breweries," said Marcel Kreber, Director of the Brewer's Association. According to Kreber, large producers (i.e. international concerns) brew

TABLE 9.1 The Swiss beer market and beer consumption (table does not include non-alcoholic beers)

Year[1]	Domestic production[2,3] (in hl)	Imports[2] (in hl)	Total consumption (in hl)	Per-capita consumption[4] (in liters)
1990/91	4,183,358	661,422	4,844,780	71.0
1995/96	3,596,388	708,885	4,305,273	60.6
1999/00	3,613,986	580,718	4,194,704	58.3
Calendar year				
2000	3,586,026	575,929	4,161,955	57.8
2001	3,536,823	617,023	4,153,846	57.4
2002	3,493,536	633,897	4,127,433	56.6
2003	3,665,888	668,486	4,334,374	58.7
2004	3,560,825	701,723	4,262,548	57.3
2005	3,416,991	715,064	4,131,055	54.8
2006	3,494,309	793,713	4,288,022	56.5
2007	3,531,828	838,094	4,369,922	57.1

Notes

1 Time frame: October 1 to September 30 of the respective years.
2 Source: Swiss Federal Customs Administration.
3 Including foreign brands that are brewed under license in Switzerland; exports not included.
4 Entire population living in Switzerland and Liechtenstein (including women and children).

beer in Switzerland using Swiss employees. The traditional brands – Calanda, Haldengut, and Eichhof – belong to Heineken, while the well-known Feldschlösschen and Cardinal operate under the umbrella of the Carlsberg Group.[4]

Nearly half of imported beers (48 percent) came from Germany, 17.3 percent from France, and 12.3 percent from Portugal. Supermarket retail in particular sells a great deal of imported beer, which the locals enjoy drinking from the can. Around 24 percent of beer is filled into non-refundable bottles, and 26 percent into cans (see Figure 9.1).[5]

Although the Swiss beer market is increasingly being taken over by the major foreign breweries, Swiss breweries in the regions near Liechtenstein are successfully making their mark with niche products, specialty brews, and their proximity to the customer. The main player on the Swiss market is the Schützengarten brewery in St Gallen. In 2007, it sold 2 percent more beer than in the previous year. With 163,600 hectoliters, Schützengarten and Löwengarten beers hit a new record mark. In spite of the loss of the Volg private label, overall beer production for the retail market remained steady at the previous year's level of 176,100 hectoliters, down only by 0.1 percent. While beer sales in Switzerland increased by 8.7 percent in the past 10 years, Schützengarten sales increased during the same time period by 29 percent. And if the sales by the Löwengarten brewery that was acquired in 2006

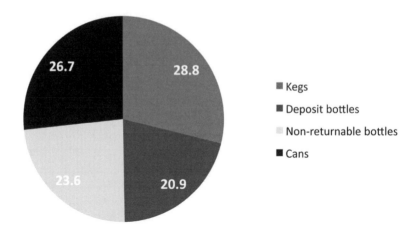

FIGURE 9.1 Beer market in Switzerland – unit sales

are included, this increase is even higher at 34.5 percent. Along with the leading Klosterbräu brand, the Schützengarten lager enjoyed the greatest sales increase. Six-packs of half-liter bottles were launched for the retail market.[6]

Market trends

An increasing segment of the population is becoming more health-conscious, and as a result is drinking less beer. Companies have taken note of this, and have responded by producing more bottles and kegs of non-alcoholic beer. When asked how the Liechtenstein Brewing Co. had responded, Güntensperger explained:

> Our main market is the regional one. Here, these kinds of specialties make up less than 5 percent of sales. So producing a non-alcoholic beer for this tiny segment is simply not an option. To make it worthwhile, we'd have to start selling beyond the market we mainly operate in. Purchasing this kind of beer or a similar product from another brewery would be an alternative.

Another point to keep in mind is that, for example, the success of beers mixed with cola or other soda pops are generally subject to what is "in" at the moment, and are promoted towards very specific target groups as the latest trend. Güntensperger explained:

> That's not really something we're interested in. We're a small town, not St Gallen, Zurich, or Chur. This kind of product needs a lot of advertising and marketing to get itself noticed among the international competition that's out there.

His strategy in this case would be to have more of a focus on local stories and history, and produce a *Naturradler* that combines beer together with cider, for example.

Marketing strategy and mix

Corporate design

The primary visual elements of the Liechtenstein Brewing Co. are the lettering, logo, and signet that apply a yellow, gold, and black color pattern. The "Liechtensteiner Brauhaus" logo is used for official communication (letterheads, etc.). The signet with the B in the circle stands for the words *Brauhaus* or *Bier*. It is a key graphic visual for the company's communication (see Figure 9.2).

FIGURE 9.2 Company logo

When the time came to decide on the lettering and color for the company logo, great importance was placed on the right balance between tradition and modern. For the color palette, two varieties of yellow are used for the signet, along with a radiant gold, which aim to symbolize the freshness of the product. Black offers an ideal contrast to the radiating colors, while at the same time signifying the modern elements of the product. Figure 9.3 shows how the design is used on the bottle labeling, coasters, and company vehicles.

The product

Fresh is what counts the most for this beer. It is brewed according the *Reinheitsgebot* (purity law) of 1516, which stipulates that beer may only be made from water, malt, hops, and yeast. It is not pasteurized, is stored only for very brief periods, and travels short distances to its final destinations. All of this ensures that the beer the customer drinks is fresh from the brewmaster's tap.

The company also maintains a simple "4 plus 1" product portfolio. Four beers are offered year-round, while an additional beer is offered seasonally or for particular events and occasions for one month.

The first two Liechtenstein Brewing Co. products entered the market on December 1, 2007: *Brauhaus Helles*, referred to as "Hell's"[7] for short, and *Brauhaus*

Vehicle sides and lettering

Coasters and labels

FIGURE 9.3 Uses of the company design

Weizenbier or "Weiza."[8] Güntensperger was clearly happy. "The brewers produced a masterpiece. It's quite a refreshing beer that really hits the spot." The *Kellerbier* was introduced towards the end of 2008 as another year-round beer in the Liechtensteiner selection.

The *iisi* beer is an example of a seasonal product (see Figure 9.4). Launched for the 2010 summer season as a somewhat lighter lager in a new package (*iisi* is a Germanic phonetic invention based on the English word "easy"), *iisi* lager contains 30 percent less alcohol than the full-bodied Liechtensteiner beers. With *iisi*, the Liechtenstein Brewing Co. was aiming to meet the increased demand on the market for lighter beers. It is just as pure as the company's other beers, and contains no preservatives or antioxidants. It also has to be stored away from light. "*iisi* tastes best right out of the fridge," says Bruno Güntensperger.

With its "take it *iisi*" slogan, the Liechtenstein Brewing Co. makes clear the character of its new beer: light, refreshing, exciting, lively, and effervescent. It's a cool beer for all kinds of occasions that lives up to its name as it makes life just a little "*iisi*er."

Other seasonal examples include *s'Narrabier* (Carnival beer that is offered during the carnival season) or *s'Bockbier* (Malbu-Bock), which is a beer that fits with the cold winter times. *S'Fäscht-Bier* (Celebrating beer) is an autumn specialty and is specially brewed at the time when the October Fest in Munich (Germany) takes place.

Although all of the Liechtenstein Brewing Co.'s beers are brewed in the tradition of Liechtenstein beer-making, their ingredients are not exclusively local. The Liechtenstein Brewing Co. would be more than willing to use only native brewing barley, but there are a few things working against this, as Güntensperger explains:

FIGURE 9.4 *"iisi"* beer

There's the first problem of quantity. We buy in volume from Bamberg in Germany. Liechtenstein simply doesn't have enough barley for us. The second issue is the climatic variations that sometimes occur here. This leads to quality fluctuations that we're not able to offset.

(www.ruggell.li/presseartikel.aspx?showarticle= 337649&cid=&year=&search)

In spite of modern technology, quality fluctuations still occur. Güntensperger describes how:

when you're in a phase where you're working under continual pressure, mistakes occur . . . that we then have to smooth out. We don't have the 100 years of brewing experience that other places do. We've learned a lot, and continue to learn. Not too long ago, we were having problems with the labeling process that we had never seen before. It was ultimately the service repairman who explained what was going wrong – now we know the weak spots of our individual pieces of equipment . . . having equipment also teaches you that you need to operate it for a year before you really know its ins and outs. Throw into the mix other factors like the different kinds of yeast and raw materials, not to mention the new employees . . . and it's no wonder that mistakes can occur.

The new brewery enjoyed national success at the start, which then budded into international recognition after that. After receiving the "Swiss Beer of the Year 2009" as well as the "Newcomer of the Year" award from an association of the Swiss breweries, the company's Hell's beer then won the prestigious gold medal at the *Deutschen Landwirtschaftsgesellschaft* (DLG) annual beer-tasting competition. This is the highest honor a company can receive for top quality. Conducting international tests in all areas of the food industry, the DLG is a European leader in quality assessment, and certified in accordance with international standards. A total of 712 different beers from breweries around the world were tasted at this contest. Purity in taste, bitter qualities, full flavor, and freshness were the main criteria according to which the beers were judged. The beer also needed to maintain its flavor during and after storage. Along with the blind taste test, rigorous lab analyses tested the beer's foam quality, extract and alcohol content, original wort qualities, color, and shelf-life. Güntensperger was thrilled:

> This award makes clear that we're on the right path. Our efforts and investments in additional facilities and processes last year are starting to bear fruit. Along with our popular Weizenbier, the Swiss Beer of the Year 2009, our Hell's has also found its place among Europe's best. We're going to do everything we can in the future to continue brewing fresh beer from Liechtenstein at an absolute top quality.
>
> (www.vaterland.li/index.cfm?ressort=liechtenstein
> &source=lv&id=6988)

Target groups and pricing

The regional market is the main focus of the Liechtenstein Brewing Co. The Liechtenstein beer market is estimated as having an annual consumption of 20,000–21,000 hectoliters. This market share is, however, difficult to estimate, with Güntensperger himself admitting that he doesn't know the exact market size.

The Liechtenstein Brewing Co.'s different beers are sold at beverage and retail stores, as well as a number of restaurants, bars, and catering companies. Its prices are slightly above those of the competition (see Table 9.2).

With every new product introduction, the market is first skimmed with high prices. After a few weeks, the prices are then reduced to being (still) comparably slightly above competitors' pricing. The retailers and partners are granted specific pricing arrangements, depending on the quantity of the beer purchased weekly and the duration of the contract.

Increasing costs of raw material have put pressure on to big breweries; small breweries like Liechtenstein Brewing Co. have been noticing this for several years. However, the company has confirmed that its beer prices would not change in the future.

The founder, values, and brand

The company founder Bruno Güntensperger holds a Ph.D. in food science from the ETH Zürich. Before his decision to start his own company, he worked for HILCONA, a Liechtenstein-based company offering convenience food products. Güntensperger started his career in the product development area, where he led about 25 people. From there he moved into the marketing area where he developed new business areas such as "food on the go." Subsequently, Güntensperger moved

TABLE 9.2 Pricing of Liechtenstein Brewing Co.'s beers

10-bottle case:	
33 cl Hell's	CHF 14.00/deposit CHF 10.00
50 cl Hell's	CHF 17.00/deposit CHF 10.00
33 cl Dunkel's	CHF 16.00/deposit CHF 10.00
50 cl Weiza	CHF 21.00/deposit CHF 10.00
33 cl seasonal beer	Price and availability on request
20-bottle case:	
33 cl Hell's	CHF 28.00/deposit CHF 15.00
50 cl Hell's	CHF 34.00/deposit CHF 15.00
33 cl Dunkel's	CHF 32.00/deposit CHF 15.00
50 cl Weiza	CHF 42.00/deposit CHF 15.00
33 cl seasonal beer	Price and availability on request
10-liter CoolKeg (self-cooling):	
Hell's	CHF 59.00/deposit CHF 150.00
20-liter keg:	
Hell's	CHF 76.00/deposit CHF 50.00
10-liter party keg:	
Hell's	CHF 48.00/deposit CHF 100.00
2-liter big bottle:	
Kellerstoff	CHF 39.00
Refill	CHF 13.00
Auxilia Schaan design wooden case	CHF 59.00

Source: www.liechtensteinerbrauhaus.li.

into sales and finally was responsible for two major key accounts. In total, his time with HILCONA gave him more than 12 years of leadership experience. Güntensperger has his own leadership philosophy:

> First, I do not expect more from my employees than what I myself can live up to. Second, the worst thing that you can do to your employees is to never give them any feedback. I have always been trying to give both, positive and negative comments. Third, a leader is only as excellent as his or her employees. I am convinced that leaders need to empower their followers in such a way that they are able to take over your job.

For the marketing task of his own company, Güntensperger engaged the services of the largest local advertising agency, Leone Ming Est. to develop a marketing concept for the introduction of his beer. This was a unique step, as this agency works almost exclusively with entrepreneurial marketing tools such as viral marketing, buzz marketing, and social networks.

The marketing campaign for the future national beverage of Liechtenstein began with "story telling" at regulars' tables at the "in" pubs, bars, and restaurants, where rumors about a new beer had been spread. Smartly applying viral marketing, a certain amount of curiosity was created among the local population, which began to grow. PR at the same time was used as an instrument in a two- or three-week rhythm to permanently establish the idea of a new beer in the country. The day before the official launch, the beer was delivered to a number of events within Liechtenstein without disclosing the brand name. In addition, a countrywide billboard teaser campaign aroused even more curiosity (see Figure 9.5), and revealed the new brand name for the first time on the day of the official product launch.

It is essential that the founder stands for his brand name and values. This is most important when taking care of the customers, who for Güntensperger would become even more significant in the future. There needs to be a congruency between what is important to the founder and what the company communicates to the public. In Güntensperger's opinion:

> It's hard for a lot of people when, for example, a company that's conservatively run starts to sell a trendy product, and then itself has to be trendy all of a sudden. It's kind of a hard juggling act, and that's where most of the employees have their difficulties.

Güntensperger's wife, who works in the company's administration and is a member of the board of directors, also helps him organize his thoughts and decision-making.

The Liechtenstein Brewing Co.'s beer needs to be a specialty, something that has its place in the local culture, and a beer that people enjoy. Real, honest, fresh, authentic are the values it needs to convey. Bruno Güntensperger describes what "authentic" communicates: "Authentic means that the beer is truly from the region. But this doesn't mean it's a down-home brand. After all, we're trying to strike a balance between traditional and modern." An overall goal of the company, as Güntensperger explains, is to create a "glass brewery":

> We want to work in a way that lets everyone have a look behind the scenes. In a market where the international brands dominate, and only a few local products are in business, it's very important for our success that our customers trust our products and company. So if we can connect the regional and modern aspects with a high level of quality, that's how we're going to set ourselves apart. If we don't get this right, we're in trouble. Without this, we're not going to be able to grow and develop or become a stronger brand.

The (German) company name was clear right from the start – the *Liechtensteiner Brauhaus*. With this name, Güntensperger was deliberately selecting a "simple" brand name that could be remembered easily. The connection to the country of Liechtenstein and brewing an own, independent quality beer are the company's focus. "Brauhaus" makes a direct reference to the craft of beer brewing as it conveys notions of "small, accessible, and authentic."

But what about everything else, including how the communication should be done? This was where Güntensperger had to stop and think for a while, at which point he asked an external consulting agency for assistance. The questions that needed to be answered were in the areas of market entry, visual design, and communication.

Communication and PR

The company's communication strategy is based on the simple slogan *Ein Land. Ein Bier.* ("One country. One beer.") This embodies the intention that is behind the company and product idea, and makes the slogan the company's pathway at the same time: unique, authentic beer from Liechtenstein, for Liechtenstein and the region.

Viral communication

Speaking with local regulars in bars, and with patrons of the "in" pubs and restaurants helped get the word out about the new beer. It wasn't long before there were enough people who knew at least something about it: its name, the shape of the bottle, the label colors, etc. Güntensperger remembers:

> The brewmaster back then was in a bar somewhere across the border in Germany near Lake Constance. He overheard somebody saying that the Crown Prince himself was opening his own new brewery. This example shows that people were talking about us, with plenty of things that were true, and plenty of things that were not so true. And that was the whole idea behind this, simply trying to spread information around. We didn't spread false information. But the more information that got around, the more people were talking about it. Things really did start to spread like a virus.

This led to a dynamic and exciting perception in the population that kept turning the spiral of expectations farther upward. The external agency and Güntensperger were confident that a lot of viral action also required classical marketing support to achieve a long-lasting effect. One sensational piece of information can soon be yesterday's news. Only when a viral idea is accompanied by the right instruments can a sustained, concerted action emerge. Güntensperger explained:

> Our topic was interesting and exciting for the newspapers – just about anyone can find something to say about beer. After all, it's part of the culture. So we found ourselves being warmly welcomed as the new brewery. Liechtenstein is so small, that when there's an article in the local paper, it's automatically known about throughout the region.

FIGURE 9.5 Teaser campaign

The excitement that was noticeable among the population was maintained by well-placed PR. Reported on every two or three weeks, the brewery's beer was continually maintained as a topic of discussion. There were articles on every milestone such as the delivery and installation of the brewery equipment. Six weeks before market entry, a teaser billboard campaign presented the corporate design to the market (see Figure 9.5).

Every two weeks an article was featured speculating when the first batch of beer would finally be brewed. A countdown was started on the homepage showing the days left until the launch. One day before market entry, the new beer made an appearance at a few official local events. Word about this exclusive promotion made the rounds throughout the country hours before the official start.

Güntensperger knew how hard it is to be and stay on everyone's mind:

> We didn't really do that much in 2009. We were too busy with working on the quality problems in our processes. In 2010, we made inroads into reaching people with our communication strategies. We did a lot of advertising during that summer for our *iisi* beer, and later on did a DUMB campaign. Here we posed the question 'Does beer make you dumb?' Everyone had a chance to participate and send in an answer, and once again, we had people talking about our product. This was a help in increasing our recognizability.

Social media

The Liechtenstein Brewing Co. runs a Facebook page that currently has 1,958 fans (as of November 2012 – see Figure 9.6).

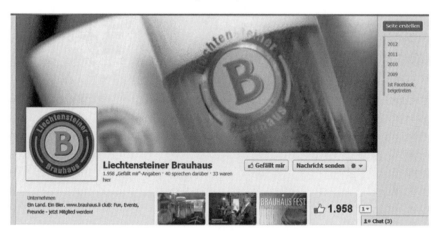

FIGURE 9.6 The use of social media – Liechtenstein Brewing Co.

Güntensperger makes clear that being on Facebook provides the company and brand with an up-to-date, modern image. Being on Facebook addresses and reaches the target group between the ages of 16 and 50. It's a medium that allows the specific spread of information at a cheap price. Güntensperger recalls how "At our founding in 2006, nobody really knew Facebook . . . it only became a topic starting in 2008 . . . we started a group, and people kept showing me how many friends we were getting, which made clear to me to stay with it . . . ." When asked whether he personally looks after the page, Güntensperger honestly admits that he himself is not an active Facebook member. Instead, an employee takes care of the postings on the site and participates in its discussions. Güntensperger still is a bit skeptical about the loyalty and willingness to buy on the part of the users: "Facebook is great for increasing awareness and recognition of the product, but in spite of this, I can't really tell whether our Facebook friends are actually 'better' than those of our competition."

Where the beer is brewed

The brewery itself was officially dedicated with an open house that welcomed thousands of visitors. Keeping in line with the idea of a glass brewery for the customers and company stakeholders, visitors to the Liechtenstein Brewing Co. are shown how their beer specialties are brewed, and learn some fun, interesting facts about the products. In the "ProBiar Stoba"[9] visitors have the chance to taste the beer fresh from the tap. There's also a full selection of fan items on sale such as T-shirts, glasses with the brewery logo, bottle openers, etc.

FIGURE 9.7 The brewing copper

The company today and where it is heading: the expansion strategies of a new name brand

The Liechtenstein Brewing Co. has grown by 15 percent since its founding in 2007. Güntensperger explained:

> It will probably "only" be 8 percent in 2010, because we didn't have that good a summer. All of the big festivals like the *Fürstenfest* were literally washed out by the bad weather. For a better picture of things, you actually have to look at how the other breweries in the region are growing . . . only then can you tell whether you're successful. Unfortunately, it's only our competition themselves who know these figures.

He can no doubt be happy with how his company has developed so far, which currently has five full-time employees and three part-time workers on its payroll.

Expanding the product assortment

January, 2011 saw the introduction of the "4 plus 1" product concept:

> We noticed that our existing product portfolio was not reaching a specific market segment. We reacted by introducing a new lager. It's positioned at a lower price. Hell's is going to be our premium brand, while the lager aims more at the "9 to 5," blue-collar market segment.

What is interesting in this instance is how demand for this beer was determined. Güntensperger describes it as follows:

> The recipe for this lager is a result of the market research we did. We first asked customers why they drink beer, why they don't drink beer, and what they would like to see added to our assortment. We then made a test brew that we tasted together with around 30 people in two sessions. Question forms were filled out which we then evaluated. After that, we took a new look at our existing product portfolio and compared it to what the competition has.

The feedback and suggestions for improvement from 1,500 different responses were analyzed and evaluated. The lager beer was developed according to the Liechtensteiner "Gusto" method of brewing, which strengthens the company's brand value of "brewed in the tradition of Liechtenstein beer-making."

Very recently, the product portfolio was extended with Schnapps, called the *Liechtensteiner Bierbrand*. Highly particular about this new product is that it is burned based on a specific mixture of 100 percent Liechtensteiner Brewery Beers. This is done by a local distillery that chose a traditional distillery technique with wood. This makes the Schnapps particularly mild and intensive in aroma. The Schnapps is free of any chemical additives.

FIGURE 9.8 The Schnapps

Export

Efforts are currently underway to internationalize the company and brand. Güntensperger explained:

We've got feelers out in Asia right now. Higher-end specialties have the potential to work well on the export market. When it comes to this, you have a bonus as somebody from Liechtenstein or the nearby parts of Switzerland. We have the advantage of being small. Our product comes across as a high-quality gem that's delivered directly from a monarchy in the heart of Europe. On the other hand, this would bring no real advantage if our goal was to export our beer to Germany, Austria, or other parts of Europe.

The international target group is mainly those originally from the region who are now living in Asia, and who "like to do nice things for themselves every once in a while; who know a thing or two about specialties like our beer; and of course who have the disposable income to pay for it." Güntensperger here specifically has in mind expatriates and restaurant owners, knowing all the while that successful export will in any case strongly depend on finding the right sales partners.

In spite of the success that Güntensperger has enjoyed so far, he and his beer face a few unanswered questions.

Case study questions

1   In a geographically small market like Liechtenstein, the boundaries of natural growth are quickly reached. What growth opportunities are available to the Liechtenstein Brewing Co. beyond the national borders? Develop a brand-based internationalization strategy. What target markets would you prefer to supply, and what brand(s) would you sell there? What things about the local culture would you have to keep in mind while doing this?

2   With the assistance of the marketing agency Leone Ming Est., the Liechtenstein Brewing Co. was able to apply a number of entrepreneurial marketing elements, particularly when it came to introducing the product (viral marketing, buzz marketing, social media marketing). In your opinion, is this approach to marketing more effective for startups than the "classic" (4Ps) forms of marketing and advertising? What advantages and disadvantages can entrepreneurial marketing bring with it? Do you think it makes sense to switch back to classical marketing once a certain company size has been achieved? If so, why? Where does an "authentic" brand fit in with the overall approaches of marketing?

3   Experience shows that beer-makers bind restaurants and bars to their product with long-term exclusive contracts, which include the provision of all kinds of promotional material (e.g. advertising banners, signs, beer taps, coasters, sunshades) with the logo of the respective beer on them. This is very expensive to do, and financially even downright impossible in some cases for small breweries. What are some things the Liechtenstein

Brewing Co. could do to go up against the "heavyweight" Swiss beer brands in the theoretical case where they would attempt to drive Bruno Güntensperger's small operation out of the Liechtenstein market (e.g. with so-called "killer prices")? Develop a defensive strategy for this kind of possible future scenario.

Notes

1   "The little beer house" in the local Liechtenstein/Swiss dialect.
2   An *Apéro* is a kind of cocktail party in Switzerland where cakes and drinks are served.
3   Available at: www.bier.ch/deu/kennzahlen-biermarkt-entwicklung-ch.html.
4   Available at: www.vaterland.li/index.cfm?id=56323&source=sda&ressort=home.
5   Available at: www.bier.ch/deu/kennzahlen-wussten-sie.php.
6   Available at: www.vaterland.li/index.cfm?ressort=home&source=sda&id=57010.
7   *Helles* is a lager beer; "Hell's" is how it is spoken in the Liechtenstein dialect.
8   *Weizenbier* is a wheat beer, or Weiss beer; "Weiza" is how it is spoken in the Liechtenstein dialect.
9   This is a wordplay using the Liechtenstein dialect. "ProBiar Stoba" is Liechtenstein dialect for the High German "Probierstube," which means "tasting" (*probieren*) and "room" (*Stube*). Notice the double play on words with *Probierstube* that manages to slip the word "beer" into the name.

10

EAT & ENJOY –
THE NETHERLANDS

Maryse Brand and Evelien Croonen

Franchising as an entrepreneurial growth strategy

In 1998, Marc Peterson,[1] a Dutch interim manager and consultant, was travelling through Germany on an assignment for one of his German customers. Marc was a sociable person with a lot of international retail experience, and had just turned 50. One of the meetings that he had during this trip would cause a major shift in his career.

Marc met Gunter Brand, a supplier of bottles of oil and vinegar. Gunter complained that Dutch consumers bought his products for ornamental purposes only. At this time, olive oil and fine vinegar were virtually unknown in the Dutch cuisine. This was in sharp contrast with Mediterranean countries, where olive oil and vinegar were traditionally being used for many cooking purposes. Marc thought that if potential customers could actually taste the oils and vinegars before they would buy, they would probably start actually using the products for cooking purposes and, most importantly, come back for a refill. As there was no such business concept in the Netherlands, Marc smelled an entrepreneurial opportunity and approached Susan Van der Bilt. Susan was also a very experienced marketing professional, with extensive knowledge of culinary business. In September 1999, Marc and Susan opened their first store in Breda, in the south of the Netherlands. Two weeks later they opened a second one about 100 kilometres further in Amstelveen, in the western part of the Netherlands. Their business concept 'Eat & Enjoy' (E&E) offered a wide range of international food and cooking products. The products were presented in a Mediterranean style and could all be tasted before buying.

Although Marc and Susan liked to have direct contact with customers in their stores, they both agreed that their goal would be to develop a successful retail chain with a focus on the Netherlands. Since they did not have enough money to finance such an entrepreneurial venture, it was also clear that the growth would mainly take place through franchising. Marc and Susan developed a business model that would be sustainable and profitable for all involved. The franchise would be a very centralized franchise system, in which franchisees would have a low level of decision rights. The franchisees were required to invest in their physical unit (about €130.000^2), pay an entrance fee (between €13.000 and €25.000), and pay sales-based periodical fees (9 per cent of turnover). As residual claimants, these franchisees would be motivated to use their managerial, entrepreneurial and local knowledge in order to make their stores successful.

The E&E concept became so popular that it won the most prestigious retail prize in the Netherlands. Furthermore, it became the best innovative retail chain in the Benelux (Belgium, the Netherlands and Luxembourg) in 2001. Two years later, E&E was elected Dutch franchise chain of the year and Marc was chosen as best Dutch franchise manager. In 2006, 7 years after startup, E&E already had nearly 40 stores in the Netherlands and around 50 stores in a dozen different countries, almost all of which were franchised stores. Newspaper clippings of that period showed that E&E's management was still announcing further growth. However, the success story of E&E started to show serious cracks when in May 2006 a group of unsatisfied franchisees organised themselves and started legal actions towards E&E for reproachable bad management. The success even came to a complete halt in the summer of 2007 when the E&E franchisor was declared bankrupt.

What caused the fast international growth of E&E? Why did the E&E concept fail in the end and even go bankrupt? What entrepreneurial mistakes did Marc and Susan make?

How Marc and Susan achieved Eat & Enjoy's local success

Marc had just passed the age of 50 when he had the idea for the E&E concept in the late 1990s. He had 25 years of international management experience in South Africa. After his return to the Netherlands in 1989, Marc worked as an interim manager and consultant in the Dutch retail industry. He also started his own wholesale business in kitchen textiles. As the owner of this company, he met the above-mentioned manufacturer of bottles of olive oil and vinegar to whom he suggested that potential customers should be able to taste the products. Triggered by this idea, Marc contacted Susan Van der Bilt, who he had met when she was a general manager at a large wholesale business for kitchen appliances. Susan was a few years younger than Marc and had 20 years of entrepreneurial experience leading her own public relations company. Her parents used to own a hotel, which is where she became passionate about good food and drink. Susan was very interested in Marc's ideas.

Marc and Susan seemed to complement each other very well as a startup team. People often characterized Marc as a passionate and charismatic salesman with a clear vision. Susan had a feeling for trends in fashion, high-cuisine and lifestyle.

She also had an eye for detail, was reliable and precise. People characterized Susan as a woman who was able to pick up trends, translate them into exciting products and to find the right suppliers to deliver the products.

In the autumn of 1999, Marc and Susan launched their first E&E stores in the Netherlands, which they ran themselves. When these stores turned out to be a big hit, Marc and Susan soon decided to grow Eat & Enjoy into a national chain with perhaps some stores in adjacent regions of Germany and Belgium. They aimed for all the stores to be within a one-day travel distance; this would make it easy to monitor and supply them. Marc and Susan also started dividing their tasks; Marc became responsible for concept development, financial issues, public relations and marketing. Susan devoted her time to product development, purchasing and logistics, visual merchandising and human resources management. In the first years after startup, both Marc and Susan kept working in their own stores for a few days a week. Because of their age, Marc and Susan also discussed possible exit strategies. Both Marc and Susan intended to build the new company and sell their shares in about six to eight years. They also promised each other that they would always work as a team, because that was what made their success.

Marc and Susan further developed the E&E concept and positioned it as a 'culinary gift shop', selling more than 25 varieties of olive oil, numerous kinds of vinegar, dressings, olives, dried tomatoes and herbs. Consumers could sample and taste the products, have their own oil and vinegar bottles (re)filled, get expert advice and have gifts wrapped in a very nice way. Besides food products, one-third of the stores' assortment consisted of related non-food products, such as ceramics and cookery books. Marc and Susan argued that the 'experience' they created for consumers made them want to buy the relatively expensive products (e.g. one litre of olive oil was priced between €12 and €15).

Just one year after opening their first E&E store, the first franchisee started its operations. By the end of 2001, there were 15 E&E stores located in the Netherlands. An external agency was hired to analyse potential retailing locations (e.g. in terms of customer traffic and competition) on which sales forecasts could be based. A series of low-budget market studies (often performed by university students) demonstrated that the concept attracted customers of all ages, ranging from students to families and the elderly. People bought the luxurious products as gifts, as a special treat for themselves or for use in the preparation of that special dinner party with close friends. Marc and Susan initially took up the joint responsibility to find the right franchisees. They put some advertisements in trade magazines and visited tradeshows, but a large part of the franchisees almost literally knocked at their door spontaneously after visiting one of the brand new stores. Winning the retail prize in 2001 really boosted the expansion of E&E. Marc and Susan took care that the quality of the franchisees was high; franchisees were selected on the basis of their enthusiasm and love for the concept. Naturally, prospective franchisees also needed to possess money to invest in the concept. This entailed about €20,000 each (and an additional €130,000 in bank loans or other sources). Many of these franchisees had rather unrelated backgrounds. For example, some people had been laid off in the banking or consultancy sector, whereas others were hobby cooks or ICT experts who had decided to make a career change.

Growing in units also meant growing in staff at the head office. Marc and Susan hired a team of rather young, enthusiastic and inexperienced people to support the franchise organization. At various commercial events, business partners thought that Marc and Susan had taken their children with them, while actually these people were the headquarters' staff! As a result of the retail prize, Marc and Susan were invited for international retail shows and events. Soon, the first parties showed their interest in bringing the E&E concept to international markets. As a result, E&E had its first international outlets before the summer of 2002.

Setting up a new chain and expanding it rapidly required some considerable financial resources. Although Marc and Susan had some savings of their own, external investors were needed from the start. Unfortunately, Marc and Susan did not succeed in obtaining any substantial amount of money from the bank. The banks had difficulties positioning the new E&E concept in a specific retail sector because there was no distinct sector fitting with their concept. The banks regarded the concept as just a new supermarket formula, and supermarkets were not considered attractive investment opportunities at that time. Marc and Susan bridged the first period by paying their main supplier in shares instead of cash. Additionally, in 2001 – after E&E won the big retail prize – a number of professional investors were eager to get on board this successful ship. Two investors provided part of the needed capital and also Johnson Logistics, E&E's main logistics partner, stepped in by agreeing to finance and manage all the logistics, including stock keeping.

In 2002, Marc and Susan hired William Jones, an accountant by profession and an acquaintance of Marc's wife. William developed a new 5-year business plan to lead the firm to grow from 15 Dutch stores to about 230–250 units in north-western Europe. William himself proved to be an active financial manager. The legal entity of E&E was split up in a whole set of limited companies and new investors were found who could enable E&E's growth plans. However, the introduction of powerful external investors who had clear financial objectives did not work out well. Marc and Susan felt that more and more people were beginning to interfere with them managing the company. Within about a year (mid-2003), the external investors were largely bought out and William's own investment company entered as one of the new shareholders. While William became responsible for financial management issues, Susan remained involved with the bookkeeping process, personally checking all payments. Eat & Enjoy seemed to be ready now for further development.

Eat & Enjoy in the Netherlands

'Culinary gift shops' and related sectors in the Netherlands

When Marc and Susan started their 'culinary gift shop' concept in the late 1990s, the concept was so new that it was difficult to define the retailing sector in which they were operating. Since Marc and Susan considered being trendy and fashionable as a core aspect of their concept, they intensively looked at the fashion industry and high-end restaurants to obtain ideas and inspiration for the E&E concept. In the early years of the E&E concept, Marc and Susan felt that there were no competitors. For this reason, they had difficulty positioning their concept in a specific retailing sector in a clear way. Besides the problems with banks (who did not really understand their entrepreneurial venture), this resulted in difficulties with analysing market developments and (potential) competition. For example, E&E was not like other specialty food stores, such as delicacy stores and stores selling foreign food products. These latter stores were mainly traditional stores selling, for example, Chinese or Turkish food products. These stores were mostly targeted at immigrants and not at the luxurious, trendy, fun-shopping segment of consumers that E&E was targeting. Additionally, E&E was not like other luxurious gift stores that offered high-priced products that people buy to spoil themselves or others (e.g. stores selling gifts such as cooking products, cosmetics and perfumes, or home decorations) because all these others did not sell *food* products. Marc therefore often referred to E&E as 'The Body Shop, but then for the body's inside'.

Marc and Susan tried to monitor developments in retailing in general, in specialty food stores and in luxurious gift shops. It was difficult to obtain market data for the gift shops since Dutch research agencies (e.g. Statistics Netherlands and the Dutch Association for Retailing) did not consider these as a specific group. Table 10.1 presents data on developments in the Dutch retailing sector in general and on specialty food stores.

TABLE 10.1 Figures on the Dutch retailing sector in general and specialty food stores (1998–2007)

Year	Growth							
	GDP*	Number of retail companies**	Retailing in general*			Specialty food stores*		
			Value	Price level	Volume	Value	Price level	Volume
	%		%	%	%	%	%	%
1998	3.9	87.284	6.8	1.9	4.7	3.2	2.5	0.6
1999	4.7	85.674	4.6	1.4	3.1	1.8	1.5	0.3
2000	3.9	85.550	4.6	0.9	3.7	2.4	0.9	1.5
2001	1.9	80.691	5.9	3.1	2.7	3.5	7.7	−3.9
2002	0.1	79.123	2.7	1.6	1.1	0.0	3.6	−3.5
2003	0.3	78.933	−1.7	−0.7	−1.0	−4.2	2.1	−6.2
2004	2.2	82.325	−1.5	−1.6	0.1	−4.9	−0.9	−4.1
2005	2.0	82.702	0.7	−0.8	1.5	−1.0	0.4	−1.3
2006	3.4	78.797	5.4	1.0	4.3	2.1	1.8	0.3
2007	3.9	79.522	3.9	0.9	3.0	0.3	1.1	−0.9

Sources: * CBS statline ** www.ondernemerschap.nl (database financed by the Dutch Ministry of Economic Affairs).

As Table 10.1 demonstrates, the years 2003 and 2004 were bad years for retailing in general, and especially for specialty food stores. However, the E&E chain still opened new units in the Netherlands. Additionally, the turnover levels of extant E&E stores did not really seem to suffer from the economic downturn. Marc and Susan's explanation for this phenomenon was that people were spending more time at home than in restaurants and bars. Second, Marc and Susan thought that people wanted to use their creativity to create a cosy atmosphere at home. Another explanation was that the E&E products made customers relive their holidays in Mediterranean countries. In the meantime, supermarkets and department stores had started to sell Mediterranean products as well, only at a lower price and quality level. This clearly demonstrates the need for E&E to add value and to remain innovative in order to justify E&E's relatively high price level.

Even though the E&E concept was very popular in the Netherlands, in such a small country there are only a limited number of locations suitable for a luxurious retail concept. Marc and Susan estimated that in the Netherlands, there would be room for a maximum of 40 E&E stores. Therefore, if they really wanted to grow, they needed to adjust their initial strategic plan – which focused mainly on the Dutch market – and enter international markets.

Franchising in the Netherlands

In the decades after the Second World War, franchising became an increasingly popular business strategy in several Dutch industries, such as food and non-food retailing, services and hospitality (see Table 10.2). In the early 1970s, this development resulted in the foundation of the Dutch Franchising Association ('Nederlandse Franchise Vereniging', or NFV), which still exists today. This voluntary self-regulatory body represents the interests of Dutch franchisors in various sectors. The NFV's main objective is to stimulate a healthy and professional development of the Dutch franchising sector. The NFV organizes seminars and manages the quality of franchisors and their franchise systems. On top of this, the NFV mediates in case of conflict between franchisors and franchisees. Franchisors can become a member of the NFV and gain access to NFV's benefits when their franchise system meets certain criteria. Additionally, franchisors need to agree with the European Code of Ethics for Franchising. This code is a self-regulatory set of ethical standards that was developed by the European Franchise Federation (EFF) in 1972. All member associations of the EFF (including the Dutch NFV) commit themselves – and in turn their respective franchisor members – to respect and promote the principles written down in this code. The code aims to prevent behaviours that are detrimental to the image of franchising. For example, it contains clauses on the rights and obligations for both the franchisor and the franchisee, and the minimum terms that should be included in franchise contracts.

As opposed to other countries such as the US, the Netherlands has never had specific franchising regulations. Instead, several types of Dutch company law may apply, such as intellectual property or contractual law. Finally, for franchises in

TABLE 10.2 The development of franchising in the Netherlands

	1981	1990	1998	2002	2005
Franchised systems (i.e. members of the NFV)	147	302	358	434	498
Franchised units	3,500	10,200	14,100	18,000	21,400

Source: NFV.

European Union member states the EU Antitrust Law applies – for example, regarding exclusive territories and pricing agreements.

The internationalization process of Eat & Enjoy

Although Marc and Susan had been quite ambitious with their enterprise right from the start, internationalization was not part of their initial strategic plan. However, early in 2002 they received so many positive signals about the E&E concept and opportunities to expand internationally that internationalization became one of E&E's major strategic goals. An experienced Belgian entrepreneur became E&E's first international master franchisee (i.e. a franchisee who had the right to subfranchise the E&E concept to other franchisees in a certain territory). This Belgian entrepreneur planned to open a first store in Mechelen and to take business further from there. After Marc and Susan, as winners of the Dutch Retail Award, had been invited to an international retail fair in Cannes, things started to move very quickly.

The business plan that E&E developed in spring 2002 demonstrated the shift to an active internationalization strategy. Table 10.3 shows the sales projections included in that plan. The plan indicated that in 2003 E&E would start to make a real profit and that profits would grow rapidly after that. To realize this strategy, additional investments were needed, and a major part of these would have to be made by master franchises in the targeted countries.

A group of investors from the United Kingdom were highly interested in the concept. Hence, they proposed to buy one or more master franchises in the UK. Naturally, Marc and Susan were very excited about these positive reactions, and

TABLE 10.3 Projected turnover in 000s euros

	2001 (actual)	2002	2003	2004	2005
Turnover Netherlands	961	956	1,494	1,963	2,192
Turnover abroad	0	283	760	2,347	5,036
Turnover total	961	1,239	2,254	4,310	7,228

Source: Business Plan, E&E, spring 2002.

it did not take long before the contract was signed. The idea was developed that larger countries such as the UK would be divided in several same-sized master franchises. This would limit the individual power of each master. E&E also decided to buy shares in every master franchise arguing that this would let E&E share in expected future profits. Besides the fact that this would require considerable investments by the E&E franchisor, this decision also influenced the relationship between the masters and E&E. On one hand, E&E showed that they were positively committed to the master franchisees. On the other hand, this arrangement also gave E&E more power because it offered the company the legal opportunity to interfere with the masters' business directly.

The British market seemed really attractive. In 2001/2002, the British economy showed consistent growth and consumer confidence was high. After the opening of the first store in Glasgow, the number of stores in the UK grew fast and soon there were three master franchises covering most of the country. In these prosperous economic circumstances real-estate prices had been growing steadily. This provided opportunities because many prospective franchisees were able to come up with the needed investment by taking an extra mortgage on their private homes. Unfortunately, high real-estate prices also means high rentals. For this reason, it was really difficult to develop a profitable model for some of the E&E locations. Nevertheless, British franchisees, customers and press remained charmed by the new exciting E&E concept that perfectly fitted the trend towards Mediterranean foods, resulting in a further growth of E&E in the UK. One of the first stores to open in the UK saw more than 30 people visiting the store during the first few weeks, who showed interest to become a franchisee themselves. As the year 2003 began, E&E consisted of 29 units, entered the Belgian and the UK market, and was ready to open another 4 UK stores (also see Table 10.4). When in April 2003 the small firm loan guarantee scheme was extended to the retail sector, opportunities for growth in the UK seemed even greater.

In the meantime, Marc was in his element travelling around, meeting new people and convincing some of them to join the E&E adventure. In accordance with his strong sales personality, Marc ran into interesting opportunities everywhere he went. As a result, in 2003 new master franchises were opened in Germany, Sweden, Ireland and Portugal. By the end of 2003, E&E consisted of about 42 units in 7 different countries and plans were announced to open 10 more Dutch and 20 more UK stores. Indeed, by the end of 2004 a total of about 71 stores was reached, including a first store in the US. That same year, E&E again won two important awards: the Franchise of the Year (in the Netherlands) and America's best new shop formula. In January 2005, E&E announced that a US consortium of private investors would pay €30 million for the right to open 124 E&E stores in the US in the next 3 years. Marc openly talked about a possible Initial Public Offering (IPO). Even more countries were added to the E&E chain. At the end of 2005, E&E consisted of about 85 stores in 12 countries: the Netherlands, Belgium, Germany, France, Sweden, Denmark, Norway, the UK, Ireland, Portugal, Spain and the US. Still, Marc was talking with new potential master franchisees from South Africa and

Australia. In 2006, a prestigious contract was signed to open an E&E store in a luxurious shopping centre in Dubai. The opening of this store took place in February 2007.

Eat & Enjoy turns sour

E&E's development: 2002–2005

As shown before, the first few years of E&E were an overwhelming success. However, in 2002, the first growing pains surfaced in the distribution network and within the management team. By 2002, some of the E&E suppliers could not deliver the quality and quantity of products that E&E needed. As a result, Susan had to take great efforts to find new reliable suppliers. On top of this, several of the E&E stores were not as successful as expected. For example, a number of Dutch stores had to be closed down, sold or had disappointing results. Additionally, when looking back, this was also the period in which Marc and Susan started to grow apart.

Marc was not worried about the little setbacks and openly celebrated E&E's success. He continued developing new plans, which required huge invest-ments, such as the set-up of a new headquarters (Marc referred to this as the 'Eat & Enjoy Academy'). Furthermore, E&E changed its logo three times within three years, thereby burdening the franchisees with large costs. Marc also started expensive projects without proper consultation with his peers. For example, he really liked the idea of producing a luxurious E&E magazine and spent money to put this idea into practice. However, there was no market research or other objec-tive information justifying such expenditure. There were also a number of anecdotes about Marc meeting people at shows, aeroplanes and other places to find new business partners who possessed considerable financial resources. Nevertheless, most of these contacts led to nothing, leaving Marc disappointed and blaming others. From time to time, he became entangled in fierce arguments and Susan became the one to calm everybody down and to patch things up. Susan started to feel rather uncomfortable as she felt that different stakeholders became the victim of unprofessional management. Payments to suppliers were overdue, potential franchisees were put under too much pressure, current franchisees were neglected, etc.

In 2003–2004, serious problems developed. At first these problems were not visible to the outside world, but later they became apparent as more and more stores closed down and legal disputes were published in newspapers. A first important development was that the board of directors had grown to four people (including Marc and Susan) and important strategic decisions were made by this group. The majority of the board now consisted of largely growth- and profit-oriented people. In the summer of 2003, the board agreed to Marc's plans to expand further into the US and Japan. This decision was not unanimous, but Susan no longer had a deciding vote. More and more, Marc became the one to represent

E&E in the media, usually announcing new growth plans. Susan moved to the background, trying to keep operations going.

When entering the US market, E&E encountered serious problems. Because of Food and Drug Administration (FDA) regulations, containers were delayed at the border. FDA approval for specific products required adapted labelling or even an extensive approval procedure, including laboratory tests. Besides, transportation was organized by E&E's Dutch logistical partner who was not able to realize promised delivery times. The main warehouse was set up in New York, while the first store was located in Montana, 3,000 km away. Obviously, being a transportation expert in a small country such as the Netherlands is very different from being one in the US.

In 2003, the penetration of the UK market was really taking off and master franchises in a handful of other European countries were sold. In the meantime, the dream team consisting of Marc and Susan started to fall apart. As the UK stores continued to have problems becoming profitable and Marc's selling strategy became more and more aggressive, Susan felt she was losing control. She thought Marc was running away from the operational problems to ever new opportunities. Franchisees also began experiencing major issues. Although E&E's size and purchasing power were growing, the purchasing prices franchisees had to pay for their products were not declining. Additionally, suppliers were not able to meet the fast growth and out of stocks occurred regularly. Some franchisees got stuck at too expensive locations; E&E did not have enough money to finance all this growth, while innovation and constant renewal of the E&E concept were crucial. Since every new master franchise meant buying shares, every new country posed an extra burden on the financial resources of the E&E franchisor. The first problems hit the Dutch newspapers in 2004 when a dispute about the closing of an unsuccessful location became public knowledge. This particular store was located in a small town in a rural area in the northern part of the Netherlands, which was not exactly the type of location Marc and Susan had had in mind earlier.

At the same time, the economic situation in Western Europe became less bright. Around 2003, consumer confidence started to decline in most European countries, a trend that continued for several years. More specifically, E&E's troubles in the UK continued and became even worse. By mid-2004, two of the three UK master franchises discontinued their contract, resulting in E&E buying back its own shares. The same happened in Germany, the Netherlands and the US. In the press, these transactions were presented as a strategic move in preparing the E&E company for sale.

Also in this period, a new company headquarters equipped with modern training facilities for all new staff was built in the Netherlands. Adjacent to this head office, E&E's logistics partner Johnson Logistics built a brand new warehouse and acquired a number of shares in E&E and thus became an even more important strategic partner.

In November 2004, Susan announced that she intended to sell her shares and leave the company. To the outside world, personal circumstances were the main reason for this decision. However, in reality the developments within E&E played a major role. Susan's departure from the company had a big effect on the franchisees who really trusted her, appreciated her creative ideas, the new products she developed and the good relationships she had developed with suppliers. Who was now going to fulfil this important role?

E&E's development: 2005–2008

What follows is a period with two faces. Externally, the growth strategy was still promoted and declared as being successful; new countries were still added to E&E's territory. Internally, problems with present franchisees within and outside the Netherlands became worse. Out of stocks were rising and there were on-going disputes about the quality of new campaigns, the ban on franchisees purchasing locally and about financial prognoses. At the beginning of 2005, the first closure in the UK was a fact. In 2006, more than 25 stores were closed down or handed over. The last of the 17 stores in the UK terminated its activities in January 2007. Table 10.4 summarizes the development in the number of units of the E&E franchise chain.

In spring 2006, a group of dissatisfied (master) franchisees joined forces and asked the director of the Dutch Franchising Association to mediate. However, this did not work out. As a consequence, a legal procedure was started against E&E in the Netherlands, a process that was reported extensively in the press. The franchisees accused E&E of mismanagement, consisting of providing too optimistic sales prognoses and the damaging of E&E's brand reputation, which had directly hurt the franchisees. An example of such a damaging act is that E&E had started buying inferior, cheap products from Asia that were detrimental to a chain positioning itself as selling high-quality Mediterranean products. The dissatisfied franchisees also openly complained about Marc's arrogant behaviour and lack of communication. Mismanagement, however, could not be proven eventually.

In this period, financial problems kept on growing. Although on chain-level realized sales were usually above projected sales, E&E made its first small profit in 2002 only (about €9,000) and its first decent one in 2003 (about €400,000). However, managing and controlling a complex and global chain requires a lot of time and money. Also, most master franchises simply did not yield sufficient profit. Eat & Enjoy seriously needed new investors and in March 2006, E&E asked a well-known Dutch consultancy firm to assess the financial situation and to develop possible solutions. This consultancy firm concluded that the company had become too complex. About €10 million were needed to successfully grow to about 150 stores, a size that was deemed necessary to be profitable. However, even with this report in hand, no new investors could be found. In June 2006, Marc came in contact with a large Portuguese investor. Although several documents were drawn up and signed, all kinds of communication problems arose. In spring 2007 it became

TABLE 10.4 Estimates of closings and openings of Eat & Enjoy

Year	Openings	Closures/ handovers	Number of stores by end of the year
1999	2	0	2
2000	1	0	3
2001	12	0	15
2002	15	2	29
2003	25	6	42
2004	30	6	71
2005	20	9	85
2006	12	26	81
2007	1	31	57

Source: Bankruptcy files, E&E (information collected by one of the master franchisees). Even though these estimates were presented in an official document, the figures do not add up precisely.

clear that the Portuguese deal was off. It seemed that Marc had seriously mis-interpreted a potential investor's intentions.

In 2007, E&E's operations went downhill fast. Caused by a serious shortage of cash, more and more products were not being supplied to the stores. Franchisees started doing their own purchasing and paid for it from their daily revenues. In July 2007, one of the suppliers presented a bankruptcy petition, which was granted by the court. When the appointed liquidators studied the documents it emerged that in the course of time a complex system of legal entities and financial structures had been developed, which even they could not get a clear picture of. It became obvious that in its present form, E&E was not sustainable. Eventually, a Dutch investor, who had experience in saving and restructuring troubled retail chains, bought the concept. He closed down about half of the remaining stores and restarted the business almost from scratch. Currently, both Marc and Susan are no longer involved in E&E. A large part of the money that Susan should have received for the shares she sold in 2004 were lost in the bankruptcy. In total, shareholders lost €7 million. Looking back, it can be concluded that the rise and fall of Eat & Enjoy has been a roller-coaster ride, which leaves a bitter after-taste for everyone involved.

Case study questions

1   Why is franchising a potentially attractive (international) growth strategy for entrepreneurs with a successful business concept? Do Marc and Susan's motivations for using franchising match with the reasons that are mentioned in the literature?

2   What kind of strategic and managerial challenges did Marc and Susan face in setting up and developing their chain of culinary gift stores in the Netherlands?

3   What kind of strategic and managerial challenges did Marc and Susan face in entering the different international markets?

4   How do you evaluate Marc and Susan's strategic and managerial plans and their way of implementing them?

5   Which factors ultimately led to E&E's bankruptcy in the year 2007, and what could different stakeholders have done to prevent this?

Notes

1   All names are pseudonyms.
2   1 euro is worth approximately 1.30 US dollars.

Bibliography

The following is suggested reading that students and lecturers can use to analyse the case from a more theoretical perspective:

Bradach, J.L. (1997), Using the Plural Form in the Management of Restaurant Chains, *Administrative Science Quarterly*, 42(2): 276–303.

Combs, J.G. and D.J. Ketchen (2003), Why Do Firms Use Franchising as an Entrepreneurial Strategy? A Meta-Analysis, *Journal of Management*, 29(3): 443–465.

Kaufmann, P.J. and S. Eroglu (1998), Standardization and Adaptation in Business Format Franchising, *Journal of Business Venturing*, 14(1): 69–85.

Winter, S.G. and G. Szulanski (2001), Replication as Strategy, *Organization Science*, 12(6): 730–743.

11

WHALE WATCH KAIKOURA – NEW ZEALAND

Chellie Spiller and Sanjay Bhowmick[1]

Kaikoura is a small township on the east coast of the ancient land, Te Waipounamu (Greenstone Island), which most New Zealanders call the South Island. Kaikoura is wedged between the Seaward Kaikoura Ranges (rising to a height of 2,885 metres) and the Pacific Ocean, which within 500 metres of the shore drops 1,300 metres to the ocean floor into the vast depths of the Kaikoura Canyon. Snow-covered often for nine months of the year, the Kaikoura Mountains provide the backdrop for what has become one of nature's most powerful signatures – the graceful flick of a tail of the sperm whale that goes "fluke-up, fluke-down".

The warmer waters from the north meet cooler flows from the south, creating a nutrient-rich up-welling that supports many forms of marine life, from krill to the sperm whale's food delight, the giant squid, which spawn and thrive in the Kaikoura waters.[2] In an area of 25 square kilometres off Kaikoura, tourists are now virtually guaranteed to see whales all year round.[3] From a total of 79 species of whale and dolphin in the world, over 15 have been identified off the Kaikoura coast. Although sperm whales are the main attraction, the right, humpback, minke, blue, fin, sei, killer, beaked and pilot whales are regularly sighted. Also frequently seen are New Zealand's small native, Hector's dolphins.[4] For the whales the attraction is the wealth of food.

"Two years to film the trilogy, millions of years to build the sets": these advertising slogans appeared at the centre of action during the Oscar season in the *Los Angeles* and *New York Times*.[5] New Zealand film director Peter Jackson and actress Keisha Castle-Hughes had promoted New Zealand to the world through their remarkable achievements. Jackson's blockbuster *Lord of the Rings* had scooped 11 Oscars and Castle-Hughes was making headlines as the youngest ever Oscar nominee for her lead role in *Whale Rider*. The stunning landscapes of the *Lord of the Rings* and the riveting cultural story of *Whale Rider* had done wonders for marketing New Zealand. Whales and New Zealand's sensational scenery were making waves around the world.

The Kaikoura Mountains are the scenic backdrop for one of New Zealand's most remarkable business tales – Whale Watch Kaikoura (WWK). WWK had been on the growth curve of an entrepreneurial success story and was now preparing to commit to another major step – building a $120 million virtual reality whale centre and 250-bedroom world-class hotel.[6] However, it was facing concerns from a number of stakeholders, including environmentalists, about the impact of tourist numbers on marine life, "green" tourists' concern that Kaikoura would turn into another overcrowded destination, and tribal members were anxious that outside investment could shift control to external money-bags. From the start, WWK was an entrepreneurial initiative with a difference; it had been generated by the community. Today, Wally Stone, a highly regarded entrepreneurial director and strategist and chairman of WWK, carried the responsibility for the community as much as he did for WWK's investors. Needing to respond to these stakeholder concerns, Stone and the WWK board were now required to come up with answers that would demonstrate a sustainable way forward, showing how WWK's sustainable development journey would progress beyond a successful entrepreneurial startup stage. That was also what the community looked for.

Living on the edge

In the 1980s, Kaikoura was a sleepy fishing village of about 2,000 inhabitants and a couple of motels. Kaikoura's only attractions were its "kai koura", or "meal of lobster", a little known seal colony and rusting relics from the whale-hunting era. The township suffered widespread unemployment and the community's high dependence on state welfare. Kaikoura's farm incomes had plummeted, social fabric was severely frayed, and local Māori, the Kati Kuri, a tribe who are members of the larger tribe Ngāi Tahu, were especially hard hit by economic restructuring.[7] "In 1988, we used to say that people came here because they got lost," said Stone.[8] The town's already high unemployment rates had been growing steadily as a result of government reforms, and was estimated at 90 per cent among the Māori community, with total employment dropping 15 per cent between 1986 and 1991,[9] a disproportionate number of people earning less than $15,000 per annum, with many less than $10,000, in 1996.[10] Limited local incentives saw a high rate of migration of Kaikoura's youth.

Seeds of transformation

It happened without "smart" money or outsiders. It happened using the resources and people who live on the town's doorstep. The initiative centred on descendants of the whales that were exploited from the 1830s for their blubber and bone to power the lamps and stiffen the corsets of European and American women. These whales were survivors of those ancestors that had also been driven to the edge of existence. Some whaling continued until this century, but long before then the town had become reliant on farming for its economic base.[11]

Securing a loan to buy the first whale-watching vessel was difficult. Mainstream banks had turned away the small group who had envisioned the business dream. Banks would not even let them open a cheque account.[12] Undeterred, a group of local Kati Kuri, led by the late Bill Solomon and his sisters Miriana and Aroha, who recognised the special nature of what Kaikoura had to offer, raised $35,000 from personal savings. Four families mortgaged their houses in 1987 to launch, equip and market the first boat, a rigid hull inflatable to take ten people. They proceeded in the belief that they might break the cycle of poverty and unemployment and create a better future for their children.[13]

A retired Christchurch banker, Des Snelling, who had offered his services, recalled those dreams as "to sea with one boat, a few brochures and a lot of hope . . . As an ordinary commercial venture, it had nothing. It was what seemed to be a hare-brained idea." For Snelling, the turning point was when the Māori gave the banks personal guarantees by putting their homes on the line. "For poor people, that was a courageous thing to do."[14] Their entrepreneurship, though linked to opportunity pursuit, was not the agenda of one individual but the collective effort of a community and braided with spiritual significance. Their purpose was defined by what they sought together for the well-being of the people and the environment.

The group's financial commitment enabled them to secure a $100,000 Māori venture-capital agency loan and a $5,000 business development grant through the Marlborough Development Board. A number of staff in the first two years worked without their salaries along with volunteer workers who helped out.[15] A marketing lecturer with Christchurch Polytechnic brought his students on a whale watch field trip, which resulted in a marketing plan being delivered in May 1989, the same year that WWK purchased a second vessel.[16]

Sustainability at the heart of the business

A motivation for WWK was to create an economic base that provided for an independent future where local Māori could be in control of their own destiny.[17] The WWK story draws on the legend of the Ngāi Tahu ancestor, Paikea, arriving in New Zealand on the back of a whale. The WWK experience offered a glimpse of what the marine environment was like before tens of thousands of whales were slaughtered worldwide. "The whales are integral to our culture," said Stone. "We are talking about our lineage, about myths and legends and how they connect."[18] A special report by the International Fund for Animal Welfare investigating the socioeconomic benefits of whale watching revealed that whale-watching images attracted environmentally conscious, high-spending tourists, making such images ideal in marketing campaigns. "Our country's careful management of the natural resource is seen as a model example of how to sensibly utilise the resource," said Stone. Whales, and whale watching, he observed, can make a significant contribution when it comes to endorsing or giving effect to Tourism New Zealand's worldwide 100 per cent pure NZ international marketing campaign.[19]

Because of the rejuvenation WWK brought to the town's economy, the Kati Kuri were held in higher esteem and played a more positive role in local affairs.

At the level of the tribal group, as at the level of the wider community, the venture exceeded all expectations, and the company made a conscious decision to contribute to the community, believing firmly that a successful company in a small town has to help make the town successful. Even though WWK were the "largest sponsor in the area by miles", they did not actively promote their contributions to enhance brand value and public perception. They stressed that they did "those things because they believed in them". They believed it undermined the mana (honour) of others to use their contributions as a marketing tool. Shareholder profits[20] were used to take young people off welfare payments and give them skills and a future, and in the eyes of some tribal members, one of the greatest achievements of the business was that some of the profits contributed to an alcohol and drug rehabilitation programme.[21] Both Māori institutional shareholders in WWK approached the social challenge of creating employment and building social capital through highlighting the goal of cultural sustainability, by explicitly recognising that some assets have cultural significance for Māori and were not subject to the same earnings or investment criteria as other investments.[22]

Green globe co-evolution: business, society, culture and the environment

Adopting a far-reaching solution was the way in which the township embraced Green Globe 21 (GG21). The Kaikoura District Council and local tourism operators, including WWK, collaborated to develop and measure performance indicators for Kaikoura. In July 2001 the Kaikoura District Council developed an environmental and social sustainability policy. In 2002 the region became the first community in New Zealand to be recognised as GG21 benchmarked. This global benchmarking and certification system for sustainable travel and tourism was based on Agenda 21 principles for sustainable development. The GG21 process used straightforward accreditation criteria based on continuous environmental improvement and was developed for entire destinations as well as individual companies.[23]

Kaikoura was chosen to be one of three international pilot studies under the GG21 project. Kaikoura District Council received numerous awards for their resource and waste-management practices. The community's vision for Kaikoura was "that of a sustainable future", with "tourism providing an economic benefit and local amenities, but not at the expense of the natural or social environment".[24] A strict and comprehensive range of natural and social environmental commitments was undertaken in order to be a GG21 benchmarked community. These commitments included monitoring greenhouse gases, energy management, air quality, freshwater resources, waste minimisation, social and cultural impact, land-use management and ecosystem conservation. The council committed to undertake responsible energy management to minimise pollution, encourage the protection of ecosystems, to encourage the use of environmentally friendly products and educate the wider community on sustainable issues (see Exhibit 11.1).[25]

The benefits of Kaikoura's GG21 involvement were significant. Due to their success with GG21, Kaikoura, too small to get publicity otherwise, was reported in the media across New Zealand and internationally. Even government departments, other councils, university researchers and state bureaux such as the Japanese Travel Bureau travelled to Kaikoura to examine and report on their GG21 approach. Other benefits have been economic, including reduced costs, such as less waste, to residents and businesses as efficiencies were improved.[26]

In November 2004, Kaikoura became the first local authority in the world, and the second community in the world, to achieve Green Globe certification, and have maintained their certified status since. Community clubs, societies and committed individuals in Kaikoura rallied together to maintain its status as the first local authority area in the world to be Green Globe certified.[27]

Also, if success is measurable in international recognition, then WWK had done remarkably well. In 1995 it won the British Airways Tourism for Tomorrow Award in both the Global and Pacific region categories. In 1997, it received the Pacific Asia Travel Association Gold Award in the heritage and culture category. In Berlin in March 1997, WWK was awarded a Green Globe Achievement Award with Distinction. This award recognised outstanding progress towards the "implementation of environmental programmes which demonstrate excellence". In 2009 they scooped up two major awards: the Supreme Award at the 2009 Responsible Tourism Awards in London and a few months later the Community Benefit Award at the Tourism for Tomorrow Awards, hosted by the World Tourism and Travel Council (WTTC) in Beijing China. WWK remained modest in claiming any single-handed transformation of the town, and said they had only been a catalyst in developing confidence within the local community. They stressed that they and the community together were strategic investors and "players" in the future of the town.

Values-based systems

New Zealand is an OECD country dominated by Western institutions of commerce and a Western philosophy in entrepreneurship. Reflecting this wider commercial system, WWK was a private company owned by Ngāi Tahu Holdings Ltd and the Kaikoura Charitable Trust, and its activities were governed by the Companies Act 1993.

However, although Māori organisations seek to create profitable, economically sustainable enterprises, they differ from the conventional business norm by viewing profit and economic well-being as a means to serve broader social, cultural, environmental and spiritual well-being goals. Thus, traditional Māori protocols for the conduct of trade that meet the needs of the individual and the collective have endured despite the enormous impact of colonisation from the 1800s. At the heart of Māori business are Māori values (see Table 11.1) and this values-based ethos was reflected in Stone's observation that "any potential conflict is resolved by adherence to clear principles and values". He noted that when difficulties arise they would always go back to their values to gain clarity and a way forward. Stone also believed that their phenomenal success had enabled them to be more Māori focused:

> As a business we have a unique ownership structure and philosophy and we are able to give effect to these values and culture because we are successful

TABLE 11.1 Introduction to Māori values

The Treaty of Waitangi partnership, a covenant between the Crown and Māori, seeks to ensure that Māori remain able to protect their cultural practices and participate fully in New Zealand society, as Māori. This can only occur if Māori remain able to exercise *tino rangatiratanga* (self-determination) in relation to their values and cultural practices. The Treaty of Waitangi principles are *Kotahitanga* (Partnership), *Kaitiakitanga* (Protection) and *Urunga-Tu* (Participation).
Māori place a high value on *whakapapa* (genealogy), where all people and life forms descend from a common source. This forms the base for kinship with the natural world as all things are considered to have a *wairua* (spiritual dimension), a *mauri* (life force) and all things have a relationship with each other. The life force of *taonga* (natural resources) are protected by *kaitiaki* (guardians). The rules governing the management framework are called *tikanga*, and it is through *kawa* (protocol) that the rules, life force and spirit are pulled together.
Māori feel a strong sense of guardianship of natural and physical resources and protection of *taonga* (treasures) and access to these by all tribe members.
Whanaungatanga focuses on engendering a sense of belonging. When operating in a framework of *whanaungatanga* individuals expect to be supported by the collective group who in turn expect the support and help of its individuals.
Utu, or reciprocity, in Māori thinking is when an individual or group will reciprocate anything they receive, whether good or bad, because the challenge of such an act represents *mana*, or the potency and authority of a person. The thing received is not inactive, even if it is an act and not tangible as such, and contains something of the person who gave it. This thing is attached to a chain of users and itself possesses a "soul" or *wairua*. To give is to give a part of oneself, and to accept is to accept a part of the other. Everyone and every act then become linked and bound by *mana*. To keep taking without giving back is to deplete the other and the *wairua* of things.
Taonga Tuku Iho is knowledge passed down from the ancestors – Māori place a high value on this knowledge.
Unlike the European enlightenment which brought forth "I think therefore I am", the Māori view is "I belong therefore I am".
Whānau (family), unlike the liberal Western system that places supremacy on the individual, are the units of Māori society. An economy based on *whānau* capacity embraces the capacity to share, guardianship, empower, plan ahead and growth.

Source: Mead, H. M. (2003). *Tikanga Māori: Living by Māori Values*. Wellington: Huia Publishers, pp. 28, 42. Henare, M. (2001). *Tapu, Mana, Mauri, Hau, Wairua: A Māori Philosophy of Vitalism and Cosmos. Indigenous Traditions and Ecology: The Interbeing of Cosmology and Community.* J. A. Grim. Harvard: Harvard University Press. Douglas, M. (1990). *The Exchange of Gifts and the Obligation to Reciprocate.* Kent: Biddles. New Zealand Institute of Economic Research. (2003). *Māori Economic Development.* Wellington, pp. 3, 44. Durie, M. (2003). *Launching Māori Futures.* Wellington: Huia Publishers, p. 24.

– we are empowered to make decisions. Success enables the company to reflect its values and this is empowering . . . We can do what we want – when we want to – the things we want to do reflect who we are. We are a company owned by Māori and proud of it. We are not owing to anyone and have control over ourselves spiritually, and economically.[28]

In 2011, the value of the Māori economy was estimated at $38 billion and consisted of increasing numbers of Māori entrepreneurial firms, tertiary institutions, with health and other service providers also making significant economic contributions. New Zealand had always scored high on entrepreneurial intention measures according to the Global Entrepreneurship Monitor studies. Māori were identified as having the world's seventh most entrepreneurial mindset, exceeding the United States, Ireland, Canada and Australia. Furthermore, Māori women had a more entrepreneurial mindset than other New Zealanders.

Growing the business

To expand operations, the Kati Kuri went with an investment proposition to Ngāi Tahu, the larger tribal group they belonged to. The board of the Ngāi Tahu Holding Corporation agreed with the proposition and bought a shareholding in the expanding company and by 2002 held a 43 per cent stake in WWK. The company's capital came from the Kati Kuri founding families and Ngāi Tahu Holding Corporation who also had their directors on its board. Income and tribal finance entirely funded WWK. In 1997 WWK turnover was said to have been NZ$3 million a year, with assets worth NZ$2.5 million and shareholders' funds of NZ$2 million. One commentator even speculated that by 2002 the whale-watching industry in Kaikoura had directly generated $25 million of revenue a year and one-third of the town's full-time jobs. WWK became the single largest employer in Kaikoura, employing up to 70 mainly Māori people in peak season and supporting many extended Māori families.

A remarkable transformation had occurred in just over 15 years. Kaikoura had become a boom town. High unemployment had shrunk and the divisive racial tensions that marked a struggle for survival and identity had eased under a renewed sense of joint purpose and togetherness. In 1987, the 3,400 visitors through Kaikoura's Visitor Information Centre had increased to 191,443 by 1995. In 1998 academic research put actual numbers visiting Kaikoura at 873,000 and today, according to Lincoln University research, visitor numbers were estimated to be around 1 million annually, and growing. In 1998, overnight visitors were mainly international and stayed 1.8 days with a daily average spend of $45.73 per overnight visitor. While employment continued to decrease in the railway, communication and agricultural sectors, it rose 25 per cent in the service and hospitality sectors between 1991 and 1996. That growth was attributed to increased tourist numbers and specifically to WWK that was conceived of in 1987 and fully operational in 1989. In 2002 unemployment in Kaikoura was down to just "six people" and there had been a "quantum shift" in personal income with a new majority group earning $30,000–$40,000 a year, and significant increases in numbers of people earning more. These days, a queue often winds its way from the doors and down the steps of the renovated railway station booking office, now called the "Whaleway Station".

Over time, visiting Kaikoura became cheaper and easier, with international flights direct to the city of Christchurch just a two-and-a-half hour drive away and brave investment decisions like a 55-employee New World supermarket store planned. The "World of Whales" virtual reality centre showcasing the whales in the Kaikoura canyon would use the same technology developed for the New Zealand America's Cup regatta virtual spectator graphics.[29] The visitor centre complex hoped to boast a 250-bed world–class hotel with exclusive accommodation lodges, a winery and an 18-hole golf course.[30]

Growth and sustainability

"One of the magical things about Kaikoura is it's still a small village," said Stone. "Because of the sense of space and quality of experience, people go away and rave about it, and more people come. But we can't destroy what we have."[31] While tourist numbers brought economic returns by contributing 30 per cent of the district's employment, and although negative impacts had not manifested widely, considerable pressure was nevertheless being placed on the infrastructure, and natural and social environment.

The potential of overcrowding was a significant risk, threatening the qualities that attracted people to the town. The delightful charm of a small coastal village, combined with the breathtaking landscape and unique marine life, could lose its socially and environmentally harmonious appeal. In 1997 Kaikoura had a tourist density of approximately 250 visitors per resident, compared to Rotorua, one of New Zealand's busiest tourism destinations, who had a tourist density of 45 per resident.[32] Some locals were concerned that the needs of the visitor would subsume their own. They were worried that different kinds of social ills would replace those experienced in Kaikoura's "dark days". Furthermore, an impact study in 1998 had already observed inappropriate human behaviour towards seals and recommended that the approved viewing distance of 5 metres be extended to 20 metres.[33] Adverse human behaviour and over-utilisation were threats. In 2002 the first rahui was established. This traditional Māori sustainable management technique closed a portion of the sea to the collection of any marine life within that area. Another rahui would be placed on a different section later, moving around the coast and thus allowing the sea to rejuvenate.[34]

Stone, of Ngāi Tahu descent, unemployed and living on the streets, was destined to help fulfil the vision of tribal elder Bill Solomon, who first recognised the special nature of what Kaikoura had. When Stone was elected as chairman of the national tourism marketing board, Tourism New Zealand, the appointment was hailed as "recognising him as one of the country's most outstanding entre-preneurial businessmen". The mayor of Christchurch observed that "the very innovative techniques that equipped Stone to survive on the wrong side of the tracks are those that make him brilliant on the other". The mayor was referring to a time in Stone's youth when he was an unemployed Māori street kid with a string of convictions, marginalised from mainstream New Zealand.

However, on this day Stone was immersed in a dilemma. Breathing in the pure ocean air on the top of the Kaikoura peninsula, he looked out to the ancient ground where Kati Kuri ancestors had built their pa (fortified village) to keep unwelcome visitors out of Kaikoura. Once the WWK land there was zoned "tourism", as he expected, work could begin on building a $120 million virtual reality whale centre and 250-room world-class hotel. Stone reflected on his present problem: how to attract and accommodate more visitors than ever before to generate greater economic returns while continuing to create and preserve environmental, social and cultural wealth?

One solution for managing the pressure from tourism was to restrict growth. This could be beneficial if they could encourage tourists to book well in advance. Surely, Stone observed, the ultimate in sustainability is a waiting list.[35] This would also enable local tourism operators to plan better on their existing capacity with higher occupancy levels.[36] WWK had made a conscious decision not to increase their vessel size beyond 20 metres – never bigger than a whale – to keep "the magic" of the journey, and also limited vessel capacity to fewer than 50 people. Although restricting supply did not automatically lead to increasing yield, WWK endeavoured to increase value through ensuring quality of experience through these self-imposed restrictions. "The bottom line," Stone said, "is people should have no regrets about the money they have spent."[37]

WWK undertook a two-year consultation process with "every group within the community we could find".[38] In its development vision to the Kaikoura community, WWK recommended a rate-neutral cost, i.e. that its project would ensure that its success did not send residents' and retailers' property rates sky high. At public meetings, concerns were expressed that outside investment might engender external control much less committed to local development than local owners. For instance, there were concerns about housing shortage. However, since farmland had been subdivided to make way for 600 sections to be sold over the next few years at reasonable rates, those concerns subsided.[39] Nevertheless, while some wondered how much development Kaikoura could absorb without impacting the natural and social environment, most of the town's retailers and the Kaikoura District Council[40] supported the project, and the development proposal outcome provoked no objections to the council.

While many in the town, especially businesses servicing tourism, welcomed the development, other stakeholders had expressed concerns to WWK's board. Some members of the community were worried that outside investment might shift control into the hands of those much less committed to Kaikoura than locals. Others were anxious and wondered if the town's social and natural environment could cope with much larger numbers, and if their own needs would be subsumed by those of tourists. Some tourists, hearing of the proposal, expressed concern that the small town would become just another tourism "factory" and wondered whether that would spoil the destination. It was important to "green" tourists in particular that not only did they get value for money, but that they could feel good about participating on a tour with a company that demonstrated commitment to strong social, environmental and cultural values. A number of environmentalists were worried about the impacts of tourism and human behaviour on the marine ecosystem. The board had acknowledged that the company and the community had come a long way already down the sustainability path. However, they wanted reassurance that Stone had a plan to successfully navigate the way forward before approving the new development.

Stone reflected on WWK's mission: "To maintain a global reputation for delivering a unique marine and cultural experience in one of the world's last unspoiled, natural wildernesses" and their philosophy to "only undertake activities that are culturally acceptable, economically viable and environmentally sensitive." He saw WWK objectives "set in the long term rather than short term" and he said they want to live there for another 950 years. He believed his people were "agents of change rather than victims of change" and that assets and profits are "like oxygen, necessary for life, but not the purpose of life". Even a pure profit motive would be difficult to translate into action for WWK, which, to be in business in the first place, depended on the fine balance of natural cycles that attracts the magnificent whales. Entrepreneurial growth opportunity, for WWK, came with great responsibility.

Stone wanted the company to be an even greater international success, but were growth and sustainability compatible? Stone pondered the Māori proverb that "we walk into the future backwards, because the only thing that is certain is the past". An important starting point for Māori when solving problems is the past. Stone sat underneath an old cabbage tree once used by the ancestors as trail markers and reflected on the path of the past for inspiration.

Back to the future

In terms of ideal leadership, Stone was adamant that "a leader must be visionary, a long-term planner and possess entrepreneurship".[41] He believed we "need to create an environment to encourage those that are actually committed to this country, committed to its lifestyle, its value system and are long-term players for New Zealand, and not there purely for the balance sheet". Stone suggested rewarding entrepreneurs and risk takers and celebrating their success, but also ensuring that their success is the country's success, so they should stop underselling the country and underpricing products and services. "The more we value New Zealand the more valuable it becomes. Take tourism – while each day the world gets more complicated and more polluted, the more desirable we become."[42]

Stone would know. He – like Kaikoura, like the whales, like his people – had been to the edge and looked over. Now they flourished. He saw the virtual reality whale centre and the 250-bedroom, world-class hotel, as critical for the future.

However, he also knew that a sustainable future required stakeholder support. He decided to begin his paper to the board with key questions to demonstrate a sustainable way forward for WWK.

1   What are the core principles that underpin WWK's quadruple bottom line?
2   What are the sustainability practices being currently applied at WWK and what will be done to address stakeholder concerns about the virtual reality whale centre and the world-class hotel developments?
3   What performance measurement criteria will WWK use to demonstrate its quadruple bottom line?
4   How do you reconcile the Māori belief that you "walk into the future backwards, because the only thing that is certain is the past" with the Schumpetarian concept of "creative destruction" in entrepreneurship theory?
5   How does the quadruple bottom line revise Venkataraman's (1997) widely accepted definition of entrepreneurship as involving the nexus of lucrative opportunities and enterprising individuals?
6   How do you see individual entrepreneurial motivation in the context of Māori entrepreneurship through the story of WWK?
7   What are your recommendations on the listing of WWK on the stock exchange? Why? How?
8   Can you generalise your recommendations and ideas for any business by drawing lessons in entrepreneurial innovation from them, and outline an idea for sustainable entrepreneurship?

While many challenges lay ahead, Stone thought that living and doing business on the edge was a great place to be, and that sustainability would come from inclusive entrepreneurship.

EXHIBIT 11.1 **WWK conservation policy**

Whale Watch is committed to providing a quality whale-watching experience while carefully managing the use of a rare natural resource. We are visitors to the world of the whales and respect it as such at all times. As a Māori-owned company, Whale Watch cherishes the twin values of hospitality to visitors and reverence for the natural world. It is a philosophy that embraces people, the land, the sea and all living things as one. Perhaps this is why so many of our visitors tell us our tours provide them with a spiritual experience.

Since arriving in the Kaikoura area in AD850, Ngāi Tahu have formed a sustainable relationship with Kaikoura's entire ecosystem, including the marine ecosystem that maintains the whales in their natural environment. Nothing within that sustainable philosophy will allow Ngāi Tahu to harm this ecosystem that keeps the whales close to Kaikoura. For dozens of generations over many centuries this view of life has been fundamental to our ancestors. There must always be enough – more than enough – to sustain life in its entire spiritual and physical sense. Thus, for Ngāi Tahu and Whale Watch, the word 'sustainable' has both a physical and spiritual meaning. It goes to the heart and soul of being Māori. It is a core principle of the whale-watching experience we share with our visitors. Ngāi Tahu have lived with whales for over a thousand years. We intend to live with them for another thousand years.

All Whale Watch vessels are specially designed for whale watching. Our modern catamarans are powered by inboard diesel engines and equipped with Hamilton propulsion units that minimise underwater noise. All on-board toilets are self-contained and never allowed to pollute the sea. Detailed records are kept for each trip, covering personalised identification of every whale seen, its location and any unusual whale behaviour. This information is part of the ongoing contribution to scientific research by Whale Watch. Some sperm whales that visit Kaikoura regularly appear to recognise and trust the Whale Watch boats and do not mind being approached. New whales, though, prefer the boats to keep further away. Whale Watch skippers recognise individual whales and adjust operations to suit each whale.

Whale Watch is proud of their many awards that recognise their commitment to the preservation of the environment. Whale Watch Chairman Wally Stone says, "Whale Watch isn't about to do anything which will adversely affect the whales that provide year-round income, or drive them from the coast. We have the most to lose, so we won't be doing anything to jeopardise the whales in our waters."

Whale Watch is a staunch ally of the marine conservation movement. Wally Stone points to the support that Whale Watch gives to the ongoing international fight to protect whales from a renewal of commercial killing and the resumption of trade in whale products. Japan and Norway continue to vigorously lobby members of the International Whaling Commission to reintroduce commercial whaling. Both nations still take hundreds of whales each year for "scientific purposes" when, in fact, the whale meat ends up in fish markets. Wally Stone says the Whale Watch "experience" sends a powerful message to those who wish to slaughter whales. "We see our business as reinforcing the anti-industrial whaling message. This in turn reinforces whale preservation, the Southern Oceans Whale Sanctuary and the whale protection stances adopted by many members of the International Whaling Commission." It remains a sad fact that the very same whales seen aboard Whale Watch tours may be killed by commercial whalers once outside New Zealand waters.

Source: www.whalewatch.co.nz

Notes

1 Adapted from the original case by Chellie Spiller and Ljiljana Erakovic "Flourishing on the Edge: Case Study of Whale Watch Kaikoura, an Indigenous Sustainable Business", which first appeared in Wilson, M. (2005). *Best Case Scenarios*. Auckland, The University of Auckland Business School. Reprinted with kind permission of GSE Press, Auckland, New Zealand. All information in this case is from published sources. Special thanks are due to Wally Stone, Chairman, Whale Watch Kaikoura and Ian Challenger, Environmental Development Officer, Kaikoura District Council for their valuable time in assisting with fact-checking and providing useful insights for the original version of the case study.

2 Whale Watch Kaikoura. (1997). *Bigger than Moby Dick*. Retrieved 10 April 2004 from www.whalewatch.co.nz

3 Ibid. Whale Watch operates every day except Christmas Day. While humans prefer the warmer summer months for viewing whales, whales feed in the canyon all year round.

4 Ibid.

5 Dye, S. (2004). Middle-earth puts NZ on top. *The New Zealand Herald*, 3 March.

6 The dilemma presented in the case is not an actual dilemma. Its purpose is to facilitate understanding of how sustainability can be applied to assist business success.

7 Whale Watch Kaikoura. (1995). *History of Whale Watch*. Retrieved 10 April 2004 from www.whalewatch.co.nz

8 Whale Watch Kaikoura. (1997), op. cit.

9 McNicol, J., Shone, M. and Horn, C. (2003). *Benchmarking the Performance of the Tourism Community in Kaikoura*. Landcare Research New Zealand Limited and the Tourism Recreation Research and Education Centre, Christchurch: Lincoln University, p. 79; see also Kaikoura District Council. (2004). Green Globe: Kaikoura's Path to a Sustainable Future: Kaikoura. p. 5.

10 Kaikoura District Council (2009). Long Term Council Community Plan 2009–2019. *Kaikoura Today*, available at: www.kaikoura.govt.nz/council_documents/ltccp/, accessed 1 October 2011.

11 Whale Watch Kaikoura. (1997). op.cit.

12 Ibid.

13 Ibid.

14 Ibid.

15 Ibid. Also, Wally Stone, personal communication.

16 Federation of Māori Authorities and Te Puni K_kiri (2003). Te Hei Whakatinana i te Tūrua Pō: Business Success and Māori Organisational Governance Management Study.

17 Whale Watch Kaikoura. (1997). op. cit.

18 Ibid.

19 Whale Watch Kaikoura. (10 December 2003). *The World of Whales: Tourism Background*. Retrieved April 2004 from www.arl.co.nz/whalewatch

20 As a private company any profits are distributed back to the shareholders, the Kati Kuri founding families and Ngāi Tahu Holdings Corporation, to use as they see fit (confirmed by Wally Stone, personal communication).

21 Whale Watch Kaikoura. (1997). op. cit.

22 Te Runanga o Ngāi Tahu. (2002). *Ngāi Tahu 2025*. Christchurch. It is useful to note that Te Runanga O Ngāi Tahu released a document *Ngāi Tahu 2025*, which is a "tribal map" explaining their social, cultural, environmental and financial policies and investments.

23 McNicol, J., Shone, M. and Horn, C. (2003). op. cit.

24 Green Globe 21. (2004). *Kaikoura District Council Case Study*. (Online). Retrieved April 2004 from www.greenglobe21.com

25 Ibid.

26 Kaikoura District Council. (2004). op. cit., p.17

27 Kaikoura District Council. (2009). op. cit.

28 Federation of Māori Authorities and Te Puni Kōkiri (2003). op. cit.
29 Whale Watch Kaikoura. (2004). Whale Watch Kaikoura goes to new depths. Retrieved April 2004 from www.arl.co.nz/whalewatch
30 Devereux. M. (2004) op. cit. (additional information confirmed by Wally Stone, personal communication).
31 Oram, R. (1 July 2002). op. cit.
32 Kaikoura District Council. (2005). Tourism Strategy for the Kaikoura District: Kaikoura., p. 16.
33 Simmons, D. and Fairweather, J. (1998). Towards a Tourism Plan for Kaikoura. Christchurch: Tourism Recreation Research and Education Centre, Lincoln University, p. 22. The viewing distance is set at 10 metres.
34 Kaikoura District Council. (2005). op. cit., p. 42 and Kaikoura District Council. (2004), op. cit., p. 7.
35 Wally Stone, personal communication.
36 Oram, R. (1 July 20002). op. cit.
37 Wally Stone, personal communication.
38 Thomas Kahu in Devereux, M. (2004). op. cit.
39 Affordable homes, however, remain a challenge for the community going forward (emphasised by Wally Stone, personal communication).
40 Kaikoura District Council is the local authority covering an area of 2,048 square kilometres from Kekerengu in the north, to the Hunderlee Hills in the south. The districts' population makes Kaikoura the smallest territorial local authority on mainland New Zealand.
41 Te Puni Kōkiri (2005). op. cit.
42 UnlimitedNet. (1 December 2003). Five years on. *UnlimitedNet*. Retrieved April 2004 from www.idg.net.nz/unlimited.nsf

Bibliography

BERL (2011). *The Māori Economy Science and Economy*, report prepared for the Māori Economic Taskforce, Wellington.
Devereux, M. (2004). Kaikoura enjoys hard-won boom. *New Zealand Herald*, 27 March.
Dye, S. (2004). Middle-earth puts NZ on top. *New Zealand Herald*, 3 March.
Federation of Māori Authorities and Te Puni Kōkiri. (2003). Te Hei Whakatinana i te Tūrua Pō: Business Success and Māori Organisational Governance Management Study.
Frederick, H. and Chittock, G. (2006). *The Global Entrepreneurship Monitor: Aotearoa New Zealand*. Unitec New Zealand's Centre for Innovation and Entrepreneurship Research Report Series, Vol. 4, No. 1. Auckland: Unitec New Zealand.
Green Globe 21. (2004). Kaikoura District Council Case Study. (Online) Retrieved April 2004 from www.greenglobe21.com
Kaikoura District Council. (2004). Green Globe: Kaikoura's Path to a Sustainable Future: Kaikoura.
Kaikoura District Council. (2005). Tourism Strategy for the Kaikoura District: Kaikoura.
Kaikoura District Council. (2009). Long Term Council Community Plan 2009–2019, *Kaikoura Today*, available at www.kaikoura.govt.nz/council_documents/ltccp/, accessed 1 October 2011.
McNicol, J., Shone, M. and Horn, C. (2002). Green Globe 21 Kaikoura Community Benchmarking Pilot Study. Landcare Research New Zealand Limited and the Tourism Recreation Research and Education Centre, Christchurch: Lincoln University.
McNicol, J., Shone, M. and Horn, C. (2003). Benchmarking the performance of the tourism community in Kaikoura. Landcare Research New Zealand Limited and the Tourism Recreation Research and Education Centre, Christchurch: Lincoln University.

Oram, R. (1 July 2002). Wicked brew. UnlimitedNet. (Online) Retrieved April 2004 from www.unlimited.co.nz/unlimited.nsf/UNID/421B2A9FEC773FE0CC256BDF001683C8

Simmons, D. and Fairweather, J. (1998). Towards a Tourism Plan for Kaikoura. Christchurch: Tourism Recreation Research and Education Centre, Lincoln University.

Spiller, C., Erakovic, L., Henare, M. and Pio, E. (2010). Relational well-being and wealth: Māori business and an ethic of care. *Journal of Business Ethics*, 98, 153–169.

Te Runanga o Ngāi Tahu. (2002). Ngāi Tahu 2025. Christchurch.

UnlimitedNet. (1 December 2003). Five years on. UnlimitedNet. Retrieved April 2004 from www.idg.net.nz/unlimited.nsf/0/AC0F8EABB5C3B64DCC256DE1007366EB

Venkataraman, S. (1997). The Distinctive Domain of Entrepreneurship Research: An Editor's Perspective. In J. A. Katz (ed.), *Advances in Entrepreneurship, Firm Emergence, and Growth* (Vol. 3, pp. 119–138). Greenwich, CT, US; London: JAI Press.

Whale Watch Kaikoura. (1995). History of Whale Watch, retrieved 10 April 2004 from www.whalewatch.co.nz

Whale Watch Kaikoura. (1997). Bigger than Moby Dick, retrieved 10 April 2004 from www.whalewatch.co.nz

Whale Watch Kaikoura. (10 December 2003). The World of Whales: Tourism Background, retrieved April 2004 from www.arl.co.nz/whalewatch

Whale Watch Kaikoura. (2004). Whale Watch Kaikoura goes to new depths, retrieved April 2004 from www.arl.co.nz/whalewatch

12

INDIGENOUS ENTREPRENEURSHIP IN NIGERIA

Growing from scratch

Henrietta Onwuegbuzie

Madu's family home was a mansion by any standards. He had certainly come a long way from his very humble beginnings. His wife, Stella, recently concluded a second university degree. This time she studied Law in order to support her husband's growing enterprise. Over the years, the business had grown to become more successful than Madu had ever imagined and it was getting more and more important to harness the legal aspects of the business. Having experienced less than desirable results from some of the lawyers Madu had engaged, Stella decided she would take the bull by the horns and become her husband's in-house lawyer. Madu totally approved and encouraged this move.

Madu constantly scanned the environment to discover unmet needs and inno-vated corresponding solutions. The lingering challenge, however, was that Madu had no formal management team and directly managed the different aspects of his business. His leadership style was fine when the enterprise was still a small business, but given the growth and international dimension it had attained, it was becoming a challenge to manage it effectively in the same way he started.

While Madu had several apprentices and shop-floor administrators in his employ, none of them was anywhere close to a rank that could be termed executive management. Having no formal business or management training, Madu had not found it necessary to consider building a management team, and so far, he had his personal method of managing the business. As Madu continuously developed new product lines based on problems he identified in his environment, his products were greeted with huge market acceptance, which led him to shift from retail to wholesale trade. His business continued to grow rapidly and it was becoming a challenge for him to manage efficiently with only the support of his wife and apprentices. Going forward, Madu was now wondering what to do about managing the business effectively as it continued to mature.

Context

The context of the case is a rural community in the eastern part of Nigeria. Nigeria is located on the west coast of Africa (see Figure 12.1). It was created in 1914 and formed by an amalgamation of the northern and southern protectorates by Sir Lord Lugard, the appointed British colonial Governor General at the time. The country achieved independence in 1960 and is home to a population of 168 million people (National Bureau of Statistics Nigeria, 2010), making it the country with the highest population in Africa and the seventh most populous country in the world.[1] The hugely multicultural population of over 200 ethnic groups spreads over 36 states (see Figure 12.2) and covers a land area of 923,768 km^2 (National Bureau of Statistics Nigeria, 2010).

The country operates a federal structure of administration and has an urban–rural population distribution estimated at 50.5 per cent and 49.5 per cent respectively.[2] As in most emerging economies, the informal sector represents a significant portion of the country's economic activity, and is estimated to be worth $187 billion.[3] As at 2012, Nigeria is the third largest economy in Africa (after South Africa and Egypt),[4] with a year-on-year growth rate of 8.9 per cent between 2001 and 2010. The IMF recently declared Nigeria to be the third fastest growing economy in the world after Mongolia and China, with a growth rate of 7.68 per cent.[5]

FIGURE 12.1 Map of Africa showing where Nigeria is located

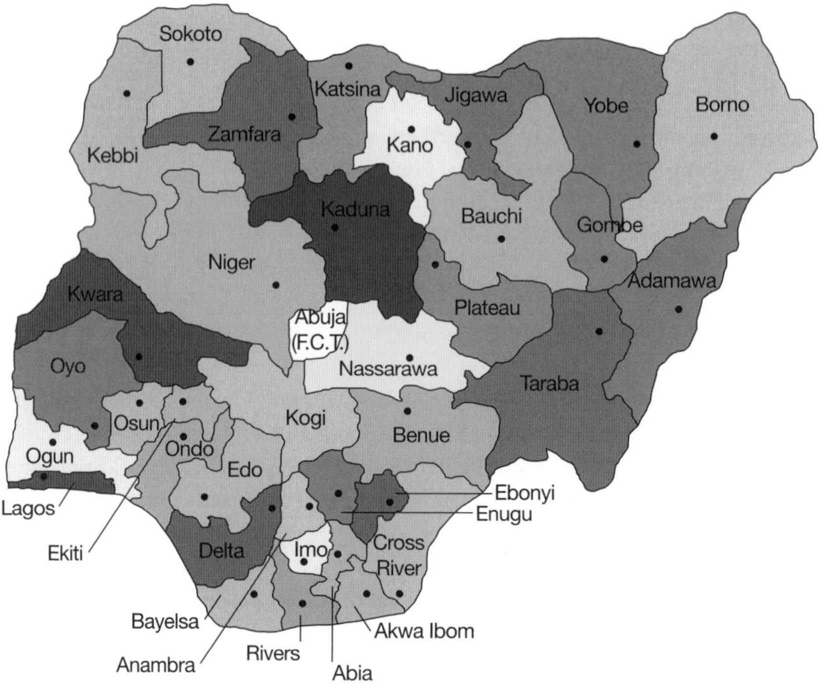

FIGURE 12.2 Map of Nigeria showing its 36 states

Nevertheless, huge income disparities continue to exist between the rich and the poor, giving rise to sharp contrasts in lifestyles. While the more affluent societies live predominantly Western lifestyles, the lower income communities tend to maintain traditional survival mechanisms that lead them to organising themselves differently. For instance, in the lower income brackets and most rural areas, apprenticeship either with parents, relatives or other members of the community form the principal means through which children and teenagers are prepared to earn a living in adulthood. Families in this cadre usually cannot afford to educate their children beyond primary or secondary levels, and so use apprenticeship as a means of skill acquisition. Consequently, the children of a herbal healer or blacksmith, for example, will usually grow up practising the same vocation as their parents. More affluent families, on the other hand, ensure that their children are educated in the best schools, right up to tertiary levels and beyond.

Madu's town, Adazi-ani in Imo state, was generally known to be a very enterprising region of the country. Traditionally, vocational skills were obtained and transmitted through apprenticeship. In more recent years, however, drawn by the higher standards of living, more people migrate to the urban areas in search of paid employment. This has contributed to rising unemployment, a situation that did not exist in the traditional system. Madu's upbringing was typical of the traditional system of entrepreneurship.

Madu's background

Madu is from a family that could not afford to educate him beyond primary school level. The practice in the rural community in which he was raised, in eastern Nigeria, was to send children on apprenticeship to learn a skill or trade of their choice, once they had attained the level of education their family could afford. Some children are fortunate to get to secondary school level before they are sent to work as apprentices with any family or acquaintance known to practise the chosen vocation for a period of about six years. In some instances, a community decides to come together to sponsor a particularly bright child so they can attend university.

This rural system of training is in sharp contrast with the practice among the higher income earners in the cities, where it is taken for granted that not only will children continue their education to tertiary levels, but that most of them are likely to continue their education abroad at some stage, after which they can get highly paid jobs or start a business of their own if they so prefer. The disparity in family income levels, a common feature in most developing countries, gives rise to these contrasting systems of preparing children for the future.

Madu's parents, however, lived in a rural community and Madu was the only son out of seven children. Considering the cultural premium placed on male children, his parents were anxious that he should be successful and put all the means they could to ensure that he, at least, got primary level education before sending him on apprenticeship. The apprenticeship system entails entering an agreement between the parents or guardians of the apprentice and the master regarding the tenure of the apprenticeship, which is usually for six years. During this period, in return for an opportunity to learn a skill or trade, the apprentice is expected to serve his master by helping out with all sorts of errands and household chores, especially if he is living with his master. In turn, at the end of the apprenticeship period, the apprentice earns his "freedom", a term the community uses to express the celebrated fact that an apprentice has become independent. The master is expected to start off the apprentice by renting a shop for him and partially fund his initial stock as a send forth package. The apprentice also receives some funding from his family and relatives to commence his business. Having acquired at least six years of experience, the apprentice is expected to run his/her business success-fully. This local system prepares individuals to earn a living in adulthood and sustain their families.

Madu's apprenticeship

Madu concluded his primary school education at the age of 13 in 1973. Since this was all the education his parents could afford, following with tradition Madu's parents asked him what trade or skill he would like to learn. Madu told them he wanted to learn the vehicle spare-part trade as his older cousins and uncles in the city who were involved in this trade were earning a good living. They came back to the village for the Christmas holidays in flashy cars and had built beautiful homes in the village, and Madu wanted to be like them.

While trying to find a vehicle spare-parts dealer Madu could apprentice with, his parents sent him to work with a relative who bought and sold used clothes in Oturkpo, Benué State (located in the middle belt of Nigeria). After six months with this relative, Madu returned home thoroughly dissatisfied and told his parents that he was not at all interested in that trade. His parents were eventually able to find someone in the motorcycle spare-parts trade who agreed to take Madu on as an apprentice. After Madu's experience with the used-clothes trader, he was more willing to make do with the motorcycle spare-parts trader, although this was not his primary interest.

Madu's new master lived in Ebonyi State. He had a motorcycle repair workshop attached to his spare-parts store, and it was located right beside a vehicle mechanic workshop. Madu was delighted with the arrangement as it gave him an opportunity to learn not only about the spare-parts trade but also about mechanical repairs. From time to time, Madu was asked to give a hand in the mechanic workshop and he did this very willingly.

However, Madu was not happy with the ill treatment he received in the home of his new master with whom he was living. After two years of trying to bear with his master's maltreatment – although he enjoyed what he was learning – he decided to leave and return to his parents. While with his parents, he wondered what else he could do. As luck would have it, one day, while walking along the road, he bumped into one of his relatives who was fond of him. He greeted Madu warmly and wanted to know what he was doing. Madu admitted that he was not engaged at the time. He then asked Madu if he would like to come to work with him as an apprentice in his vehicle spare-parts trade. Madu could not believe his ears, as this was exactly what he had always wanted. He agreed to work for his relation as an apprentice for four years, since he felt he had already carried out two years' apprenticeship elsewhere. Madu's parents gave their blessing and he went to live with his new master, Emeka, who lived in Lagos. In the four years Madu spent in his new apprenticeship, he learnt a lot about the trade and developed good selling skills. The knowledge gained from the motorcycle and mechanic workshop made him able to advise and make recommendations to customers who came to buy vehicle spare parts. He was also hardworking and honest, and his master was pleased with him.

During this period, Madu read a lot of books. Two books that signalled the turning point in his life and way of thinking were *The Power of Positive Thinking* by Vincent Norman Peale and *The Magic of Thinking Big* by David Schwartz. According to Madu:

> These books made me realise that I could become whatever I wanted to be, once I put my mind to it . . . and that if my dream was big enough, not even my enemy could stop me. I started dreaming about my future and thinking big.

By December 1979, the apprenticeship period was finished and Madu's master offered to make him a business partner, putting him in charge of a shop he planned to open in Nnewi, a town located six hours away from Lagos, Nigeria's commercial nerve centre. However, Madu had bigger plans and wanted to remain in Lagos. He felt that Lagos, the commercial capital of Nigeria, presented better opportunities to actualise his dreams if he was in Lagos and that going to a smaller town would limit his ability to achieve his plans. He thus politely declined the partnership offer, preferring to receive the customary separation package in cash, so that he could rent a shop in Lagos and start his own business there.

Madu's master was surprised that he would reject an offer he thought was an opportunity his apprentice would jump at. He interpreted Madu's rejection of his offer to be a result of large savings Madu must have made while apprenticing with him. He therefore gave Madu a paltry sum of money as a parting gift. The amount Madu received was not sufficient to rent a shop, no matter how small. Worse still, Madu had no savings at all. The fact however, was that Madu had no money besides what he had now been given. He, however, accepted it, preferring to maintain a cordial relationship with his relative than to demand his full rights. Madu then had to think of a survival strategy if he was to remain in Lagos and start a business.

Surviving in the city

Madu had a friend who owned a vehicle spare-parts shop in Lagos and this friend agreed to let Madu stay with him until he could acquire his own shop. During this period Madu tried to find a means of making money. Every morning, he would go to his friend's vehicle spare-parts shop and hang around. In between helping his friend with attending to customers or assisting with whatever was needed, he found a way to make some money for himself by helping customers who called in for items not available in his friend's store. He would immediately offer to help such customers by going into the rest of the market to find it for the customer. Madu added a small margin on all such transactions. Over time, he developed a knack for helping customer's locate goods they could not find. He saved up almost every penny he made, surviving on only one meal a day, which he had at night. Within six months, Madu had saved up enough money to rent a shop of his own. His reputation for being honest and hardworking made it easy for suppliers to trust him and give him goods on credit. Madu had been careful to stick to only legitimate forms of business. While people in Madu's town were generally known to be friendly, they were not exactly refined in their manners. For example, in their bid to attract a potential buyer's attention, they could actually reach out to touch people passing by their stores, just to make them notice their store and the goods they carried. Madu's refined friendliness therefore made him stand out. According to Madu, "I try my best to be very friendly with everyone. When you are friendly with people, they don't find it difficult to help you."

Besides his industriousness, Madu's congenial character drew him close to many people. After some years of buying goods from suppliers, one of his acquaintances who imported vehicle spare parts from Taiwan for sale in Nigeria, offered to take him along on one of his trips to Taiwan and teach him the business.

After a few trips with his friend, Madu felt comfortable enough to take orders from people and bring in exactly what was requested as opposed to buying goods and expecting that there would be a demand for them. Unfortunately, his first transaction did not work out as expected. The customer, who requested the goods Madu imported, insisted on paying an amount that was lower than what the goods had cost and Madu found himself stuck with goods that were difficult to sell to anyone else. Consequently, Madu learnt his first hard lesson:

> I learnt my first lesson in importation – I should only buy goods that have widespread demand. Even when I take orders from customers, I will only agree to buy goods I can easily sell in the wider market in case there are issues with the customer who ordered them.

Over time, Madu transited from importing commonly available spare parts to importing parts, which were not easily found in the local market but were essential for the functioning of cars. He was also careful to ensure that the parts he chose to bring in were not too expensive.

> I wanted to deal in goods that would give me a command of the market and control of the price of the goods. So I stopped going for commonly available items and chose to import those parts that were essential to the functioning of cars such as kick bushings or the key and cork, which are necessary for cars to start. These are hidden items that require a good knowledge of how vehicles work. I was able to make a margin of 150 per cent on these items.
>
> At one point, I brought in 50,000 pieces of kick bushings and sold them within two months. Then I imported 150,000 pieces and sold them within a month and a half. Then imported 1 million pieces and sold them in 3 hours as people had made advanced bookings for them. Even when I topped the price to a 180 per cent margin, the goods were still in high demand and I made a lot of money. I got these ideas from the book *The Magic of Thinking Big*.

Madu made bold steps and his business grew in leaps and bounds. By the end of the first year of his business, which started in 1980, he made a turnover of ₦8,000 ($15,545). By the end of the second year of his business in 1981, his turnover had tripled to ₦24,000 ($39,344). He bought his first car, a pick-up van, which he used in transporting his goods and for personal purposes. Madu, now 21, made the transition from retailing to wholesale, selling mainly to distributors. By 1982, his turnover had more than tripled again to ₦60,000 ($89,552). Madu was well known for importing goods that were in high demand and rare to find in the market. After several trips to Taiwan, Madu had gradually become acquainted with the production process of the plastic-based vehicle parts he imported. It then occurred to him that the parts he had been importing could be locally produced by manufacturers of plastic products in Nigeria if they had the mould. The mould was made from steel but unfortunately, the steel plant in Nigeria had been dysfunctional for several years. It then occurred to Madu that he could get the moulds from Taiwan and try to find plastic products manufacturers who would be willing to produce vehicle parts.

Changing the industry structure

In discussions with the plastic manufacturers, Madu told them that the same quantity of plastic, which they used in making plastic bowls, could be used in making vehicle spare parts that sell at a much higher margin per unit. It was not difficult to convince them to start manufacturing this product line, which was new to them, but would more than double their profits. Madu imported the moulds and soon, local manufacturing of the hitherto imported products began (Figure 12.3).

This took Madu's business to an even higher level and changed the pricing structure in the vehicle spare-parts industry. Having eliminated freight cost and clearing charges, the cost of the goods to Madu's customers was significantly lowered. Other vehicle spare-parts suppliers could no longer compete favourably with Madu,

FIGURE 12.3 Madu standing beside samples of the plastic vehicle spare parts manufactured locally

FIGURE 12.4 Façade of Madu's family home in Lagos, Nigeria

who was now a clear market leader and was enjoying much higher sales volumes and profits.[6]

To remain competitive, other suppliers had to either buy from Madu or begin to manufacture locally. Thus, Madu had transformed the business model of the industry and had tremendously brought down the price of the vehicle parts he sold.

By this time, Madu, who was operating from three different locations and owned a large warehouse, married and could now afford to live in a high-income neighbourhood in Lagos (Figure 12.4). Besides other staff, Madu usually had at least four to five apprentices working with him to learn the ropes. At the end of the apprenticeship period as was customary, he was expected to set them up to run their own independent ventures. They could choose to become distributors for the products Madu supplied or do whatever else they preferred. Madu also had a strategy of looking for new product ideas based on the needs he identified.

The innovation imperative

Madu continually sought new product ideas based on the needs he identified. He also constantly developed new product ideas, even going out of his core industry: "My strategy is to create markets by solving problems. I don't go for what others carry. I try to think of what is needed or how I can solve a problem and my ideas usually sell."

One of his new products was a stackable shoe-rack. He realised from personal experience that it was difficult to keep shoes in order and that if one had many pairs, there should be a convenient way to find the needed pair without having to search for long. He created the design of a shoe-rack that made it easy to keep several pairs of shoes in order and in view. Considering the design requirements, he realised that it might be easier to manufacture it in China rather than locally as it required a process that was not as straightforward as the mould process. He also conceived the shoe-rack as a potential gift item if it was collapsible and nicely packaged. He took the design to China and got it manufactured in varying capacity ranges (6 pairs, 12 pairs, 20 pairs and 50 pairs) and it was branded exclusively in his company name, "Accord-Addidas Special Quality Products".

The first consignment supplied to distributors in Nigeria sold out quickly. Madu realised he had hit the jackpot and ordered even larger volumes to be manufactured. This brought down the unit price further and increased his margins in spite of the low prices he was offering his distributors. Seeing how successful this was, Madu was encouraged to keep thinking.

It then occurred to him that he could actually create a range of related products. Based on this idea, he created a design for a collapsible wardrobe on wheels, which could be used to instantly increase an existing wardrobe capacity or be used as a mobile wardrobe facility. He had the product manufactured in China, imported it to Nigeria and again, it sold out fast. Next, he designed a clothes-rack that could be used for various purposes, including an indoor laundry (see Figure 12.5).

FIGURE 12.5 Products designed by Madu and manufactured in China

All these products were simple, low-priced and effective in fulfilling their functions. Over time, competition replicated some of these products in the market. Madu, however, held a competitive advantage resulting from the economies of scale due to the large volumes he ordered, which lowered his cost significantly.

As Madu's new product ideas were many, he created a list of new product ideas for the market, and executed them gradually.

> My latest design in the family of gift items (referring to the product series of shoe-racks, mobile wardrobes and clothing-racks) is a hanger for bags and belts. It will allow one to keep bags in a way that maintains the shape, while making it easy for them to find the bag they want to carry at any time. I haven't seen it anywhere, but I know people need it and that it will sell.

Madu continued to come up with products that were readily accepted by the market. His humble store, which started in 1980, had subsequently transformed into a problem-solving and wealth-generating venture. Madu gradually grew the business to an annual turnover of over ₦1 billion ($6.5 million) by 2011.

In spite of the decline in demand for vehicle spare parts due to the increase in the purchase of new cars in Nigeria, Madu's business continued to grow. His new product ideas sold well and the business generated a higher turnover every year. Madu was, however, interested in diversifying into other areas. By early 2012, he started investing in real estate. He wanted to preserve his wealth and grow it, while waiting for his children, who were still relatively young, to eventually come into the business and take over from him. Madu thought real estate provided a safe opportunity to shield his wealth from economic upheavals and did not need much attention, so he started investing in properties.

Madu found it difficult to trust other people to manage his business. Although it had been growing beyond the reach of what he could manage alone, past betrayals made Madu wary of entrusting any part of the business to others to manage. It was now time to think of how best to solve this problem if he wanted the venture to keep growing.

Case study questions

1   Do you think Madu's apprenticeship years were a good preparation for his eventual business success?
2   How would you compare the preparation from apprenticeship with classroom preparation for business venturing? Are there synergies to be drawn from both models?
3   Does training in values matter for entrepreneurial success?
4   What specific factors do you think were critical to Madu's success?
5   What can be considered as key learning points from Madu's story?

Notes

1   United Nations Development Programme. (2011). "Human Development Report 2011". New York: Palgrave Macmillan.
2   Ibid. 2.
3   International Labour Organisation. (2011). "*Informal Sector*". Available at www.ilo.org/public/english/protection/secsoc/areas/policy/informal.htm (accessed 23 November 2011).
4   Accessed 29 November 2011.
5   *Daily Times*, Nigeria, 2012. Available at: www.dailytimes.com.ng/article/nigeria-3rd-fastest-growing-economy-idb (accessed 15 September 2014).
6   In Nigeria, entrepreneurs are reluctant to reveal profit figures. However, one can get an idea of the growth in income of Madu's business considering his accomplishments.

13

THE CULINARY ARTS ACADEMY – TURKEY

Cagri Bulut, Ahmet Murat Fiş and Duygu Seckin Halac

Mehmet Aksel,[1] age 44, is many things – college drop-out, professional race-car driver, serial entrepreneur – but a cook is not one of them. A man of fine tastes, Mehmet's limitations in the kitchen led him to see early on that there was a dearth of highly skilled restaurateurs and chefs in his native Turkey. In 2004, he started Mutfak Sanatları Akademisi (MSA),[2] which translates literally into The Academy of Culinary Arts, to fill this gap. His vision was to meet the demands of the growing hospitality sector and the country's unemployed people, which typically generate 700,000 new jobs per year, including the agriculture sector, in spite of a population with 12 million youth.

Over the last six years, with the mission "to be recognized as a worldwide leading culinary institution, and set a new standard for vocational education in Turkey", MSA has grown from a one-kitchen studio into a state-of-the-art culinary academy. Located in the prime business district of Istanbul, MSA is now the only culinary school with both international and domestic accreditation, offering courses certified by the UK's City and Guilds Agency as well as the Turkish Ministry of Education (MoNE). MSA boasts a 90 percent placement rate at the top restaurants and hotels in Turkey, and Mehmet expected to graduate 750 culinary professionals in 2011. Founded in 2004, MSA currently employs 44 people, owns 5 state-of-the-art professional kitchens, Turkey's first "professional kitchen auditorium – the Electrolux Auditorium" with a capacity of 150 seats and the highest technology audio–video functionality, a food-and-beverage library with over 4,000 publications, an R&D lab, training restaurant, one corporate hall, and US$3 million worth of equipment in a 4,000 square meters of space, including a 3-floor stand-alone building with an annual sales volume of about $7.5 million.

The context

In spite of lacking a strong economic and cultural infrastructure to support an entrepreneurial environment, with the contribution of the ongoing European Union membership process, a thorough transformation both in social and economic terms is being observed in Turkey. There has been a dramatic shift from a predominantly agricultural economy (from 43 percent of GNP in the 1920s to 8 percent in 2009) to an increasingly industrialized and service-based economy. The working culture of Turkish firms has started to become a mixture of Western and Eastern values and systems (Aycan *et al.*, 2000).

Unemployment and education are two important issues for this young and highly populated economy. Vocational and technical education is especially important in Turkey. Some 60 percent of the population is under the age of 29, and the average age is 28, according to the Turkish Statistical Institute (TUIK, 2011). With an overall unemployment rate of 14 percent, and new graduates' unemployment rate of 33 percent, it is often hard for young people to get a job without formal training. Despite growth in many sectors (restaurant and hospitality included), the Turkish Employment Agency (ISKUR) shows that there is a continuous gap in the market for a skilled/trained workforce. According to a joint survey conducted by SVET and ISKUR, 7.5 percent of job openings across 31 cities in Turkey were in hotels and restaurants where employers challenged with filling the vacant positions as a result of unqualified applications (SVET/MEGEP, 2006). This has led to growth in vocational and certificate programs. In order to balance the general and vocational school education, non-formal education institutions have more than doubled between 1999 and 2009, and vocational training programs have increased from 355 to 392 (TUIK, 2010). Graduates of MSA's professional programs not only fuel the food and beverages industry but also overcome the structural challenges in Turkey's education system, such as a shortage of higher education options and a nascent vocational educational sector.

The food and beverage industry accounted for 19 percent of Turkey's total GDP in 2008, and the number of new hotels and restaurants opened increased from 3,167 to 3,387 between 2008 and 2009. In addition, tourism is a large driver of the restaurant sector – many of the country's best restaurants are in hotels (TUIK, 2011) – tourism expenditure in Turkey is increasing by 15 percent on average yearly. With the domestic food and beverage sector valued at US$15 billion currently, government surveys have shown that this sector has the potential for significant job creation.

Until the 1950s, cooks were taught in a master–apprentice relationship and only after the establishment of Ministry of Tourism short-term training programs were held. With the establishment of Ankara School of Tourism, a formal structure was achieved for the first time in 1962. Until 2005–2006, this institution was the only formal school teaching culinary arts under the name of a cooking department. Beginning in 2004, MSA was the first private culinary training center in Turkey and one of the leading private vocational training institutions.

Because of the high costs involved in the provision of cooking education together with the limited budgets of public vocational schools, MSA as a private vocational school has an advantage over public schools in terms of available capital. With an MSA certificate, graduates can secure higher paid jobs in the service industry. On average, 90 percent of graduates enter high-end hotels and restaurants, with starting monthly gross wages of at least US$1,000, which is 100 percent above the minimum gross wages typically earned by sector employees. To date, MSA has placed over 1,500 graduates at the best restaurants and hotels in Turkey, such as the Four Seasons, W Hotel, and Les Ottomans. In the last three years, MSA graduates have moved across the borders and you can see them working or running the leading restaurants all over the world. MSA currently have graduates working in New York, Hong Kong, Dubai, Amsterdam, and many other cities around the world.

The entrepreneur

Born and raised in Istanbul, Mehmet has taken a winding road to get where he is today. As an ambitious, driven man, Mehmet has been pursuing his own dreams since he dropped out of the University of Michigan in 1987 and has succeeded in several industries, often with the same energy that drove him in the professional car-racing and equestrian circuits. As a perfectionist, he has done nothing for the sake of just doing it. He has tried to do his best in every compartment of his life from marriage to business. Mehmet summarizes his short university education period in the US as an awareness period where he finally realized that he does not need a formal education as the general "crowd". As a "doer", his primary way of learning has always been "learning by doing". At first glance, though, this may seem a little contrary to his current business where he basically sells formal education; "learning by doing" has been one of the primary competitive advantages of the MSA education system. Yet, Mehmet sees education/training as a must for the general crowd in doing every job, even for driving on the street.

After dropping out of university, Mehmet returned to Istanbul and was a professional Formula 3, rally and touring car driver between 1991 and 2001, with a total of 100 national and international prizes. He has also been in the Turkish National Equestrian Team and won up to 300 different prizes, including the Balkan Championship in 1986. In 1991, he opened a Peugeot dealership, which was later recognized as the best-selling dealership of all years in Istanbul. However, when Peugeot set up a condition in 1994 that all of their dealerships must include a "services department", he decided against taking the dealership in that direction and became a restaurateur, opening the Café Turc and Brasserie D'oeuf restaurants.

After nearly a decade in the restaurant business, Mehmet built up relationships with suppliers and other restaurateurs. He also noticed that the traditional way of becoming a cook is a master–apprentice relationship, and there was only one college program and one vocational school running in Turkey. Thus, cooks had serious educational needs, which included dietary issues, side dishes, plate presentation, etc. as well as being specialized in country menus. Aspiring to make a real impact on the food and beverage industry in Turkey, he sold his own restaurants and ended up with a sum of US$350,000 to invest in training the next generation of Turkey's top chefs and restaurant owners.

With his lens as a restaurant owner and manager – as well as a fine-dining enthusiast – he built MSA to reflect the highest standards of global service in achieving change in the food and beverage industry. To him, this was also the best way to have an impact on society.

The business

With no experience in the education business, Mehmet rented a single kitchen, hired accredited chefs to lead amateur cooking classes, and began working towards a professional culinary curriculum in 2004. In this early start-up period, he focused mostly on amateur cooking classes because of the lower financial and physical requirements. In this short period, he tried to cooperate with companies, catching sponsorship opportunities, placement agreements for course participants, and so on.

Sponsors and partners

MSA did not fully take shape until Mehmet landed corporate sponsors like the Turkish home-appliance company, Vestel, which early on provided US$120,000 in equipment and cash in return for cross-marketing and co-branding opportunities. In 2005, the MoNE approved MSA, which made it the first and only private institution permitted to issue official graduation diplomas. That same year, MSA secured a sponsorship deal with the bulk food outlet Metro and started its first professional certification program: the "Metro Professional Food and Beverage Management" course lasting two months. Within two years, MSA had emerged as the leader in culinary education in Turkey and was the only private institution, with global standards and blue-chip sponsors.

Eager to raise the bar in Turkey, Mehmet achieved a major milestone in 2006, when MSA was certified by City and Guilds. With this international stamp of approval by City and Guilds, which has issued certificates to Michelin star chefs like Jamie Oliver and Gordon Ramsay, Mehmet extended the school's operations to another building, opened two new professional kitchens, and started extending vocational programs for people who wanted to become professional chefs. Another extension to the current building was made in the same year in order to establish an excellent library specializing in culinary arts to serve all the students and the graduates as well as the sector professionals. In January 2009, the owner of Le Cordon Bleu cooking schools was so impressed by Mehmet's high-tech kitchens and high-quality curriculum that he offered to share potential business opportunities when suitable. As a starting step, Le Cordon Bleu and MSA are exchanging chefs and students today. MSA also has an exclusive joint program with the leading culinary school of Italy – ALMA – in which the MSA graduates go to the ALMA campus in Parma to take the Advanced Italian Cuisine program, which enables them to experience an internship period of two months in Italy's finest restaurants. Furthermore, MSA has many liaisons with different culinary schools around the world, through its accreditors' networks, City and Guilds and World Association of Chefs Societies (WACS).

Opportunities like these are commonplace for Mehmet, who is often approached by sponsors and potential partners. Approximately 70 percent of MSA's operating costs stem from daily food and beverage requirements, and new equipment (such as pots, pans, etc.) is procured at the beginning of each year to ensure that MSA students have the best tools. To help mitigate the high cost of procurement and also add revenue streams, MSA has two tiers of sponsorship. For the majority of its 60+ corporate sponsors, MSA is able to secure discounted rates on food and equipment, and in return MSA offers discounts on its corporate services. From a handful of more significant sponsors, MSA also offers co-branding and cross-marketing opportunities. Above the operating costs, MSA makes 67 percent profit on its sponsorship deals.

- *Tefal*, a multinational appliance supplier, has a sponsorship deal for US$1 million over a five-year period – i.e. US$200,000 annually. Tefal also provides an un-limited supply of kitchen equipment for use in amateur classrooms.
- *Unilever Food Solutions* – UniPro specifically – is under a three-year contract with MSA that will expire in 2011. In total, this sponsorship is worth US$300,000 in unrestricted funds, as well as US$68,000 in donated kitchen products. MSA has co-branded two of its professional programs as "Unilever International Professional Kitchen" and "UniPro International Pastry and Bakery".
- *Diversey*, a cleaning supplies company, provides an unlimited supply of cleaning and hygiene products. MSA estimates this sponsorship is worth US$100,000 annually.
- *Kayra*, a leading wine producer in the region, provides MSA with US$15,000 in unrestricted funds and US$30,000 per year in donations of wine for MSA events and classes.
- *Keskinoglu*, one of the biggest producers of white meat, eggs and olive oil provides MSA US$40,000 worth of these products annually.
- *Altinmarka*, the leading chocolate producer in Turkey provides US$10,000 worth of chocolate products annually for MSA's Professional Pastry and Bakery Program.

Program

Mehmet has created a vocational education institution that matches the best schools in the world and the programs grew steadily in popularity requiring him to make significant investments in capacity to meet demand. As a result, MSA now offers divergent service lines and continues to invest in a campus which may soon prove limiting. MSA focuses on providing high-quality education and training in the culinary arts to aspiring restaurant professionals, as well as amateur cooks. Over the last six years, its course offering has evolved to meet the demands of the sector and take advantage of sponsorships and partners looking to associate with Turkey's first private culinary institution. In 2009, MSA moved into a stand-alone building in downtown Istanbul, where it now offers both amateur and professional programs, as well as services with corporate clients. Today, the business also augments its service line with corporate programs and consultancy services. There are three kitchens for the professional cookery and bakery programs, one kitchen that doubles for amateur programs and corporate programs/services, and one kitchen for the restaurant management program.

MSA focuses its daily operations on the management of its training programs, and consulting and corporate programs occur on an ad hoc basis to meet specific client demand. The following model details the operations of the culinary institute:

1   *Professional programs (81 percent of sales)*: MSA's professional programs train students with global standards, as certified by City and Guilds and MoNE. The school currently offers three main courses, each of which focuses on a particular area of culinary expertise, with sponsorship provided by a well-known supplier in that particular sector. For interested students, MSA also offers a joint discount program through which students can mix and match the following professional programs:

   –   Unilever International Professional Kitchen (5 months + 3-month internship); 62 percent of professional program sales; US$7,000 per person.
   –   UniPro International Professional Pastry and Bakery (5 months + 3-month internship); 21 percent of professional program sales; US$6,000 per person.
   –   Metro Professional Food and Beverage Management (2 months); 17 percent of professional program sales; US$2,200 per person.

   Taught in Turkish, and using the very best in equipment and raw materials, MSA offers 3 semesters of cooking and pastry each year, and a restaurant management course 5–6 times each year. All courses focus on international standards and mix local and international cuisines. After being accepted into the program by one of MSA's chef trainers, students can opt into either an extended program (16 hours of class each week) or an accelerated program (28 hours of class each week), each of which have an maximum class size of 24 students. In order to graduate, students in the Professional Kitchen (cookery) and Professional Pastry and Bakery (pastry) must complete an additional three months internship in an MSA-approved restaurant or hotel kitchen. Following this internship, which is unique to MSA even among City and Guilds programs, students take exams and then receive both the MoNE certificate and City and Guilds diploma. After completing one of these programs, students can also pay an additional €8,500 to participate in the joint advanced program with the ALMA institute in Parma, through which MSA graduates can get additional training and certification in Italy. MSA sends around 30 students to Italy every year.

2   *Amateur programs (7 percent of sales)*: MSA offers approximately 15 amateur course on a monthly basis, setting the calendar about 1 month in advance and determining course offerings based on customer demand. Each amateur program lasts 3–4 hours and costs around US$50–80 per person depending on the supplies. To date, the most popular courses have been sushi-making and Italian cuisine, with other lessons, including wine appreciation, meat and meat-cooking techniques, chocolate making, Chinese cuisine, Mexican tapas, and Turkish cuisine.

3   *Corporate programs (6 percent of sales)*: MSA offers corporate firms a variety of services to motivate their teams and celebrate special events. At the MSA academy, groups of 28–30 people can participate in a customized lesson or dining event. Also serving its corporate clients, MSA chefs can cater for corporate events and showrooms (sometimes adding in a learning component) and can participate in fairs/tradeshows when suppliers organize events to promote new products. More recently (2011), MSA has also begun (on a small scale) to help their corporate clients with product testing and marketing – for example, MSA will soon begin testing glassware products for Pasabahce, a major supplier in Turkey, and is also creating a range of cookbooks for Tefal's new "Nutritious and Delicious" products. The cookbooks will showcase easy recipes using Tefal's equipment. Fees per organization vary from US$2,500 to US$4,000 depending on the number of participants and the type of activity. For its corporate programs and sponsors, some of the current clients are Coca-Cola, Vestel, Becks, Tefal, Unilever Food Solutions, Unipro and Komşufırın, a prestigious patisserie chain.

4   *Consulting services (6 percent of sales)*: MSA has recently (2011) begun to advise restaurants and hospitality providers on a variety of areas including restaurant management and administration, franchising and menu development.

The MSA curriculum differs by program but is equally interactive across all classes. The curriculum for the professional programs is designed by City and Guilds, and the amateur programs are designed and updated on a regular basis by the business development team at MSA according to customer feedback and demand. All classes involve significant time at cooking stations. After each class, MSA's chef instructors assign homework based on that week's topic. Once a month, students are gathered together for evaluations and feedback. Although amateur courses are one-off and do not involve homework or feedback, they embody the same MSA ethos of learning by doing.

In order to graduate from the cookery or pastry professional program, students must successfully complete a 3-month internship at an MSA-approved location. MSA has a very strong internship network, including the best restaurants and hotels, such as the Hyatt Regency, Radisson SAS, Four Seasons, Swissotel, Sunset, Mikla, Ulus29, Les Ottomans, and many more. MSA frequently hosts world-renowned chefs to lead special master classes and has an exchange program with the ALMA school in Italy, where advanced students can go for additional training. City and Guilds and MoNE renew their accreditation with an on-site audit on an annual basis. Following the internship, students complete exams approved by these institutions and then receive their diploma and certificate. MSA pays City and Guilds a fee of about US$110 per graduate.

Teacher sourcing and training

MSA currently employs 14 well-regarded, full-time chef trainers to teach its courses. It pays its chefs approximately US$2,100 starting monthly gross wages, which is nearly 15 percent above the industry average. Depending on the course they will be teaching, trainers must themselves pass through up to 10 certification programs, from City and Guilds, the Turkish government, HICMA, etc. Of note, MSA chefs come from the top restaurants in Istanbul, including Ritz Carlton Naples, Marriott Hotel Marco Island, Ulus29, W Hotel Istanbul, and Hilton Istanbul.

Students

The number of students per year has been rising steadily since MSA opened. MSA students tend to range in age from 20 to 35 years. Most of them are university graduates. MSA primarily targets the A and B segments, which represent annual income levels of US$25,000 and more. MSA's Operations and Administration Department coordinates prospective student interviews for all interested applicants on an ongoing basis to fill their programs. Each prospective student meets with one of MSA's senior chefs, and he/she assesses the applicant's future plans, desire to learn and general attitude. Following the interview, the senior chef makes a recommendation on whether or not the student should be admitted to the program of their choice. MSA accepts 90 percent of applicants and accepted students have some flexibility in tuition payment, as MSA accepts installment payments over a 4–6-month period. Currently, MSA is able to provide limited scholarship to students – around 3 percent of students receive some form of financial aid.

Last year, MSA trained 594 students through its professional programs, with all clients accounting for a small share of revenues. To date, MSA has graduated over 2,000 students total from its professional programs and over 20,000 students from its amateur programs. Going forward, MSA hopes to increase its client base in part by appealing to students from other socioeconomic demographics and from areas outside of Istanbul.

The market

When it was opened in 2004, MSA was the first private certificate program to start addressing the training and vocational education gap. There were no local

TABLE 13.1 The culinary training market in 2011

Competitor	Year opened	Accreditation	Strengths	Weaknesses	Size
Yeditepe University	Culinary Department opened in 2003	Turkish Council of Higher Education (standard university diploma)	• First and only 4-year culinary arts program • Courses taught in English and French • Wide range of courses covering all aspects of the industry	• Curriculum includes essay writing, math, history, etc. according to university standards • Costs US$48,000 for 4 years • No amateur or part-time courses • No sponsors – high operating costs	Capacity to graduate: around 25 students each year
Istanbul Culinary Institute	2008	Bilgi University (diploma only recognized by Bilgi University and Istanbul Culinary Institute)	• Includes a training restaurant, Enstitu, which is well regarded in the city • Thorough courses, 540 hours • Builds a feeling of culture and community – includes a coffee, wine, and food shop • Enstitu provides a natural internship experience for students • Offers 10 amateur programs – one-off 2–3 hour classes – which were recently written up in the *New York Times*	• Courses cost US$10,000 • Only operates one training kitchen • Amateur courses cost US$100 • Only has five sponsors	Capacity to graduate: 27 per year (has only graduated 27 to date)
Bolu Mengen Culinary Vocational High School	1981	Turkish Ministry of Education (standard high school diploma)	• Extremely well respected as a prestigious high school in Turkey • Detailed 4-year program • Public school – i.e. free upon acceptance • School covers a space of 9,300 m^2	• Stringent qualification standards – applicants cannot be over 17 years of age • Poor quality teachers	Graduates 104 students each year

reference points and one of the biggest challenges for MSA has been to raise awareness in the culinary industry and convince people that a career in the kitchen is both fun and rewarding. MSA has invested US$150,000 in PR activities related to this mission. Other than proving and convincing the public in general and parents in specific that university education is not the only way for pursuing career opportunities, MSA has worked a lot to increase the reputation of culinary jobs in the eyes of the public. This was a hard task in a country where chefs have mostly been characterized as potbellied men with handlebar moustaches. Although MSA has finally demonstrated that becoming a professional chef is a valid career opportunity, a similar challenge is still valid for bartending, for which MSA opened a new program.

Yet, since 2004, a handful of other vocational programs have opened to absorb the growing number of Turkish youth that are striving to enter mid-tier jobs in hospitality, tourism, and the food and beverage industry. MSA competes with three other schools in Turkey in terms of institutionalized culinary training for both amateurs and professionals. Although it was the first private culinary institution in the country, one other school has since opened (see Table 13.1).

Future challenges

Bartending courses: MSA is in the process of launching a professional bartending course, which it expects to attract 80–100 new students in 2011 and account for US$80,000 – US$100,000 in sales. Mehmet has already secured sponsorship from the French liquor company Pernod Ricard in the form of US$20,000 in annual funds and US$70,000 in beverages.

Capacity growth through graduates: This year for the first time, MSA will allow students to complete their internships as assistants at the academy. This will help MSA establish an academic career opportunity for students, so that they can hopefully go on to work at MSA or other similar institutions as professional instructors.

MSA-branded Publications: MSA aims to publish educational material to complement its coursework. Currently, MSA uses City and Guilds' materials, which are in English. Mehmet's goal is to secure the copyrights for these materials and publish them in Turkish for MSA students as well as other potential customers outside of the school. Mehmet is also personally working on a collection of rare books about the culinary world, with a vision to publish a series of prestigious books. These would complement MSA's culinary museum and library, at which over 3,000 books and artifacts are on display.

Increase school diversity and reach: MSA currently offers scholarships to 3 percent of students. These funds are typically provided by one the school's sponsors. Going forward, Mehmet would like to offer more scholarships and attract students from outside of Istanbul (and outside of Turkey) by opening up dorms.

Pricing: Increased diversity and reach may make pricing an issue. Although demand is there, the high cost can be prohibitive for many who would like to participate in culinary training programs like MSA. In order to reach a broader demographic, MSA is trying to convince related institutions (banks, corporations) to establish different models for financial aid.

Capacity constraint: MSA already occupies an impressive space in the city, which houses kitchens, communal dining spaces, as well as a culinary library and museum filled with rare books and artifacts Mehmet's collected from all around the world. Just one year after making significant investments in its current space, MSA is currently operating at 83 percent of its capacity. In the near term, MSA will be opening evening classes for those who are already employed and this is planned to expand capacity by 20 percent. MSA is currently looking into renting space near the current building and, beyond this, MSA might ultimately move to a bigger campus so that Mehmet can add professional programs to MSA's portfolio. Going forward, Mehmet wants to maintain MSA as one of the leading culinary campuses in the world. He plans to introduce new education programs in both the culinary services as well as the 'hospitality' services. This will require a larger space for additional kitchens, and classrooms for the practical training. Thus, in the long run, MSA may need to seek outside capital to make the necessary investments to increase capacity.

The issue at hand

Mehmet hired a general manager in 2009 to help manage MSA's daily operations so that he could focus more on business development and strategy. He currently serves as CEO and has a seat on the board, which is comprised of respectable chefs and gourmets and does not provide daily oversight (see Figure 13.1). Mehmet believes that MSA can grow to have a huge impact on Turkish society and he has many ideas for how this might look.

Besides the above summarized future challenges, MSA has several opportunities for future growth, including deepening its relationships with corporations and sponsors, broadening its reach and reputation in Turkey, and expanding its vocational model to other industries. In the near-term, Mehmet plans to continue to build out a culinary ecosystem and ensure that the MSA brand becomes associated with the highest quality training worldwide. In his evolving company vision, a world-recognized culinary school could be the beginning of a vocational education empire, with training programs in everything from cosmetology to eldercare. MSA is currently in the planning phase of an Internet survey that could potentially reach half a million to two million people in Turkey, which will focus on understanding the needs of the vocational education sector from the perspectives of students, HR experts, and current professionals. Based on his current assessment of the landscape, Mehmet believes that elderly care, babysitting, and other

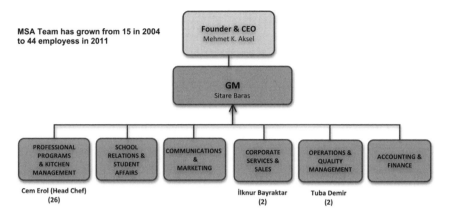

FIGURE 13.1 Organization chart

hospitality services would be worth exploring as the next MSA service lines. With its wide range of accreditation modules, MSA would likely rely on City and Guilds for certification in these new endeavors.

With limited academic experience, and no experience in the corporate world, Mehmet has been used to having full control over his swift decisions. Yet now, though he has a vision for his company and future challenges summarized above, he cannot always articulate how current business decisions and actions will bring him closer to realizing that vision. Mehmet wants MSA to grow quickly and does not always take the time to think through a clear strategy. Currently, he is at a critical point where he has to hone his future strategy and decide whether to expand into the food and beverage industry – potentially through franchising and merchandising – or apply his vocational education expertise to other verticals, or even sell MSA to a potential buyer and seek out new entrepreneurial adventures. Although he has certainly built a successful business, it remains unclear whether or not this particular business will be the platform for Mehmet's vision.

Case study questions

1   What are the mission and vision of MSA? Please make an assessment from a social and entrepreneurial perspective.
2   What competitive advantages does MSA have in the market?
3   What challenges may MSA face in the future, considering the European Union transition process of Turkey and globalization?
4   How would you assess the position of MSA in the market, using SWOT analysis?
5   If you were in Mehmet's shoes, what would your decision be about the business? Stay with MSA or go for new ventures?

Notes

1   Mehmet Aksel is one of the Endeavor entrepreneurs. We are indebted to Endeavor Turkey who not only supported the initial information but later contact with the entrepreneur.
2   See: www.msa.com.tr

References

Aycan, Z., Kanungo, R. N., Mendonca, M., Yu, K., Deller, J., Stahl, G. and Khursid, A. (2000). Impact of culture on human resource management practices: a ten-country comparison. *Applied Psychology: International Review,* *49*(1): 192–220.

SVET/MEGEP (2006). *Strengthening the Vocational Education and Training System in Turkey: Turkey's Labour Market.* MEGEP: Ankara.

TUIK (2011). TurkStat Statistics, www.tuik.gov.tr/VeriBilgi.do?tb_id=25&ust_id=8. Accessed September 5, 2011.

TUIK, 2010 National Education Statistics, Non-Formal Education 2008/2009, Turkish Statistical Institute, Printing Division, Ankara.

14

BAREFRUIT PRODUCTS

A case of entrepreneurial failure in the UK agri-food sector – United Kingdom

Janine Swail

Cope (2011) states that 'failure represents one of the most difficult, complex and yet valuable learning experiences that entrepreneurs will ever have the (mis)fortune to engage in' (p. 620). Thus, venture failure is an important concept to understand in entrepreneurship, both in terms of its causes and consequences for the individual entrepreneur, organisations and society at large. Consequently, the aim of this teaching case is to bring to life, the often untold story of entrepreneurial failure to advance students' understanding of the entrepreneurial learning process.

Barefruit seeds: the entrepreneur and the business entity

Barefruit Products Ltd (BPL), incorporated in October 2005, was a manufacturing, micro-business[1] based in Northern Ireland (NI), United Kingdom (UK), which produced a range of whole fresh fruit smoothie drinks under the brand name Puro. The brand readily gained market acceptance and was a well-recognised offering on the supermarket shelves of large UK retail chains of Sainsbury's and Tesco in NI. Product exports to the rest of the UK found the range listed in the prestigious Waitrose supermarket chain as well as in a number of specialised outlets such as Fortnum and Mason, Selfridges and Daylesford Organic. Café culture listings were secured throughout Ireland, north and south in chains such as Costa Coffee, The Streat and O'Briens.

Company's Unique Selling Proposition (USP): innovative processes

BPL focused on innovation as the opportunity to produce an already existing marketplace product, differently, and was established with the aim of becoming a market leader in the fresh fruit convenience foods sector providing healthy choices

FIGURE 14.1 Barefruit's product range

for consumers. Key criteria for successful modern food products are to satisfy the health, convenience, indulgence and ethical needs of the discerning consumer. Puro was designed to meet those needs and the brand went on to win a series of industry awards during its 35 months in operation, including 'Emerging NI Company of the Year – 2007' (awarded by InterTrade Ireland) and 'Best Small Company Award for Food Innovation – 2007' sponsored by Ulster Bank (awarded by NI Food and Drink Association (NIFDA)). Puro's competitive edge was derived from its twofold USP of superior quality ingredients (natural freshly prepared fruit versus bulk puree and/or concentrate) combined with high retention of vitamin C. This was achieved through a novel innovation process known as High Pressure Processing (HPP). BPL ceased trading in September 2008 and is now classified as a business failure. From an external perspective, BPL appeared to be a startup success and it was apparent that key stakeholders in the local business community perceived it to have grown larger and faster than it actually had.

The entrepreneur: Rose

Before launching BPL, Rose's previous career was in the financial sales service-sector where, up until 2004, she worked as the Senior Manager for NI in Standard Life Assurance. Her career decision to become an entrepreneur resulted after a national restructuring of her employment organisation led to the closure of the Northern Irish offices and subsequent imposed redundancy. Consequently, at 45 years old, Rose's steady career path became somewhat uncertain and it was at this point that she began to consider more seriously what she described as 'a sideline idea'. Throughout her adult working life Rose had notions of having her own business one day, but was unable to identify a suitable opportunity. She undertook a 'Women into Business Programme' at a regional university and began to explore the viability of various venture ideas. She had three potential ideas – a juice bar, an exercise franchise and a management/training consultancy. As she worked through each concept on the programme it became apparent that the smoothie bar was the most attractive and potentially financially lucrative option. However, retail locations with the required level of footfall were in short supply, which subsequently led to her decision to develop the idea as a manufacturing outlet as opposed to retail. Rose aired her startup intentions with friends, family and key stakeholders. Invest Northern Ireland (INI) was the first port of call for Rose. As part of the Department for Enterprise Trade and Industry (DETI), INI are the regional development agency for NI committed to supporting new and existing businesses to compete internationally and also by attracting new investment to NI. They initially showed interest in the Puro concept for three key reasons: 1) Rose's business idea promoted indigenous manufacturing; 2) it demonstrated export potential; and 3) local employment without displacement as no one else in NI was operating such a facility. In providing assistance they supported Rose to attend a brand marketing programme, which helped her to develop the Puro brand including logo, trademarks and packaging. She also developed and trademarked Petit Puro, a children's smoothie range that she planned to launch shortly after Puro entered the market.

While confident in having developed a strong brand that was beginning to be received positively, Rose recognised that in other areas she lacked the required skills and knowledge. She reflected on how her husband, who was much less of a risk-taker, questioned her startup endeavours when he gently cajoled her, 'Darling, what do you know about food, production, retail, Tesco and all the rest? You risk making a fool of yourself!' This only made her more determined to succeed, and she employed a full-time production manager to ensure that environmental health controls were in place and all key legislation was adhered to. In addition, she completed a course in food hygiene and an introduction to HACCP (Hazard Analysis and Critical Control Points), a food safety procedure required in all stages of food production. This equipped Rose with the knowledge to enable her to communicate effectively with her production manager about fundamental production processes. This knowledge also helped her to develop a novel processing technique with the assistance of the Agri-Food and Bio-Sciences Institute (AFBI) in Belfast. Once confident that there were no other competitors with similar processing technology in the UK or Republic of Ireland (RoI), she committed herself to leasing production premises. In addition to her production manager, Rose employed a second full-time employee as an operative and two part-time operatives.

In order to finance her seed-corn micro-business, Rose used several bootstrapping and informal lending strategies. She remortgaged her family home, negotiated a generous overdraft limit with her bank, borrowed 25 per cent from her sister, also an entrepreneur, and invested a small amount of her redundancy package in trademarking and relevant training. All in all, this initial outlay amounted to over £100,000 (British pounds). After nearly 18 months of idea exploration, market research, brand differentiation and R&D, Rose crossed the chasm from nascent entrepreneur to an 'actual' entrepreneur and launched her Puro brand on to the market in February 2006. She reflected on her 'tipping-point' decision at this stage:

> At the end of the day you must have the belief that your product is good, that you can bring it to market and that people will want to buy it. You also need the determination to know that you personally can make a business succeed. All that talking about it and dreaming about it and going on programmes, courses and classes, what was it all about then if I don't have the guts to go ahead with it and put the money behind it? I've put so much into this now, financially and emotionally and to not go ahead with it would be cheating myself.

The Northern Irish context: green pastures for entrepreneurship?

At a glance, NI's economic history is characterised by a reliance on a self-sufficient agricultural system, large employing firms in declining industries (e.g. shipbuilding) and a dominant public sector. Furthermore, the social and political unrest fuelled by the history of 'The Troubles' have led to a suggested 'dependency' culture, which is ultimately not conducive to enterprising activity. Therefore, it is argued that despite a number of successful entrepreneurial ventures in NI, the choice of entrepreneurship as a viable career option is not readily recognised by individuals at large. This is supported by recent Global Entrepreneurship Monitor (GEM) statistics, which reported that in comparison with other UK regions, NI has the lowest proportion of the non-entrepreneurially active population reporting that there are good startup opportunities in their local area in the next six months (Levie and Hart, 2012). In addition, 52 per cent of this group quoted that fear of failure would prevent them from starting a business (Levie and Hart, 2012). That said, INI in the last decade have gone to great lengths to encourage more positive cultural attitudes towards entrepreneurship. From 2003 onwards, the 'entrepreneurship agenda' was firmly embedding itself within economic policy development in NI, and a number of key actions were implemented under the Accelerating Entrepreneurship Strategy 2003–2006. This regional strategy aimed to position NI as an exemplar location to start and grow a business, and thus increase both the quality and volume of business ventures in NI.

The agri-food sector

This sector has grown significantly and makes a vital contribution to NI's economic development. This contribution is best represented by the sector's generation of value added, which was £580 million in 2009 – an increase of over 10 per cent – £522 million in 2007, and representing 2 per cent of total gross value added (GVA). Now the largest manufacturing industry in NI, accounting for 19.3 per cent of NI's total manufacturing sales, this sector employed over 25,000 people in 2010, representing 3.2 per cent of total employment in NI (DARD NI, 2011). The agri-food sector in NI has been a stalwart in recent years and is recognised by government and policy-makers at large as the backbone of the economy in NI.

Fighting for survival

Reaching break-even volumes

Break-even is defined as the *calculation* of the *approximate sales volume* required to just *cover costs*, below which production would be unprofitable and above which it would be *profitable*. BPL began production in early 2006 and each Puro smoothie bottle (250ml) was considered one unit and retailed between £1.85 and £2.50 in the UK market and between €2.50 and €3.50 in the Republic of Ireland (RoI) market. Puro price point was immediately aligned with Innocent brand[2] pricing as they were currently the category leaders in the supermarket multiples. Coming from a financial services background, Rose firmly understood the importance of the break-even concept and 7,500 became the magic number of her weekly operations as this was the number of Puro smoothies she needed to sell each week in order to break even. Once over this unit amount, BPL was officially making a profit.

BPL commenced operations producing 500 units per week and Rose felt that scaling up volumes within the first year to 7,500 per week was realistic and viable. She reflected at startup, 'How hard can it be to sell 7,500 in Northern Ireland every week, for approximately 50 weeks of the year?' Having conducted her market research, she knew that 100,000 sandwiches were sold in NI every day. All she needed was 10 per cent of that market to buy a smoothie along with that sandwich and she was making money! Nonetheless, the challenge of reaching break-even point quickly became apparent. Volumes increased incrementally by the hundreds, reaching 1,000, then 1,300, then 1,500, and gradually up to 5,000, but just when break-even was within reach, the financials confirmed more margin depletion due to seasonal fluctuations in raw material costs, minimum wage increases and process inefficiencies. These factors all ate into profit margins and working capital became difficult to control within the business.

Securing the multiples

The client portfolio of BPL was impressive as from the outset Rose was determined to supply to the large supermarket multiples and other outlets as she realised that this was the best chance of increasing her unit volumes as quickly as possible. Independents such as coffee and health-food shops, despite getting the product on their shelves and visible for the end consumer, could not ensure consistent weekly volumes. That said, attracting the interest of large multiples took considerable time and effort. For example, securing listings with Tesco took 18 months and nearly 2 years with Waitrose. Rose played to her strengths in sales and negotiating during this process as she describes how it was imperative to convince these influential buyers of BPL's USP. Very often she would have as little as ten minutes to explain BPL's point of difference and justify why the Puro brand deserved shelf space over other 'me too' products. Consequently, characteristic of the Fast Moving Consumer Goods market (FMCG), if the product does not move quickly enough, it will not earn enough revenue to maintain the shelf space and will simply be dropped from suppliers' lists. Therefore, gaining shelf space was only the first hurdle. The next challenge was to educate the consumer about the merits of Puro and communicate its superior quality over other smoothie ranges. The added difficulty here was when Puro was automatically being compared to Innocent, as one of Rose's mentors commented, 'Customers didn't necessarily see the value in paying for Puro over established competitor products, rather they saw it as like for like . . . even though technically Puro product was superior. Therefore, securing a premium price was problematic.'

One-woman band

Rose started her business with one full-time production manager and a handful of part-time and casual operatives. Initially, with her production manager, Tamsin, in place Rose hoped to focus on sales and strategic marketing of the business so that successful growth could be achieved. Tamsin had previously worked in quality assurance for the global alcoholic beverages company Diageo, and she was attracted to the alternative experience of working in a micro-firm and gaining hands-on knowledge of running a startup business. Rose perceived her as a good fit for BPL as being an expert in environmental health controls and changing legislation. Nonetheless, while qualified in production, Tamsin had never experienced the physical day-to-day management of production. After a year working in BPL, she realised that production management was not her forte, so she decided to move back into quality assurance with a larger organisation. With her wedding approaching and a signing for a new mortgage, she wanted to be sure that her medium-term employment was secure, a luxury that could not be guaranteed at BPL. This left Rose directly responsible for manufacturing and while she recognised the need to find a qualified production manager, she could not afford the time to recruit the right person, while getting orders out the door, securing new listings, managing the accounts – essentially, running the business. In addition, she opted to save on payroll overheads by subsuming the role of interim production manager. She reflected how at this point:

> There was no room for thinking . . . that would have been a luxury! I went from one thing to the next . . . and sometimes strategy just happened through a reactive response to something. For example, I began processing fresh orange juice because Costa Coffee asked me to and they were a key account.

On the periphery

Supply-chain logistics was a day-to-day operation that Rose had to deal with. Operating a manufacturing business in NI that ships products to mainland Britain presented distinct challenges and increased costs. When Rose initially secured the Waitrose account, her delight at adding a prestigious account to her portfolio was soon marred as they placed a modest first order of 4 pallets, which were distributed to only 35 out of the 180 stores in England. Subsequent pallet orders fluctuated from one week to the next, when upon doing the sums Rose realised that she was losing money in distribution costs because the volumes she was supplying to Waitrose in England were not large enough to reduce the shipping costs. In addition, Waitrose demanded 45 days before any credit payment, yet Rose had to pay on a monthly basis for every pallet she shipped.

With working capital stretched, Rose had to be meticulous with keeping on top of her financial commitments and quickly became expert at juggling and prioritising her creditors. She lived in hope from week-to-week that she would eventually secure all 180 Waitrose stores and start shipping larger pallet sizes and therefore the short-term profit loss would eventually be recouped. What is more, she recognised that the strategic legitimacy of a key account such as Waitrose would lead to increased brand value, so this was a risk worth taking. The added issue that Rose encountered was the fact that Puro smoothies had to be transported at a required (chilled) temperature, which resulted in a shorter product shelf-life and ultimately incurred greater logistic costs than dry products. The large multiples often insisted on a minimum of a 15-day shelf-life, which had to be considered for every shipment. Often external factors beyond Rose's control, such as broken-down lorries and inclement weather conditions, which resulted in boat cancellations, caused delivery delays and subsequent wastage.

One way of reducing the logistical challenges was to identify a distributor in England who would act as an agent for BPL and take responsibility for the initial storage and subsequent sales and distribution, for an agreed profit margin. Rose became convinced that in the absence of a sales team to enable her to grow the volumes, engaging several distributors in England, Scotland and the Republic of Ireland was the solution. After visiting some trade shows and doing research, Rose identified distributors in the regions with most potential, but initial approaches were fruitless as it quickly became apparent that without a sizeable marketing budget, distributors were reluctant to take Puro on to their portfolios. However, perseverance paid off and eventually Rose found a willing distributor who also listed Innocent Drinks. Despite successful negotiations, a few days before the planned launch they withdrew and it emerged that Innocent had exercised their dominance by telling the distributor that it had to be either Innocent or Puro, but under no circumstances could they represent both.

A blind courtship

Despite the challenges of the day-to-day running of the business, BPL was perceived as a startup success, particularly with respect to brand marketing and developing innovation. Rose even featured in INI's Start a Business guide as a local female entrepreneur who had successfully taken the plunge. Indeed, Rose realised that without an allocated marketing budget for advertising and other promotional activities, she had to be creative in generating positive PR for her organisation. A key way to do this was to enter as many relevant industry awards and competitions that normally involved presenting to a panel of influential stakeholders and submitting a structured business plan. Despite a time-consuming process, these sponsored competitions had formidable PR machines and BPL was able to piggy-back on much of the advertising as they progressed to competition finals. In addition, through participating and featuring in these competitions, Rose met many experienced individuals who came from various investment, banking and production backgrounds. Thus, in addition to generating PR for her business, Rose benefited from receiving expert advice about how to best grow her business.

In order to achieve growth, external investment became essential, as scaling up production was too slow and eating away at her bottom line. In addition, Rose accepted that she could no longer continue as a 'one-woman band' and needed to formalise her fledgling business structure by identifying a management board and putting a team in place. Consequently, a combination of investment and expertises in the key areas of production, distribution, sales and marketing was required to successfully grow her business. Shortly after winning an award for Best Small Company Award for Food Innovation and the significant media coverage that followed, BPL attracted the attention of Coca-Cola Ireland, who directly expressed an interest in the brand. Discussions ensued over the following months with an initial view to forming a strategic alliance and a possible eventual buyout. Rose was excited at the prospect of an exit strategy and focused her energies over the next few months on developing the relationship with Coca-Cola, providing detailed financial projections, attending meetings and presentations, and hosting plant visits. This protracted process went on for over a year, during which time the financial position of the business was deteriorating rapidly. Rose was desperately holding out for Coca-Cola to follow through with their initial expression of interest, but as each quarter came to an end they failed to communicate a decision and reassured her that they would be raising it at the next board meeting. Desperation turned to fear as Rose knew the business was running out of cashflow and, despite the gradual increase in sales volumes, break-even was still far off. At this point, she felt physically and emotionally drained and, as she faced the potential failure of her business, she reflected,

> I don't want to fail . . . I started the business with such confidence and optimism and I am still very passionate and I believe I have an excellent product and that I can I fill a really good niche in the market place. It still

is the best smoothie you can buy that goes into a package and the healthiest one you can give your body. But probably the energy and drive has been knocked out of me. You just come up against so many hurdles and obstacles all the time and disappointment.

A much needed ski vacation in the French Alps, away from the stresses of production, distribution and sales provided some perspective for Rose. Despite being on holiday she emailed her courting partner, emphasising that the business had reached a 'critical' stage and urged them to make their final decision on whether or not the required financial investment would be made and a subsequent joint venture partnership created. With the vulnerability of the business exposed, the response was far from desirable as Coca-Cola withdrew their interest, asserting that 'the business was in decline and the size of the transaction was too small', but nonetheless offered Rose a lump sum to clear the debts of the business and invited her, along with the Puro brand, to come and work with them. Rose felt sick to her stomach as her business went into tailspin and urgently needed capital investment. She realised that she needed to think and act quickly if she had any chance of saving her business, so she approached INI for advice and was referred to a business angel network. She met with a number of angels but none were particularly attracted to invest. She went on to secure the services of a management consultant and together they prepared a 'Prospectus for the Sale of Barefruit Products', with the aim of attracting an investor interested in acquiring the business in part since Rose, despite everything, still wished to be at least a part owner. Thirty pertinent, desirable businesses throughout Ireland were targeted as potential suitable 'business partners' and issued with the prospectus towards the end of April 2008. Eight of these businesses registered their interest and a round of meetings ensued. A number of these interested parties were perfect as potential investors, in that they could fulfil a core function of the business such as sales and marketing or chilled distribution, while providing the much needed strategic input. However, one by one they withdrew their interest and the final potential investor withdrew his keen interest in September 2008, citing the reason as: 'the current economic climate is not good and unfortunately I need to retain any investment capital for my own businesses'.

The economic recession had taken hold in NI during summer 2008 and that particular investor was Rose's final hope. Her accountant advised her that she was technically insolvent, in that she did not have enough cash-flow to sustain the day-to-day running, and as company director she was obliged to stop business operations. With immense emotional difficulty, she had to make the hardest decision in her life and ceased trading some two weeks later.

The aftermath of failure

Enduring entrepreneurial failure should not be underestimated and the process of reinventing oneself and finding the physical and emotional energy to apply oneself to other opportunities requires significant character and strength. Rose was doing a part-time Masters in Agri-Food Marketing and she reflected how for nearly six months she was unable to share with her student peers that her business had ceased trading and instead, when drawing on her BPL experiences for classroom discussion, she spoke in the present tense.

> After I 'shut the doors' I couldn't deal with it. I couldn't deal with them (student peers) asking me, 'Why? What happened?'. Eventually, I began to share piecemeal details, but I mostly told them I didn't want to discuss it. I didn't want word spread around, but eventually it did.

The perceived and/or actual lack of credibility was difficult for Rose to deal with immediately after the failure of BPL, especially as from an external stakeholder perspective the business appeared to have a strong brand, appearing on the supermarket shelves of key multiples and showing steady signs of a growing manufacturing small- and medium-sized enterprise (SME). 'I had so much outward success. People were asking me to come and speak at dinners and networking events, but inside I was fighting for survival.'

The financial debt that Rose became exposed to post-BPL was another pressure that had to be dealt with. In total, she estimated that she had lost nearly £150,000 (British pounds). She had already remortgaged once and, having maxed out several credit cards to keep the working capital in the business flowing, she had to quickly remortgage for a second time to clear the credit card debt. This seemed like the best option as she knew she would not have an income for the foreseeable future. She also cashed in a pension to partly pay off a large bank overdraft and they continued chasing with relentless pressure for the full amount, as she reflected, 'If you owe the bank millions it's their problem, and if you owe them thousands it's your problem!'

The pressure of financial debt led to feelings of extreme guilt that she had exposed herself and her husband Tim to this debt and eroded their retirement savings. In addition, the social stigma attached to failure was recognised by both Rose and Tim as they both drew comparisons between how failure was perceived in the US and NI. Tim reflected,

> I think the Americans are more readily able to give people money who have failed because they can sit down and look through the business plan and say, 'well, you failed'. And they say, 'yeah I failed because of this, this and this . . .' and they say, 'Well, you'll not do that again . . .?' 'No!' They know they're not going to make the same mistakes twice. So the Americans would be willing to give people more of a chance second time around. This country won't.

Rose alluded to the Northern Irish mindset that people take pleasure in someone else's misfortune and felt that some people she encountered post-BPL exuded the impression of 'I could have told you that it would not work!' However, no one ever explicitly said it. She also noticed that none of her close friends acknowledged the failure of her business and almost avoided any conversation about it, but Rose was quite happy with that as she herself did not want to discuss it.

Regardless of what people thought Rose knew, she had to move on. She knew she had withdrawn a bit from her social and professional networks and in some respects her mind was still processing the experience she had just come through. Eventually, she began to re-engage and contacted two consultancy partners that she used to freelance with. She was glad that, despite being distracted by her business for the last three years, she had maintained her professional relationship with these organisations and completed the odd project for them. She was now able to approach them again for some larger projects. 'Needs must! I needed to go and get some money in, especially when I knew what I had cost us. So I couldn't sit about feeling sorry for myself.'

In addition, she threw herself into completing her Masters in Agri-Food Marketing and found that experience strangely therapeutic as she continuously reflected on BPL and she began to process various reasons why it did not work.

> It has all been a fantastic learning curve, but a very expensive one! This experiential learning, consolidated with my academic learning, has provided me with a greater and sharper business skills-set than I had when I embarked on my business idea in 2004. So, like they say, it is wholeheartedly better to have tried and failed, than never to have tried at all.

Conclusion

This chapter has presented insights of the entrepreneurial process and the obstacles faced by the entrepreneur, with a particular focus on entrepreneurial failure and the factors leading up to that point. Rose faced many challenges as she launched and sustained her business, but there were insurmountable challenges, which eventually lead to failure. Despite a difficult time, the aftermath of failure afforded Rose the space to reflect on the critical incidents and she acknowledged the learning she had accrued, leaving her with a sharper set of entrepreneurial tools for the future.

Case study questions

1   Consider the challenges facing Rose as she launched and operated Barefruits Ltd. Which challenges do you feel were successfully overcome and which were not? Of those insurmountable challenges, detail those which you perceive influenced the failure of the business and justify your arguments accordingly.

2 In mapping the case of Barefruits from nascent-to-operational-to-failing, list the critical incidents over the life-course of the business. Reflect on Rose's behaviour when dealing with these critical incidents and consider those actions and decisions which both facilitated the development and growth of the business and those which were more detrimental.

3 Consider the external factors which led to the failure of the business. To what extent could each of these factors have been controlled and what actions (if any) could Rose have conducted in order to minimise their impact?

4 Rose's concluding comments reflect on the 'fantastic learning curve'. What key learning experiences do you think Rose has accrued as a result of coming through entrepreneurial failure?

Role play/presentation

You are a management consultant and BPL becomes one of your client companies in January 2008, six months *before* the business officially ceased trading. Your remit is to intervene and provide consultancy advice on a turnaround strategy for the company. In groups, consider the key points of address that you would include in such a strategy and what advice would you offer to Rose for implementation. Prepare a short 10-minute presentation report for delivery to the rest of your seminar class and be prepared to answer questions defending your recommendations.

Potential seminar debate or practical exam question

Do you agree or disagree with the following statement?

'If entrepreneurs paid greater attention to the danger signs – dwindling cash flow, slowing debtor payments and pressures on sales and margins – and took early advice, many of these insolvencies could be avoided.'

In the light of your learning developed in this case, provide a 500-word response to the above quote, providing justification for your arguments.

Task

Identify an entrepreneur in your network or community who has come through prior business failure only to start over. Do some initial research on this individual and then email/call and invite them to talk to you about their entrepreneurial failure and learning experiences. Reconvene with your study group and share (in confidence) your empirical insights.

Notes

1   UK definition of a micro-business is less than 10 employees.
2   See: www.innocentdrinks.co.uk

References

Cope, J. (2011) Entrepreneurial learning from failure: An interpretative phenomenological analysis. *Journal of Business Venturing*, 26(6): 604–623.
Dard, NI. (2011) Available online at: www.dardni.gov.uk/ni-agri-food-sector-key-statistics
Levie, J. and Hart, M. (2012) The Global Entrepreneurship Monitor, United Kingdom, 2011 Extended Report. Aston Business School and the Hunter Centre for Entrepreneurship, University of Strathclyde.

15

WYNKOOP BREWING COMPANY – USA

John Mueller and Clay Dibrell

The case focuses on the craft brewing industry and how the first brewpub in the US state of Colorado, Wynkoop Brewing Company, has leveraged a customer counterculture against the mainstream culture associated with the large, mass, national brewers through innovative craft brewing of quality beers and a unique perspective on fun and growth to successfully compete in the consolidated US beer industry.

Beer industry

Beer has been an important part of civilization for a number of years, dating back to ancient Babylonian, Egyptian, and Chinese societies.[1] However, the development of the beer industry in the United States has been go, stop, and go, as seen in the implementation of prohibition, which outlawed the sale of all alcoholic drinks for personal consumption in 1919 before being repealed in 1933.

The beer market in the US is sizable, but has been declining over the last couple of years and is highly concentrated, consisting of only three very large competitors. The US market accounts for 16.5 percent of the global market value. After years of growth, the beer market declined by 1.5 percent in 2009 to reach $77.6 billion in sales in 2009, and shrank 1.9 percent in terms of market volume. The market is highly concentrated, with the top three companies having a combined market share of 79.8 percent of the total market volume. These companies are Anheuser-Busch Inbev, SABMiller, and Molson Coors Brewing Company. These companies may offer premium beers; however, most of their business involves mass-market products.[2]

Overall beer consumption has declined in the US, and along with a weakening US dollar, has led to an increase in the consolidation of the US beer industry. Miller Brewing Company was acquired by South African Breweries in 2002 from Philip Morris for $5.6 billion to form SABMiller.[3] Coors merged with the Canadian brewing company Molson in 2005, with the new company having approximately $6 billion in sales.[4] In 2007, SABMiller and Molson Coors merged their operations in the US and Puerto Rico with the new joint venture having $6.6 billion in annual sales.[5] Finally, Anheuser-Busch was purchased for $52 billion in 2008 by the Belgian InBev.[6] For the purposes of clarity, the names of Miller, Coors, and Anheuser-Busch will be used to identify these larger corporations.

The dominant culture of the beer industry in the USA has been established and supported by several of the largest brewers, including Anheuser-Busch, Coors, and Miller, which focused on mass-produced lagers for the mass market at a low price. This culture was most evident in the late 1970s when there were less than 50 breweries in the US. However, since 1985, a movement with the craft brewers has emerged, which has set up two distinct cultures in the industry. The craft brewing industry is a subset of the overall beer industry. The three largest brewers represent and mold the dominant culture in the industry through their marketing campaigns and beer distribution networks, with the craft brewers exhibiting a counterculture with their attitudes and servicing a distinct and more educated customer base. Craft brewers range in size from brewpubs to microbreweries, with each being independently owned and producing less than 6 million barrels per year.

In 2010, the US beer industry produced 180 million barrels (1 barrel = 31 US gallons),[7] which is a 1.5 percent decrease from 2009. Of the 180 million barrels, 1,753 craft brewers produced an estimated 10 million barrels (4.9 percent of the total industry production). The production of craft brewers increased by 11 percent from 2009 to 2010, which is in contrast to the decline in the overall industry production. When examining the market by dollar value, the craft brewers' market share makes up a greater share of the market, at 7.6 percent of the overall market and employ over 100,000 employees, including staff, in the US. In terms of estimated retail sales, craft brewery sales were up from $7 billion in 2009 to $7.6 billion in 2010. As of 2011, more than 1,927 breweries existed in the US, the majority of which were craft breweries.[8]

As the three largest breweries face stiff competition in the mass market, these breweries have looked enviably at craft brewers and their loyal customers. A recent trend by these larger breweries is through acquisition of the craft brewers. Comparably, an exit strategy by some craft brewers is to get larger and then to be purchased by the largest breweries to create a liquidity event. To illustrate this point, Anheuser-Busch purchased Goose Island Brewery of Chicago, IL, for $39 million in April, 2011, with the founders and other investors gaining $23 million from the sale.[9] However, there is much concern on whether or not Goose Island Brewery will be able to maintain its loyal customer base, as some patrons are already indicating that it will become a part of Anheuser-Busch's corporate culture and lose its unique identity and counterculture to the more corporate culture of Anheuser-Busch. Other craft breweries face a comparable dilemma such as Wynkoop Brewing Company in Colorado.

Likewise, other breweries, such as Coors, eschewed an acquisition approach and instead focused on a internal corporate venturing strategy by creating their own craft brewery. Through Coors's Tenth and Blake division, Coors started Blue Moon Brewing Company @ the Sandlot in Denver, Colorado, in 1995 in an effort to pursue customers of craft beers. The Sandlot, owned by Coors, is a brewpub restaurant that is only open during the Major League Baseball season and sells only craft beers such as Blue Moon. Based on appearance, it looks like a microbrewery. Blue Moon Brewing has met with both financial and critical success since its inception. For example, the beer produced by Blue Moon Brewing Company has won 36 awards at the Great American Beer Festival,[10] as well as the 2005 Best Small Brewing Company.[11] However, in both of these situations, these companies are not considered craft brewers by definition since a large brewer now owns more than 25 percent of Goose Island and Blue Moon.

The craft brewers have become concerned that they are losing their competitive advantage to the larger producers, as these larger breweries are successfully imitating their strategy. Dick Cantwell, head brewer and founder of Elysian Brewing Co. in Seattle, Washington, stated in an interview with Andy Crouch of beerscribe.com:

> The definition of our success ensures our failure. All of a sudden our market share would drop. And yes, Blue Moon, or what we are now calling it, Blue Moon by Coors, their success and the decency of their beers—I mean twenty years ago wouldn't all of us have considered that a good thing, that one of the big brewers is actually making a beer we can drink, it is a victory in terms of sensibility but it's scary in terms of the inroads it makes on our more purely defined arena but I still think it's a victory.[12]

Further, Mr. Cantwell in the same interview indicated that the Brewers Association would respond to mass producers entering their niche markets by asking craft beer drinkers to consider who makes their beer:

> We're going to do a whole campaign of 'who makes your beer?' So that it is right out there . . . it's also going to be, 'how much of your company is owned by Anheuser-Busch?' and 'who makes this?' and what the Plank Road Brewery really means. We want consumers to go to the website or generally have it forged into their consciences so that they pay attention and give a damn where it comes from and who does it.[13]

Following this logic and presented in Figure 15.1, the Brewers Association drafted the following Declaration of Beer Independence in 2009 and every year thereafter.

The Declaration of Beer Independence draws on the symbolism of the US Declaration of Independence written in 1776, which provided the arguments for the 13 American colonies to declare independence from Britain during the American Revolutionary War. By signing the document, craft beer drinkers are engaged in practicing "the concept 'Informed Consumption,' seeking and deserving to know if my beer comes from a small and independent brewer or if it is owned by a large brewing company."

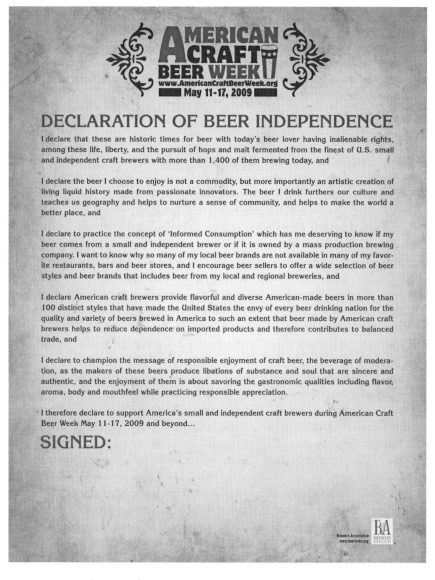

FIGURE 15.1 Declaration of Beer Independence

The craft brewers association has discovered that one of its best ways to compete against mass producers of beers is not only through a quality offering, but by tapping into the counterculture that has been cultivated by the entrepreneurs and their customers. A part of the US national culture is individualism, and to a lesser degree of the underdog or small company competing and beating the larger company. The larger company should win as they possess advantageous resources, which enable these companies to compete on national and global levels. However, when customers see that an entrepreneur with a smaller, independent and individualized company with far fewer resources is able to effectively pull its resources together to compete against these larger companies, then these same customers often pull for the small company to succeed. The Craft Brewers Association wants to tap into this counterculture movement against the mass-market brewing industry by declaring their independence from the mainstream.

Wynkoop Brewing Company

In 2010, the state of Colorado had over 100 breweries and was one of the top states for beer production, with 47,956 people per brewery. Although Colorado is the home of Coors, one of the largest breweries in the US, the state is considered to be a very conducive area for craft breweries, due to the well-educated denizens of Colorado. The first brewpub in the state, Wynkoop Brewing Company was started in 1988. The founders of Wynkoop included John Hickenlooper, an oil geologist, along with several young urban pioneers, Mark Schiffler and Ron Robinson. Hickenlooper, being the driving force for starting the brewery, had moved to Colorado from the East coast of the US in the early 1980s to work with an oil company as a geologist. Shortly after moving to Colorado the oil industry collapsed and Hickenlooper lost his job. After pondering several avenues for employment, he decided to explore the option of starting the first brewpub in the state.

From the beginning, the founders went against the dominant thought pattern of the time by being environmentally sensitive through green business practices, buying local, and supporting urban renewal. From the start, the company has recycled glass and cardboard, which was unheard of in the late 1980s. In addition, they compost their biodegradable waste and use spent brewing grains to feed local livestock. They source premium malts and hops from a large number of local producers to support the local community. As for a location, the founders established Wynkoop in the dilapidated warehouse district of Denver, the capital of the state. Locating in the warehouse district in downtown Denver went against the trendy style of other establishments, which had vacated the downtown area for more posh facilities in the suburbs. Several years after establishing Wynkoop in downtown, other establishments, including the professional baseball, basketball, and football stadiums, became main fixtures to help grow the downtown warehouse area into a thriving business area again, resulting in what local patrons call "LoDo." These decisions, which were counter to the dominant culture of the customers and the market-share leaders in the US, have turned out to be helpful in the success of the brewery.

However, there was a point where the success of Wynkoop pushed the brewery in the wrong direction. Growth was not the primary motivation of the owners initially. However, when they started experiencing success and had customers who pushed them to grow, they lost sight of their origins and the original vision. In the midst of their growth, the brewery became more predictable and less innovative as it started to cater to the taste buds of craft beers' mainstream customers, and in effect joining the dominant brewing culture. The strategic change went against the original strategic focus of bucking the dominant cultural trends of the beer industry. In trying to cater to the craft beers' mainstream customers, the brewery's reputation took a hit with their core customer base believing the brewery had lost its authenticity, the quality of the beer declined, and the brewery experienced stagnation in financial performance.

To rectify this situation, the founders restructured the ownership and operations by bringing in a new brewer, Andy Brown, with a counterculture reputation due to the unique flavors of the beer that he produced. In addition, with the original founder's move into politics, the company had lost its pitchman in Hickenlooper. To fill this void, the company brought in an experienced and savvy promoter, Marty Jones (also known as the Idea Man, Cheersleader, and Beer Evangelist). It also helped that owners, Lee Driscoll (CEO), Mark Shifler (co-founder, COO), and Ron Robinson (co-founder, General Manager), who were also part of top management (owner-managers), were supportive of their move and were also part of the counterculture themselves.

Over the past few years the brewery has focused on going back to their roots of brewing quality beer for people who like good-tasting beer. In 2010, they brewed 35 craft beers that catered to their core customer base. This list consisted of some of their original beers, as well as experimenting with new beers. The move back to their roots has helped them rebuild their reputation while still growing; they have been able to "bring back old fans (customers), draw new beer customers and elevate (their) status in Denver's beer culture," says Andy Brown.

With this strategic revitalization, Wynkoop produced 3,500 barrels of beer in 2010 (see Figure 15.2), an increase of 25 percent in production from the previous year, and their hand-canned and draft beers were available in over 150 bars and retailers in Colorado, as compared to only 30 locations in the previous year.

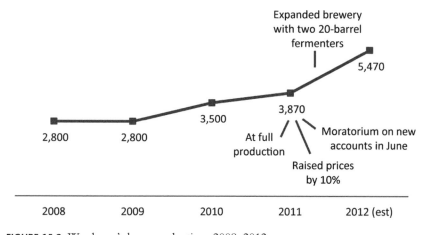

FIGURE 15.2 Wynkoop's beer production, 2008–2012

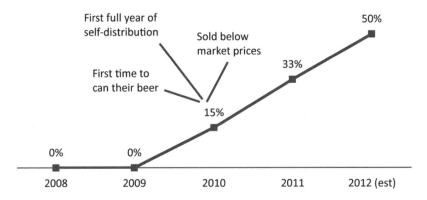

FIGURE 15.3 Wynkoop's beer sales, 2008–2012

This resulted in an increase in sales of 15 percent from 2009 to 2010, their first full year of self-distribution and canning of their beer. In 2011, the growth continued with sales growth of 33 percent, barrel production at 3,870, and 175 retailers offering Wynkoop's beer (see Figure 15.3).

Even with these increases, growth was hindered due to the company reaching full production capacity. This resulted in management putting a moratorium on new retail customers in June, 2011. The number of retail customers grew from 150 to 175 retail outlets, as shown in Figure 15.4. Thus, the brewery added two 20-barrel fermenters in the latter half of 2011 to support further growth in 2012, which is estimated to produce enough Wynkoop products to supply a total of 250 outlets. As such, production and sales are expected to increase by 50 percent and 41 percent respectively.

As stated earlier, the customer base in the craft beer industry is more educated, both in general education and education about beer. This is evident in the customer base of Wynkoop. As such, the brewery spends a large portion of their marketing dollars on programs to help educate the customers on what good beer is. They do this via various methods, including getting involved in high-profile events like the governor's bash (Hickenlooper is now the governor of Colorado), hosting events like the Beerdrinker of the Year contest, participating heavily in beer festivals, and being involved in the local community. By being engaged in events and participating in local community events, they continue to be engulfed in the culture they sell to; this enables them to cater to an educated and proactive customer base that spreads across socioeconomic demographics. A benefit by being part of the counterculture, they are able to attract loyal customers and create a community of beer drinkers who support their initiatives. In the end, the individuals at Wynkoop feel they are producing "liquid art" with each of their beers and keeping the counterculture alive.

Wynkoop is facing another dilemma due to its success. The entrepreneurs who started Wynkoop have been very successful in creating a winning formula of high

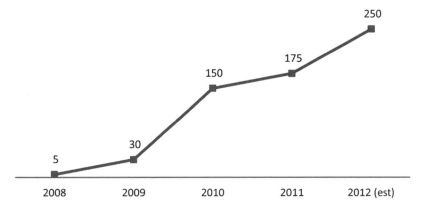

FIGURE 15.4 Wynkoop's retail customers, 2008–2012

quality beer in a counterculture customer environment. After a previous failed attempt to ramp up growth, Wynkoop has challenged the mainstream market to focus on its competitive niche of craft brewing. With this renewed focus on brewing a quality craft brew, the company's retail sales, production, and manufacturing capacity have all increased. As this company continues to grow and, with the larger breweries looking to acquire craft brewers, the entrepreneurs of Wynkoop will need to decide on how best to maintain the business' increasing growth trajectory while sustaining their counterculture legitimacy or look for a liquidity event, such as being acquired by a large brewery in the future. In the end, the counterculture of Wynkoop may become the mainstream in the US beer industry.

Case study questions

1 To what extent does the craft brewing industry rely on counterculture? Are craft brewers able to leverage the counterculture movement to create value for the craft brewery and its investors?
2 Does a craft brewery have to grow to compete? If not, why not? How could a craft brewery compete against larger, national breweries?
3 How do larger, national breweries attempt to compete against craft brewers? To what extent have the larger, national breweries been successful in competing against the craft brewers?
4 How does counterculture enable the craft brewery industry to compete from a producer, customer, and supplier perspectives?
5 What is the motivation of the entrepreneur who started Wynkoop? How did it evolve over time? What was the motivation of the three partners in the beginning, and how did their motivation change over time?
6 How did external investors play on the Wynkoop's strategy?

7 Is Wynkoop an innovative lifestyle business? If so, why? If Wynkoop is a lifestyle business, could it be transformed into a high growth business? If so, how?

8 How did Wynkoop use counterculture to protect their competitive space explicitly or implicitly?

9 To what extent does authenticity affect the success of Wynkoop's counterculture strategy?

10 How could the counterculture strategy implemented by Wynkoop constrain future strategic initiatives for growth?

11 Should Wynkoop leverage its counterculture in an attempt to sell to one of the big three breweries in the US market? What are the potential positive aspects of this exit strategy? What are the potential negative implications of this exit strategy?

12 Could the success of Wynkoop and the craft brewing industry be replicated in your country? Why? In other regions of the world? If so, why and how? How would national culture impact the effectiveness of the counterculture strategy? How would national economic development influence the effectiveness of the counterculture strategy?

13 In your country, how could a counterculture strategy enable a small business to compete more effectively against larger, national competitors? What industries do you believe would have the best opportunity for a counterculture strategy to be successful?

Notes

1 The Beer Institute.
2 Beer Industry Profile: United States, DataMonitor, 2010.
3 Available at: http://money.cnn.com/2002/05/30/news/deals/miller_sab/index.htm
4 Available at: www.cbc.ca/news/business/story/2004/07/22/molsonmerger_040722.html
5 Available at: www.nytimes.com/2007/10/10/business/worldbusiness/10beer.html
6 Anheuser-Busch InBev.
7 The Beer Institute.
8 Brewers Association.
9 Available at: www.huffingtonpost.com/2011/03/29/goose-island-bought-by-bu_n_841990.html?ir=Food
10 Available at: http://blogs.westword.com/cafesociety/2011/09/five_things_you_didnt_know_abo.php
11 Available at: http://phx.corporate-ir.net/phoenix.zhtml?c=101929&p=irol-newsArticle_Print&ID=764263&highlight=12 www.beerscribe.com/2009/03/18/the-brewers-associations-quiet-war-on-blue-moon-leinenkugels-goose-island-and-maybe-even-elysian-new-belgium-and-your-brewery/
13 Available at: www.beerscribe.com/2009/03/18/the-brewers-associations-quiet-war-on-blue-moon-leinenkugels-goose-island-and-maybe-even-elysian-new-belgium-and-your-brewery/

INDEX

Page numbers for figures and tables are in *italics*